MW01057981

STRUGGLING FOR AIR

STRUGGLING FOR AIR

Power Plants and the "War on Coal"

Richard L. Revesz and Jack Lienke

OXFORD
UNIVERSITY PRESS

OXFORD
UNIVERSITY PRESS

Oxford University Press is a department of the University of Oxford. It furthers the University's objective of excellence in research, scholarship, and education by publishing worldwide. Oxford is a registered trade mark of Oxford University Press in the UK and certain other countries.

Published in the United States of America by Oxford University Press
198 Madison Avenue, New York, NY 10016, United States of America.

First Edition published in 2016

Cataloging-in-Publication Data is on file at the Library of Congress
ISBN 978–0–19–023311–2

1 3 5 7 9 8 6 4 2
Printed by Edwards Brothers, USA

For my children, Joshua and Sarah—R. R.

For my parents—J. L.

CONTENTS

STRUGGLING FOR AIR

Prologue: Conflict and Context

In recent years, denouncing President Obama's "war on coal" has become a favorite pastime of Republican members of Congress, coal-state officials of all political stripes, assorted trade associations, and antiregulatory theorists. Conservative media outlets have embraced the catchphrase with similar enthusiasm, pounding out a steady drumbeat of incendiary headlines:

Obama Declares a War on Coal[1]
Obama's War on Coal Hits Your Electric Bill[2]
The Casualties of Obama's War on Coal[3]
The War on Coal Is a War Against American Jobs[4]

To hear these groups tell it, while the President campaigned on a promise to end his predecessor's war in Iraq, he wasted little time in waging a misbegotten battle of his own—this one on U.S. soil—that will cripple industry, imperil access to reliable electricity, and impoverish the average citizen. As the primary evidence of this undeclared war, its opponents point to three regulations issued pursuant to the Clean Air Act that aim to reduce pollution from the nation's aging power plants. The Cross-State Air Pollution Rule, also known as the Transport Rule, prevents soot- and smog-forming pollutants emitted by plants in upwind states from creating dangerous air-quality conditions in their downwind neighbors.[5] The Mercury and Air Toxics Standards restrict power plants' emissions of mercury, which can impair neurological development in young children, as well as other toxic metals like arsenic and chromium, which can cause cancer.[6] Finally, the Clean Power Plan requires significant reductions in plants' emissions of carbon dioxide, the primary driver of global climate change.[7] Because coal generates more of each of these types of pollution than any other energy source, the new rules are expected to further reduce its already shrinking share of the domestic electricity market in favor of cleaner-burning natural gas and renewables like wind and solar power. Some might call this progress; mining companies and coal-dependent utilities consider it a siege.

In a society plagued by actual violence that kills dozens of real people each day, it's disheartening that challenges to regulatory policy—however important—so routinely rely on the vocabulary of armed conflict. And we do mean routinely: in 2012, *Mother Jones* compiled a tongue-in-cheek list of 109 different things on which President Obama had, according to pundits and headline writers, declared war—including Christmas trees, Wall Street, poor people, fishing, and, of course, freedom.[8] Perhaps the most memorable use of this rhetorical strategy is a 2010 campaign ad for the Democratic Senate candidate in West Virginia, then Governor Joe Manchin. In the ad, titled "Dead Aim," the governor raised a rifle and literally shot a copy of the climate change bill that the President was then urging Congress to pass.[9] (Not long after, Manchin won the election.)

But questions of taste and propriety aside, the biggest problem with the narrative of "Obama's war on coal" is that it is almost entirely ahistorical and, as a result, misleading. To claim that recent environmental rulemakings are "unprecedented regulatory assaults,"[10] one must ignore decades of, well, precedent.

Each of the three major "fronts" in the President's supposed war—the Transport Rule, the Mercury and Air Toxics Standards, and the Clean Power Plan—can trace its lineage not just to the policy choices of previous administrations, both Republican and Democratic, but all the way back to the dawn of modern environmental policy. Viewed in this historical context, the rules tell a very different story. The "war on coal" is exposed as neither new nor the brainchild of President Obama. Instead, it is merely the latest—and possibly final—chapter in a long-standing quest for redemption, a decades-long effort to counter the ill effects of a tragic flaw in one of our most important environmental laws.

The flaw in question? In 1970, a nearly unanimous Congress passed the Clean Air Act of 1970, which had the remarkably ambitious aim of eliminating essentially *all* air pollution that posed a threat to public health and welfare. But for some of the most ubiquitous pollutants, the Act empowered the Environmental Protection Agency (EPA) to set emission limits only for *newly constructed* industrial facilities, most notably coal-fired power plants. Existing facilities, by contrast, were largely exempt from direct federal regulation.

At first, this "grandfathering" of old plants didn't seem terribly consequential. After all, its effects wouldn't be permanent. Eventually, the plants would run out their useful lives—then thought to be about thirty years—and close down, making way for new plants that *would* be subject to federal standards, right?

Wrong. Policymakers soon realized that instituting different regulatory regimes for new and existing plants had dramatically altered the math behind plant retirement decisions. A system in which new plants are subject to strict pollution controls and old plants can emit with impunity gives those old plants an enormous comparative advantage and an incentive to stay in business much longer than they otherwise would. Under early Clean Air Act regulations, building a new coal-fired power plant required either a substantial investment in an end-of-stack pollution "scrubber," which cost millions to install and operate, or the use of low-sulfur coal, which, in some parts of the country, was an equally expensive proposition. Continuing to run an old plant, meanwhile, carried no such costs. Thus, a statute designed to prompt technological innovation ended up favoring old, obsolete, and very dirty generators. Today, some communities are still drawing power from coal plants built in the 1950s.

By the late 1980s, it was clear that the central promise of the Clean Air Act—safe air for every American—would never be realized if grandfathered coal plants were not more stringently regulated. Every President since then, whether Democratic or Republican, has taken meaningful steps to slash pollution from these plants. Furthermore, most of these efforts have relied not on new legislation but on previously neglected provisions of the Clean Air Act itself. The statute has, in this sense, held the keys to its own salvation.

The Transport Rule, the Mercury and Air Toxics Standards, and the Clean Power Plan follow in this bipartisan tradition—all were promulgated under Clean Air Act sections that have been on the books for decades. And aided by a booming market for low-priced natural gas, these three rules look set to overcome the seemingly intractable legacy of grandfathering once and for all: the vast majority of pre-1970 coal plants are expected to retire in the next decade, and the rest will have to reduce their emissions substantially to continue operating. Redemption for the Clean Air Act's tragic flaw may finally be at hand.

What could go wrong? Quite a lot. Natural gas prices are famously volatile, the EPA has already been hit with a barrage of lawsuits (with still more to come), and Republicans in Congress are attempting to block the agency's most important rule, the

Clean Power Plan, with appropriations riders and other legislative maneuvers.

Even if courts ultimately uphold the Clean Power Plan and Congress fails to derail it, that rule's success in cutting pollution will depend largely on state efforts to implement it. And Senate Majority Leader Mitch McConnell has urged governors and state legislators not to cooperate. The EPA has statutory authority to impose direct federal controls in noncompliant states, but given the regulatory timeline, that won't happen before the 2016 presidential election. If a Republican takes the White House, recalcitrant states are likely to get their way, at least for a while.

Overcoming grandfathering's harmful legacy will thus require continued political resolve on the part of the Obama Administration, thoughtful rulemaking by the EPA and its state partners, and savvy lawyering by the Justice Department. But it will also require a healthy dose of luck, subject as it is to the varied whims of energy markets, federal judges, state officials, and voters.

No one said redemption was easy.

The remainder of this book proceeds as follows.

Chapter 1 offers a brief primer on coal—what it is, how and where we get and use it, and why it's so environmentally problematic.

Chapter 2 examines the evolution of the "war on coal" as a conservative catchphrase, mapping its spread from Appalachian editorial pages to campaign rallies and Capitol Hill hearings.

Chapter 3 travels back to 1970, chronicling the bipartisan negotiations that led, laudably, to the passage of the Clean Air Act and, regrettably, to the tragic error of grandfathering. We also consider and criticize the traditional defenses of grandfathering offered by legal academics and investigate whether federal legislators had any of these justifications in mind when they designed the Clean Air Act.

Chapter 4 explores how the EPA, often at the urging of trade associations, interpreted and implemented Clean Air Act provisions on the "modification" of old plants in ways that served to extend rather than curtail the benefits of grandfathering. We also show that when lobbying and litigation failed to yield sufficiently favorable regulations, many grandfathered coal plants simply flouted the rules that didn't suit them.

Chapter 5 turns to grandfathering's negative impacts on public health, explaining how uncontrolled emissions from aging Midwestern and Appalachian coal plants made it essentially impossible for their Northeastern neighbors to meet EPA limits on the ambient concentration of particulate matter (commonly known as soot) and ground-level ozone (smog), leading to the needless premature deaths of hundreds of thousands of Americans. We then describe the innovative but aggressive market-based policies that the administrations of George H.W. Bush, Bill Clinton, and George W. Bush implemented to address this interstate pollution.

Chapter 6 considers the extent to which grandfathering has exacerbated the problem of carbon dioxide pollution in the electricity sector. We examine the pivotal role old plants played in the failure of proposed legislation to slash U.S. greenhouse gas emissions. Facilities that would have already been shuttered but for the pernicious effects of grandfathering made an aggressive push for yet more special treatment that ended up dooming the bill altogether.

Finally, **Chapter 7** looks to the potentially brighter—and cleaner—future, explaining why a happy confluence of low natural-gas prices and the Obama Administration's regulatory policies might at last succeed in closing down or cleaning up the grandfathered plants that have caused too much harm to too many Americans for far too long.

1

Coal

A Primer

This book chronicles almost five decades of efforts by the United States government to reduce the air pollution associated with burning coal, along with the often misleading political rhetoric surrounding those efforts. Given the central role that coal and its environmental consequences will play in our story, it's helpful at the outset to understand some basic facts about the fuel.

WHAT IS COAL?

Short Answer: A combustible rock.

Longer Answer: Coal is a fossil fuel—"fossil" because it's primarily composed of the preserved remains of ancient plants and "fuel" because it can be burned to create energy. Most of the coal we use today was formed hundreds of millions of years ago when large swaths of the earth were covered in swampy forests.[1] As plant life in these swamps died, it sank to the bottom of the water, where it was eventually buried under additional layers of sediment and slowly decomposed into a soggy, carbon-rich, soil-like substance known as peat.[2] As still more time passed, this peat was further transformed by heat and pressure, a process known as carbonization, into the sedimentary rock we call coal.[3]

HOW AND WHERE DO WE *GET* IT?

Short Answer: We mine it, mostly in Wyoming and Appalachia.

Longer Answer: There are two basic methods of mining coal: underground mining and surface mining. Surface mining is typically used for shallow coal beds—those buried less than 200 feet deep.[4] Miners access the fuel by simply removing (often with explosives) the trees and soil and rocks that sit atop it.[5] Underground mining, by contrast, is used to extract coal that sits between 300 and 1,000 feet deep.[6] The surface is left relatively undisturbed, and miners dig tunnels through which to enter the mine and retrieve the coal.[7]

Historically, underground mining was the more common of these two methods, but today, the majority of U.S. coal is produced at surface mines, which require far fewer workers to produce the same amount of coal.[8] In addition to being cheaper to operate, surface mines are safer: both fatal and serious nonfatal injuries occur about three times more often in underground mines.[9]

Twenty-five of the fifty states contain active coal mines, but just five of those states account for more than two-thirds of domestic production: Wyoming (39 percent), West Virginia (12 percent), Kentucky (8 percent), Illinois (5 percent), and Pennsylvania (5 percent).[10] Plenty of foreign countries produce coal as well, but the United States imports very little of the fuel (and, in any event, exports far more than it imports).[11]

Generally, surface mining is more common in Western states like Wyoming, while underground mines are dominant in the East. One prominent exception to this pattern is the Appalachian practice of "mountaintop removal mining," a highly controversial variant of surface mining in which the tops of mountains are blown off to get at the coal underneath.[12]

HOW AND WHERE DO WE *USE* IT?

Short Answer: We burn it, mostly to generate electricity and mostly in the Midwest and Appalachia.

Longer Answer: Popular for home heating and cooking in the eighteenth, nineteenth, and early twentieth centuries, coal is now primarily used to generate electricity.[13] The United States' very first power plant, opened by Thomas Edison in 1882, was coal-fired, and coal remains the electric sector's most popular fuel to this day, though its market share has been declining since the late 1980s.[14]

Generally, Midwestern and Appalachian states rely far more on coal than do coastal states. As of 2014, Kentucky, West Virginia, and Indiana, for example, each got more than 80 percent of their electricity from coal-fired plants, whereas California, Oregon, and Washington each drew less than 5 percent of their power from such plants.[15]

As for *how* utilities go about generating electricity from coal, in the most common variety of coal plant, the fuel is ground into a fine powder and blown into a combustion chamber.[16] (Pulverizing the coal first allows it to burn hotter and more completely.[17]) When burned, the coal heats water carried in tubes running through the combustion chamber into highly pressurized steam.[18] That steam is then used to turn a turbine, connected to the shaft of a generator, which produces electricity by spinning magnets inside a set of wire coils.[19] Once the steam has passed through the turbine, it is cooled back into water so the process can begin anew.[20]

Operating a coal plant can require a truly enormous amount of fuel. The Mountaineer Plant in New Haven, West Virginia, for example, burns a million pounds of coal every *hour* to supply its 1.3 million customers.[21]

WHAT DOES IT *COST* US?

Short Answer: A lot.

Longer Answer: There are serious problems associated with every stage of coal's life cycle. Extracting the fuel, especially through surface mining and mountaintop removal, disrupts wildlife habitats and can contaminate waterways.[22] It's also hazardous to the humans doing the extracting: miners can develop serious respiratory diseases like pneumoconiosis (also known as black lung) and silicosis, due to inhalation of coal and quartz dust on the job.[23]

But coal's most widespread harms occur when the fuel is burned. Coal-fired power plants are among the United States' largest sources of four major air pollutants—sulfur dioxide, nitrogen oxides, mercury, and carbon dioxide—all of which pose significant threats to both the human body and the environment.[24]

Sulfur dioxide (SO_2) is an invisible but pungent gas that irritates the mucous membranes of the eyes, nose, throat, and lungs.[25] Exposure to SO_2 is associated with increased hospital admissions for respiratory problems, particularly among vulnerable populations like children, the elderly, and asthmatics.[26] What's more, SO_2 can react with other atmospheric compounds to create microscopic particles called sulfates, which can penetrate deeply into the lungs and either cause or worsen serious conditions like emphysema, bronchitis, and heart disease, in some cases leading to premature death.[27] On top of these very serious health effects, SO_2 emissions contribute to a variety of environmental harms, including acid rain.[28]

It's worth noting here that the softer, subbituminous coal produced in Western states tends to contain much less sulfur than the harder, bituminous variety found in the East.[29]

Nitrogen oxides (NO_x) are a group of gases that include nitrogen dioxide, nitrous acid, and nitric acid.[30] As with SO_2, exposure to NO_x is associated with increased hospital admissions for respiratory problems like asthma.[31] And, like SO_2, NO_x can react with other compounds in the atmosphere to form small particles—in this case, nitrates—that can create or exacerbate serious respiratory problems, aggravate existing heart disease, and contribute to acid rain.[32] Finally, when exposed to heat and sunlight, NO_x can form ground-level ozone—commonly known as smog—which also has adverse respiratory effects.[33]

Mercury is a toxic metal found in many rocks, including coal.[34] When coal is burned, its mercury is released into the air and can eventually settle in bodies of water.[35] There, it is transformed by microorganisms into highly toxic methylmercury, which subsequently accumulates in fish that live in the water.[36] If consumed by pregnant women, these contaminated fish can cause lasting neurological damage to the women's unborn children.[37]

Finally, **carbon dioxide** (CO_2) is a greenhouse gas and the driving force behind global climate change.[38] Like the glass of a greenhouse, it allows sunlight to enter the earth's atmosphere but prevents heat from radiating back out. Over time, the warming caused by industrial CO_2 emissions is expected to have a number of extremely dangerous consequences, both in the United States and abroad, including increased drought, increased coastal flooding, and more frequent (and severe) heat waves.[39]

2

War Stories

To Representative Marsha Blackburn, Republican of Tennessee, the threat was clear: "Mr. Speaker, there is a war being waged on energy and on coal in this country. But it's not coming from another country, it is coming from our own government."[1] Her colleague, Mike Pompeo of Kansas, agreed: "President Obama's War on Coal means fewer jobs and higher energy costs for Americans."[2] Those who believed otherwise, Virginia Representative David McKinley warned, were "in dangerous denial."[3]

It was September 20, 2012, two months before a presidential election that would pit incumbent Barack Obama against former Massachusetts governor Mitt Romney, and the United States House of Representatives was preparing to vote on the bluntly titled Stop the War on Coal Act. Democrats on the Energy and Commerce Committee called the proposed legislation, which would strip the EPA of its power to regulate coal-mining operations and coal-fired power plants under a host of federal laws, "the single worst anti-environment bill to be considered in the House this Congress."[4] But the bill's sponsors argued that significantly curtailing the EPA's authority over the coal industry was the only way to prevent the President's war from claiming "even more victims."[5]

The Stop the War on Coal Act passed the House on September 21, 2012, in a 233–175 vote, with the support of nineteen

Democrats.[6] No one thought it had any chance of moving in the Democrat-controlled Senate. Instead, the House's vote, which would be its last act before election day, was "only meant to be an instrument to bludgeon Obama and other Democrats," as one commentator put it—a reminder to the coal-country electorate of the existential threat posed by the current President and his party.[7]

It hadn't always been this way. On the contrary, four years earlier, Barack Obama had enjoyed a brief, involuntary tenure as the coal industry's "spokesperson-in-chief."[8] About a month after Obama emerged victorious from the 2008 election, the American Coalition for Clean Coal Electricity (ACCCE), a "partnership of the industries involved in producing electricity from coal,"[9] released an advertisement made up entirely of video excerpts from a speech he had given at a September 2008 campaign rally in Lebanon, Virginia.[10] In the footage, Obama proclaimed that "clean coal technology" could make America "energy independent,"[11] and expressed confidence that the pollution generated by coal combustion could be dealt with: "This is America. We figured out how to put a man on the moon in ten years. You can't tell me we can't figure out how to burn coal that we mine right here in the United States of America and make it work."[12] The ad ran for months.[13]

And ACCCE wasn't alone in characterizing Obama as a coal supporter in 2008. During the campaign, coal-state Democrats had proven equally eager to brand their party's candidate as a "friend of coal."[14] Longtime Congressman Nick Rahall of West Virginia, for instance, expressed certainty that Obama would be better for the coal industry than John McCain.[15]

On the one hand, the portrayal of Obama as a cheerleader for coal wasn't entirely unfounded. He did, after all, hail from Illinois, a major coal producer. As a U.S. senator, he had cosponsored a bill with Republican Jim Bunning of Kentucky to provide up to $8 billion in subsidies for controversial coal-to-liquid fuel technologies.[16]

Earlier, while serving in the Illinois State Senate, he had publicly criticized a mercury regulation proposed by President George W. Bush that he felt unfairly favored Western coal over the variety produced in Illinois.[17] And, as the ACCCE ads emphasized, Obama *was* an enthusiastic proponent of developing so-called "clean coal" plants—that is, facilities equipped with technology that could capture at least some of their carbon dioxide emissions and then sequester the trapped gas underground where it wouldn't contribute to climate change. Indeed, the economic stimulus package Obama pushed through Congress in February 2009 included $3.4 billion in funding for pilot carbon-capture projects.[18]

But there was a corollary to the President's support for "clean coal" technology that neither ACCCE nor Rahall cared to emphasize: a belief that the status quo of burning coal *without* capturing its CO_2 emissions was environmentally unsustainable. Obama was bullish on clean coal but bearish on dirty coal. His support for coal-to-liquid fuel subsidies in the Senate, for instance, was ultimately conditioned on a requirement that the fuel's production and use generate at least 20 percent less CO_2 than the production and use of conventional petroleum.[19] More important, as a presidential candidate, he had publicly and repeatedly vowed to impose a cap-and-trade system that would cut American greenhouse gas emissions to 80 percent below 1990 levels by 2050.[20] Under such a system, any power plant that burned fossil fuels would need to buy a permit—from either the government or a fellow polluter—for each ton of carbon dioxide it emitted. This was a particularly onerous prospect for coal plants because they emit twice as much CO_2 per kilowatt-hour of electricity as their natural gas-fired counterparts.[21] In other words, coal plant owners operating under a cap would likely have to spend a great deal on permits, invest a great deal in emission-reducing technologies like carbon capture, or simply close down.

The coal industry was happy to burnish its public image by broadcasting a then very popular new President's support for the idea of "clean coal." It was happier still to accept taxpayer dollars for the testing of pollution-reducing technologies. But it had no interest in spending its *own* money on such reduction efforts. As a result, as soon as the new White House's focus shifted from doling out stimulus funds to following through on the President's cap-and-trade pledge, the coal PR machine undertook a shift of its own. With surprising speed, Obama's public image went from that of coal's biggest fan to its No. 1 enemy.

RISE OF THE RHETORIC

The first rumblings of conflict were heard in the spring of 2009, after the White House released a budget that anticipated significant revenue from cap-and-trade emissions auctions—almost $650 billion over a ten-year period.[22] At the time, a staff writer for the *Dayton Daily News* in Ohio predicted that the President's plan would "ignite a new War Between the States in Congress, pitting the coal-dependent states against those that use other forms of energy."[23] But coal country turned out to be less interested in blaming other states for cap-and-trade than in blaming the President. When the legislation overcame its first congressional hurdle, a May 2009 vote of the House Energy and Commerce Committee, Republican Congressman Bob Latta of Ohio told the press, "It almost looks like Obama and the Democrats declared war on Ohio and Indiana."[24] By the time the bill passed the full House in late June, there was no "almost" about it, at least not for the editors of the *Charleston Daily Mail* in West Virginia, who declared that the "war on coal, and the accompanying cap-and-trade mumbo-jumbo, would clobber West Virginia and West Virginians."[25]

The rhetoric snowballed from there. In October 2009, the West Virginia Chamber of Commerce deemed the "war on coal" serious enough to justify taking a hostage: health-care reform. The Chamber demanded (without success) that its home-state senators block the Affordable Care Act "until the Obama Administration, particularly the U.S. Environmental Protection Agency, back[ed] down on its campaign against coal."[26] The following spring, when the EPA tightened its Clean Water Act permitting standards for mountaintop mines, a spokesperson for the National Mining Association, Luke Popovich, suggested that the President was "parking his tanks on [mining companies'] front lawns."[27]

The "war" next emerged as a dominant theme in West Virginia's 2010 midterm elections, with Democrats and Republicans alike scrambling to prove "[w]ho love[d] coal more."[28] As already mentioned in our Prologue, the state's popular governor, Joe Manchin, gained an edge in his Senate race only after producing an ad in which he put a literal bullet through a copy of the President's cap-and-trade bill.[29] Seventeen-term Congressman Rahall, too, was forced to distance himself from the White House, only two years after endorsing Obama as "committed to coal."[30] Rather than denying his Republican opponent's claims that "Pelosi and Obama have declared war on coal," Rahall argued that his seniority in the Democratic party left him better positioned to *fight* the Administration's environmental initiatives,[31] going so far as to compare his unsung success at blocking committee votes on mining restrictions to the thwarting of terrorist attacks: "I've had to hold off many threats. It's kind of like fighting terrorism. When you are successful in fighting off the threat, but the threat is never published it isn't known."[32] Rahall managed to secure an eighteenth term, but described the race as his "toughest campaign in 34 years."[33]

Confined primarily to coal-state media in 2010, the public relations campaign for the "war on coal" went national during the

2012 presidential election. By that point, Democrats in the Senate had long since abandoned hope of passing Obama's cap-and-trade plan, but Mitt Romney nevertheless seized on coal as a major talking point, citing the EPA's recently finalized Mercury and Air Toxics Standards as the latest evidence of the President's war.[34] According to the Romney campaign, "President Obama [couldn't] claim to support clean coal while imposing regulations that his EPA admit[ted] would prevent another coal plant from ever being built."[35]

As the campaign wore on, messaging around the "war on coal" became ubiquitous. Lawns in coal-producing states were littered with signs reading "Stop the War on Coal. Fire Obama."[36] A Romney television ad titled "War on Coal" accused President Obama of "attacking [the] livelihood" of coal miners.[37] ACCCE piled on with ads of its own that criticized the EPA's "heavy-handed regulations."[38] Minutes into the first presidential debate, Romney announced, "I like coal," and suggested that people in the coal industry felt they were "getting crushed by [Obama's] policies."[39] Not surprisingly, "war on coal" reached its most heavily searched period on Google in November 2012.[40]

For all the advertising dollars spent (ACCCE's efforts alone cost $35 million[41]), the "war" narrative ended up holding little sway with voters outside Appalachia. Romney won West Virginia and Kentucky by wide margins, but he lost coal-producing swing states like Ohio, Pennsylvania, and Virginia—and, with them, the presidency.[42] The National Mining Association's Popovich would later muse that the concept of a " 'war on coal' never resonated with much conviction among ordinary Americans."[43]

But if proponents of the "war on coal" were chastened by defeat, they didn't stay that way for long. Seven years into the Obama presidency, complaints about the "war" still routinely make headlines.[44] They were, for instance, a major focus of the 2014 congressional races in coal country. In West Virginia, Congressman Rahall failed to secure a twentieth term after the National Republican Congressional Committee ran ads arguing that "a vote for Nick Rahall is a vote for Barack Obama and an agenda that includes the war on coal."[45] In neighboring Kentucky, Allison Grimes, a Democrat challenging incumbent Senator Mitch McConnell, was quick to assure voters that she didn't "agree with the president's war on coal."[46] Grimes lost anyway, and, at McConnell's victory celebration, fellow Senator Rand Paul suggested that Kentucky voters had sent a clear message to the White House: "Mr. President, the war on Kentucky coal must end."[47]

PEELING BACK THE PROPAGANDA

In his essay *Narrative Transactions—Does the Law Need a Narratology?*, literary scholar Peter Brooks examines the distinction "between events in the world and the ways in which they are presented in narratives."[48] To illustrate the idea—obvious in theory but discomfiting in practice—that "how a story is told can make a difference in legal outcomes," Brooks highlights cases in which different judges rely on the same set of core, undisputed events or actions to justify opposite conclusions.[49] The explanation for the differing results, he argues, resides in the "narrative glue" of each judge's opinion, "the way incidents and events are made to combine in a meaningful story."[50] In Brooks' view, "[n]arratives do not simply recount happenings; they give them shape, give them a point, argue their import, proclaim their results."[51]

Essential to determining the "shape" of any story, of course, is deciding where it begins. Consider the seminal affirmative action case of *Regents of the University of California v. Bakke*, which Brooks cites in an interview about his scholarship.[52] In *Bakke*, a twice-rejected white applicant to the medical school of the University of

California at Davis challenged the constitutionality of the school's race-conscious admission policy.[53] At the time, Davis reserved 16 of the 100 seats in each year's class for minority students.[54] A five-Justice majority of the Supreme Court held that the quota was a violation of the Equal Protection Clause of the Fourteenth Amendment.[55]

Judicial decisions typically begin with a recitation of relevant facts, and those in *Bakke* are no exception. But two of the Justices demonstrate very different understandings of which facts should be considered "relevant" to Bakke's claims. Justice Louis Powell's controlling opinion opens with a description of the origins of the university's admission policy:

> The Medical School of the University of California at Davis opened in 1968 with an entering class of 50 students. In 1971, the size of the entering class was increased to 100 students, a level at which it remains. No admissions program for disadvantaged or minority students existed when the school opened, and the first class contained three Asians but no blacks, no Mexican-Americans, and no American Indians. Over the next two years, the faculty devised a special admissions program to increase the representation of "disadvantaged" students in each Medical School class. The special program consisted of a separate admissions system operating in coordination with the regular admissions process.[56]

Justice Thurgood Marshall's dissent, by contrast, begins with a very different sort of history lesson:

> Three hundred and fifty years ago, the Negro was dragged to this country in chains to be sold into slavery. Uprooted from his homeland and thrust into bondage for forced labor, the

> slave was deprived of all legal rights. It was unlawful to teach him to read; he could be sold away from his family and friends at the whim of his master; and killing or maiming him was not a crime. The system of slavery brutalized and dehumanized both master and slave.[57]

Unlike Powell, Marshall recognizes that the horrors of slavery and the decades of institutionalized discrimination that followed its abolition are very much "facts of the case." Rather than assessing the constitutional merits of Davis's quota system in a historical vacuum, his dissent forces the reader to grapple with affirmative action's reasons for being, the stubborn legacy of disadvantage that Davis's admission policy sought to address. As Brooks explains, "[Marshall] just suddenly alters the whole time frame, the whole perspective on the story and you've got to say, 'Wow, this is a story that the others are not telling.' It makes you reconceptualize what the story is all about."[58]

Historical context is similarly essential to any reasoned evaluation of the EPA's recent rulemakings. To characterize them as a "war on coal," the coal industry and its allies rely on an artificially compressed time frame, beginning the story with the 2008 election and casting President Obama as the villain of the piece. In this telling, the President's environmental policies are an "ideological crusade" motivated by outright malice toward the coal industry.[59]

As evidence for this point, the "war" crowd is fond of citing an interview that President Obama gave to the *San Francisco Chronicle* while on the campaign trail in 2008. Discussing his cap-and-trade plan, Obama explained, "If somebody wants to build a coal-powered plant, they can. It's just that it will bankrupt them because they are going to be charged a huge sum for all that greenhouse gas that's being emitted." [60] He later added that under his plan "electricity rates would necessarily skyrocket."[61]

From an economic perspective, the President's statements are perfectly rational. Raising the price of electricity to reflect the social cost of its creation (namely, pollution) is a sensible way to encourage both energy conservation and the use of cleaner fuels. But the logic of Obama's position is largely irrelevant to his critics. What matters to them is the callousness that can be read into his casual mentions of bankruptcy and skyrocketing electric bills. Because the statements focus on costs (the ways that greenhouse gas limits will harm coal companies and electricity consumers) rather than benefits (the ways such limits will protect public health and welfare), they lend support to the idea that the President's environmental agenda is the product of a personal vendetta against the coal industry and those who depend on it for employment or affordable electricity.

Some, like Senate Majority Leader Mitch McConnell have suggested that this animus is a manifestation of the President's cultural elitism.[62] In a similar vein, the author of a blog post titled *Why Does Obama Hate Coal Miners and Appalachia?* speculated that the President's coal policies stem from his disdain for "those who cling to guns and religion."[63]

There's just one problem with this "malice of the elite" theory: it's hard to condemn policies as products of presidential animus when they weren't the President's idea to begin with. With the cap-and-trade bill a distant political memory, the most commonly cited evidence of Obama's "war on coal" are the three EPA restrictions on pollution from power plants that we mentioned in the Prologue: the Transport Rule, which prevents plants in upwind states from exporting dangerous soot- and smog-forming pollution to their downwind neighbors; the Mercury and Air Toxics Standards, which aim to control plants' emissions of mercury and other toxic pollutants; and the Clean Power Plan, which will limit plants' emissions of climate change-driving carbon dioxide. But the truth is that not one of these rules wholly originated with the

Obama Administration. Each was, to some extent, made necessary by the decisions of prior Presidents. Each was promulgated under the authority of the same forty-five-year-old statute, the Clean Air Act of 1970. And each is, at some level, an attempt to compensate for the same fundamental flaw in that legislation. Thus, if we are to understand fully the purpose and potential of these rules, we must first understand what the Clean Air Act itself was meant to accomplish—the old evils it sought to remedy—and the new evil to which it inadvertently gave rise. We must, like Justice Marshall in *Bakke*, go back to the beginning.

3

Congress Misses the Mark

For polluters, America in 1970 was still something of a Wild West. A number of federal, state, and municipal laws aimed at improving air quality were already on the books, but few were enforced, and pollution from the nation's ever-growing stock of motor vehicles, power plants, and factories remained uncontrolled in much of the country.[1] A passage from the Ralph Nader Study Group's *Vanishing Air*, published in May 1970, vividly illustrates the extent to which dirty air was a fact of life for city dwellers of the period:

> The New Yorker almost always senses a slight discomfort in breathing, especially in midtown; he knows that his cleaning bills are higher than they would be in the country; he periodically runs his handkerchief across his face and notes the fine black soot that has fallen on him; and he often feels the air pressing against him with almost as much weight as the bodies in the crowds he weaves through daily.[2]

New York's problems with air quality were hardly unique. In an October 1969 letter to the Senate Subcommittee on Air and Water Pollution, a resident of St. Louis expressed similar sentiments about the sheer pervasiveness of pollution in her community:

> What really made me take the time to write this letter was the realization that I had begun to take the haze and various odors for granted. Close the doors and windows and they'll be less noticeable[. I]t is very disturbing to think I've become used to the burning-rubber smell in the evening and the slightly sour smell in the morning. What does air smell like?[3]

And air pollution's costs went far beyond sour smells and dirty handkerchiefs, as a series of deadly "inversions" both here and abroad had made dramatically clear beginning in the late 1940s.

Typically, the air at higher altitudes is cooler than that below.[4] This is because the surface of the earth absorbs sunlight and radiates heat, warming the air closest to the ground.[5] That warm surface air then cools as it rises higher into the atmosphere.[6] But in certain weather conditions, this temperature pattern can be flipped. When a warm front moves in above a cooler mass of air, it acts as a sort of lid, preventing the surface air (and any pollutants it contains) from rising into the atmosphere and dispersing.[7] The longer an inversion lasts, the worse surface air quality gets, as more and more pollution becomes trapped beneath the lid.[8]

In 1948, Donora, an industrial town in southwest Pennsylvania, made national news after suffering a five-day inversion that killed 20 people and sickened 6,000 others, more than 40 percent of the town's residents.[9] Four years later came London's "Great Smog of 1952," another lengthy inversion that was estimated to have caused the premature deaths of at least 4,000 Londoners.[10] And in 1966, an inversion in New York City killed an estimated 168 people over the course of a week.[11]

Acute incidents may have drawn the biggest headlines, but scientists of the time were also beginning to understand that even "normal" levels of pollution had serious, long-term health consequences. In December 1970, the acting Surgeon General, in testimony before the House of Representatives, cited "abundant scientific evidence that exposure to polluted air is associated with the occurrence and worsening of chronic respiratory diseases, such as emphysema, bronchitis, asthma, and even lung cancer."[12]

And yet, while 1970 was not an ideal time for the actual environment, it was something of a golden age for environmentalists. On January 1, 1970, President Richard Nixon signed the National Environmental Policy Act into law.[13] Six months later, he proposed the creation of the Environmental Protection Agency, which opened for business in early December.[14] And on December 31, he capped off the year by signing the Clean Air Act, which was then—and still is—our nation's most ambitious environmental law.[15] At the signing ceremony, Nixon speculated—correctly—that 1970 would later "be known as the year of the beginning, in which we really began to move on the problems of clean air and clean water and open spaces for the future generations of America."[16]

Why did all of these green stars align in 1970? For one thing, public interest in environmental issues was growing rapidly. According to nationwide Opinion Research Corporation polls, only 28 percent of the U.S. population considered air pollution a somewhat or very serious problem in 1965; by 1970, that figure had risen to 69 percent.[17]

J. Clarence Davies, a Princeton political scientist who would go on to serve as a senior staffer for the White House Council on Environmental Quality, speculated at the time that heightened concern about environmental degradation was an inevitable product of America's post-World War II economic boom:

> The massive growth in production and in the availability of resources which has characterized the U.S. economy in the past two decades affects the problem of pollution in several

> ways. The increase in production has contributed to an intensification of the degree of actual pollution; the increase in the standard of living has permitted people the comparative luxury of being able to be concerned about this; and the availability of ample public and private resources has given the society sufficient funds and skilled manpower to provide the potential for dealing with the problem.[18]

In other words, getting rich had come at great cost to the nation's air and waterways, but, as a result of the nation's new affluence, Americans were both more inclined to care about improving the quality of their environment *and* better equipped to succeed in that effort.

The most memorable demonstration of environmental protection's newfound political salience came in April 1970 when Senator Gaylord Nelson, a Wisconsin Democrat, and Congressman Pete McCloskey, a California Republican, cochaired the first Earth Day, a "national teach-in on the environment."[19] The event drew more than 20 million participants all over the country.[20] The same month, *CBS Evening News* anchor Walter Cronkite, who would soon become known as the "most trusted man in America," began to include an environment-focused story in each night's broadcast under the provocative heading "Can the World Be Saved?"[21]

But even with strong public support for legislative action, the Clean Air Act likely wouldn't have passed when it did and in the form it did if not for the somewhat unexpected advocacy of President Nixon. According to William Ruckelshaus, whom Nixon appointed as the first EPA administrator, the President did not share the public's concern for the environment.[22] He thought the environmental movement, along with the antiwar activism of the period, "reflected weaknesses of the American character."[23] Nixon *was*, however, very concerned with staying president, and his expected opponent for the 1972 race was Senator Edmund Muskie, a Maine Democrat whose chairmanship of the Senate Subcommittee on Air and Water Pollution had earned him the nickname "Mr. Clean."[24] Nixon had no interest in conceding the green mantle to Muskie, so he set out to look even more protective of the environment than his liberal rival. Or, as the Nader report more colorfully explained, "The environmental bandwagon is the cheapest ride in town. . . . President Nixon paid his fare and jumped aboard."[25]

That January, President Nixon made the environment a major focus of his first State of the Union address:

> The great question of the seventies is, shall we surrender to our surroundings, or shall we make our peace with nature and begin to make reparations for the damage we have done to our air, to our land, and to our water?
>
> Restoring nature to its natural state is a cause beyond party and beyond factions. It has become a common cause of all the people of this country.[26]

The President vowed to present Congress with the "most comprehensive and costly program of pollution control in America's history."[27] (Apparently, in 1970, the costliness of a regulatory program was considered a selling point.)

The following month, Nixon made good on his pledge with a special address to Congress that outlined a "37-point program, embracing 23 major legislative proposals and 14 new measures being taken by administrative action or Executive Order" aimed at addressing a variety of environmental concerns, including water pollution, air pollution, solid waste management, and parklands.[28] Among those twenty-three legislative proposals were a series of amendments to the nation's existing air pollution laws that would eventually become the Clean Air Act of 1970.[29]

Nixon's bill was unquestionably stronger than one that Muskie himself had put forward the previous December, which involved little more than "minor tinkering" with the largely ineffectual Air Quality Act of 1967.[30] But rather than admit defeat, Muskie doubled down. During the summer of 1970, his Senate subcommittee developed a bill that followed the same general structure as the President's proposal but was "tougher at every turn."[31] The deadlines were tighter, and the standards were both more stringent and more enforceable.[32] Most controversially, the bill included a requirement that auto manufacturers cut emissions of carbon monoxide, hydrocarbons, and nitrogen oxides from new motor vehicles by 90 percent in only six years.[33] In September, the Senate passed Muskie's bill, 73–0.[34]

The House had already passed a bill the previous June that more closely tracked Nixon's, so a conference committee was charged with reconciling the two versions of the new law.[35] Despite heavy lobbying by the auto industry and pressure from the White House to take a less aggressive approach, particularly with regard to the auto standards, the committee hewed much closer to the Senate version, and the new Clean Air Act was passed by both chambers of Congress in a voice vote on December 18, 1970.[36] When President Nixon signed the bill into law on December 31, he invited a number of the Act's congressional architects to the signing ceremony.[37] Senator Muskie was not among them.[38]

FLY IN THE OINTMENT

The goals of the Clean Air Act were extremely ambitious. By 1975, every area in the country would be required to reduce concentrations of some of the most ubiquitous and dangerous pollutants in the ambient air—including sulfur dioxide, nitrogen oxides, and particulate matter, among others—to levels that protected public health with an "adequate margin of safety."[39] The power to set these National Ambient Air Quality Standards, known as NAAQS, was entrusted to the administrator of the newly formed EPA.[40]

Once NAAQS were in place, the baton would be passed to states to develop individualized plans for achieving the necessary reductions.[41] Upon approval by the EPA, these state implementation plans would be enforceable by both the state and federal governments.[42] Furthermore, if a state failed to design an adequate plan, the EPA could step in with a federal implementation plan.[43]

In addition to setting NAAQS, the EPA was required to establish nationally uniform limits on emissions from individual "stationary sources," the most common and highly polluting of which were power plants.[44] These "performance standards"—typically expressed as a maximum rate of emission rather than an absolute limit (so, *x* pounds of pollutant *y per kilowatt-hour generated* rather than *x* pounds of pollutant *y per year*)—were to reflect the reductions achievable using what the EPA deemed the "best system of emission reduction" for the relevant source category.[45]

But Congress placed a significant limit on the EPA's power to regulate individual sources of pollution: for NAAQS pollutants (that is, pollutants subject to ambient limits), the EPA's performance standards could apply only to *newly constructed* facilities. Existing sources were left to the states to deal with as part of their implementation plans for meeting the NAAQS.

That, to put it mildly, was a very big mistake. Imposing restrictive standards on new sources and lax or no standards on old sources, a regulatory practice known as "grandfathering," creates two problematic incentives: old plants are encouraged to stay in business longer than they otherwise would, and new plants are discouraged from coming online at all.[46]

Imagine a utility that owns a single power plant. The plant has been in service for quite a while, and its owner is thinking about replacing it. Because the utility is a rational, profit-maximizing actor, it will do so only if the benefits of replacement exceed the accompanying costs. For the utility's purposes, the chief *benefit* of replacing the plant is the reduction in operational costs that will result from running a more efficient facility. All else being equal, newer plants typically wring more electricity out of a given amount of fuel.[47] (Replacing the plant is likely to generate other benefits as well. For one, a more efficient plant is likely to generate less pollution. But a utility has no economic incentive to take this sort of "social benefit" into account, because it doesn't affect the company's bottom line.)

The chief *cost* of replacing the old plant, meanwhile, is just that: the cost of building a new, more efficient facility. Thus, a rational utility should choose to replace the old plant whenever the amount it will save on operational costs over the life of the new plant outweighs the construction bill.

An environmental regulation that applies solely to new plants alters this calculus. Why? Let's assume that the only way to comply with the regulation is to install a new emission-reduction technology. Purchasing and installing that equipment will cost the utility money, as will operating it. So the costs of building a new plant have gone up, and the benefits (avoided operational expenses) have gone down, making the project less likely to pencil out for the utility.

Consider a numerical example:

> Say that the annual operating cost of an existing facility is $100, while . . . the annual operating cost of a new facility (with the same production capacity) is $90 (*including annualized capital costs*). Assuming that [the plant owner] acts economically, [it] will choose to construct a new facility.[48]

In other words, even with the cost of construction factored in, the owner will save $10 a year by replacing the existing facility.

But what if the government has just issued a rule that will raise annual operating costs by $20? (Assume for the sake of simplicity that any capital expenditures necessary to comply with the regulation have been annualized into that $20 operating cost.) If the new regulatory costs fall equally on both old and new plants, the owner's decision won't change. Running either kind of plant will now be $20 more expensive, but the new plant still has a $10 advantage over the old plant. It's when the burden of environmental regulation falls *only* on new plants that problems arise:

> [N]ow say that the applicable environmental regulation imposes costs of $20 if [the plant owner] constructs a new facility but no cost if [it] retains [its] existing facility. The modified annual operating cost of a new facility is $110, while the annual operating cost of the existing facility remains $100. Accordingly, [the owner] will now opt to retain [its] existing facility in operation.[49]

Academics call this distortion of retirement decisions the "old plant effect," and the Clean Air Act is a paradigmatic example of the sort of policy that causes it.[50]

Soon after the Act was passed, the EPA issued New Source Performance Standards limiting coal-fired power plants' emissions of sulfur dioxide.[51] (At the time, such plants were responsible for more than half the nation's SO_2 pollution.[52]) In order to satisfy the standards, newly constructed coal-fired plants needed either to install multimillion dollar pollution "scrubbers," which rely on a chemical reaction to remove sulfur from exhaust gases as they pass through a smokestack, or to burn low-sulfur coal, which, in some Eastern states, was just as costly as installing a scrubber due to the high cost of transporting the cleaner coal from the Western mines that produced it.[53] Facilities built prior to 1971, however, could continue to pollute in unlimited quantities.

The regulatory advantage enjoyed by old plants grew even more pronounced with time, as the standards applicable to new facilities became more stringent. Starting in 1978, *all* new coal-fired plants were required to install a scrubber, even if they burned low-sulfur coal.[54] That same year also brought restrictions on the plants' emissions of nitrogen oxides.[55] And as the burdens on new plants increased, so did the incentive for old plants to delay retirement.

The eventual result was an electric generation fleet dominated by coal-fired clunkers. Prior to the passage of the Clean Air Act, the economically useful life of a coal plant was thought to be about thirty years.[56] But by 2012, more than three-quarters of the nation's coal-fired generation capacity had been in service for longer than that.[57] Indeed, almost 40 percent of the nation's coal-fired capacity was more than forty years old, and close to 20 percent was more than fifty years old.[58] Until quite recently, some operating plants dated all the way back to the 1940s, meaning they had been running for more than twice their expected lifespan.[59]

Permitted to operate with minimal or no emissions controls, these grandfathered plants have, for decades, accounted for a wildly disproportionate share of the nation's pollution.[60] As of 2002, coal-fired generating units that began construction prior to 1971, when the first New Source Performance Standards took effect, emitted SO_2 at almost twice the rate per megawatt-hour as coal units that were subject to the 1971 standards and at more than four times the rate of coal units that were subject to the 1978 standards (when scrubbers became mandatory for new plants).[61] The oldest units, those built prior to 1950, emitted at more than *six* times the rate of plants subject to the 1978 standards![62]

For nitrogen oxides, grandfathered units emitted at a 33 percent higher rate than plants built after NO_x performance standards took effect in 1978.[63] As with SO_2, the disparity increased with the age of the grandfathered unit: those built prior to 1950 emitted at a 57 percent higher rate than those subject to the 1978 standards.[64]

And grandfathered coal plants look even worse in comparison to natural gas plants, which have accounted for the vast majority of capacity since 1990, as will be discussed in Chapters 6 and 7.[65] As of 2010, plants constructed prior to 1978 emitted more than 100 times as much SO_2, 5 times as much NO_x, and twice as much CO_2 per megawatt-hour as the average gas plant.[66]

The bottom line is that the total amount of air pollution emitted in the United States has been and remains much greater than it would be in the absence of grandfathering. A 1998 study, for example, estimated that eliminating grandfathering in the power sector and requiring all existing plants to meet current new-plant standards would singlehandedly cut the nation's total SO_2 emissions by 40 percent and its NO_x emissions by 15 percent.[67]

Lest we be too hard on the Clean Air Act of 1970, we should point out that Congress built in two significant exceptions to its grandfathering. First, while the EPA cannot directly regulate the emission of NAAQS pollutants like sulfur dioxide from existing sources, it can, and indeed must, regulate the emission of what the Act calls "hazardous" pollutants from such sources.[68] "Hazardous" pollutants, also known as "air toxics," are substances that can cause cancer, infertility, or other serious health problems, even when they are not highly concentrated in the ambient air.[69] Second, the EPA must, in some cases, regulate existing sources' emissions of *un*classified pollutants—those that are neither "hazardous" *nor* subject to a NAAQS.[70] Essentially ignored by the agency for decades, these powers have received a great deal of new attention in recent years, as we'll discuss in Chapter 7.

We should also note that, on balance, the Clean Air Act has managed to do quite a lot of good over the past forty-five years. The 90 percent emissions cut for new motor vehicles that automakers protested so heartily? It was achieved by 1981, even as the manufacturers continued to thrive.[71] More generally, aggregate emissions of NAAQS pollutants fell 68 percent between 1970 and 2013, even as GDP more than tripled, energy consumption rose by 44 percent, and the U.S. population grew by 54 percent.[72] These reductions have yielded enormous dividends for the American public. A 1990 EPA study estimated that the Act prevented 205,000 premature deaths between 1970 and 1990 and that the value of these benefits exceeded compliance costs by a margin of at least 10 to 1.[73]

Congress's 1990 amendments to the Act—which, as we'll explain in later chapters, served to limit grandfathering—have yielded even larger benefits. A 2011 EPA study concluded that the 1990 amendments had prevented 160,000 premature deaths in 2010 alone and estimated that the number of lives saved annually would climb to 230,000 by 2020.[74]

And yet, despite these significant achievements, it is clear that the Clean Air Act could have accomplished much more, much sooner, if not for the terrible consequences of grandfathering.

EXPLAINING THE ERROR

Thus far, we've presented Congress's decision to grandfather existing plants as an unequivocal error. But exempting those already engaged in an activity from complying with new restrictions on that activity is common practice in a variety of legal arenas, ranging from the federal tax code to local licensing requirements for interior designers.[75] And although few would dispute that the Clean Air Act's approach—a near-complete, near-permanent exemption for older facilities—has had undesirable consequences, scholars disagree as to whether grandfathering is *always* a mistake. Over the years, legal academics have identified three reasons that a policymaker might reasonably consider offering some sort of "transition relief" to existing actors when imposing a new regulatory regime. We consider the merits of each justification below.

1. Fairness

The classic rationale for transition relief is fairness.[76] Proponents of this view argue that market actors rely on existing law when making investment decisions and, as a result, should be shielded from—or compensated for—legal changes that would decrease the value of those investments.[77] By this logic, a power plant should not be punished for lacking pollution controls if no emission restrictions were in place at the time of its construction.

But is it truly reasonable for an investor to believe that the laws governing its investment will never change? Laws change quite often, after all—often in foreseeable ways. Furthermore, as critics of the "fairness" rationale have pointed out, society doesn't protect investors from market risks, like declining demand or technological change, that might affect the value of their investments.[78] Why should regulatory risks be treated differently? Indeed, insulating investors from regulatory risks might distort their behavior in socially undesirable ways, leading them to overinvest in harmful but underregulated activities.[79]

2. Efficiency

Fairness aside, some argue that under the right circumstances, grandfathering is simply more efficient than treating new and existing sources alike.[80] A rule is more efficient in the economic sense if it generates greater net benefits for society, with net benefits being the difference between the value of society's gains from a regulation and the costs of complying with it.

Why might grandfathering be the more efficient choice? For one thing, compliance costs might be greater for an existing source than a new source.[81] Whereas a new power plant can be designed with scrubbers in mind, an existing plant might have to undertake expensive retrofits to accommodate new technology that wasn't anticipated by its original architects. Thanks to these extra "transition costs," a performance standard that is cost-benefit justified for a new source might not be so for an existing source.

Additionally, the benefits of installing a given control technology might be lower for an existing source than a new source.[82] Say, for instance, that a scrubber required by a new law will eliminate $100 of pollution-related harm over a ten-year period. Now say that an existing source already has an older, less effective scrubber in place that will nevertheless eliminate $50 of harm over the same ten years. If a brand new plant incorporates the newer scrubber into its initial design, society gets the full $100 of pollution-reducing benefit in return. But if the existing plant upgrades to the better scrubber, society gets only $50 of new benefit (because it was already getting $50 from the old technology). As a result, it's possible that the benefits of the scrubber will outweigh its costs for a new source, but not for an existing one.

But even where grandfathering looks more efficient in the short term, it may be undesirable in the long term.[83] This is because the cost advantage of running an uncontrolled old plant rather than upgrading it or opening a new one will decline over time, as deteriorating equipment results in higher maintenance costs and as pollution-reduction equipment becomes more cost effective.[84] As a result, the sort of indefinite grandfathering practiced by the Clean Air Act is particularly undesirable from an efficiency standpoint.

Furthermore, efficiency concerns can be minimized through the use of joint rather than sequential optimization. What does this mean? Traditionally, defenders of grandfathering have implicitly assumed that environmental standards are properly established in two discrete steps.[85] First, regulators set an optimal standard for new sources without taking any notice of existing sources. Next, in light of the new-source standard they've just chosen, they determine whether and to what extent existing sources should be grandfathered. With joint optimization, by contrast, both the new and existing sources standards are chosen simultaneously, with an eye toward their collective effect on emissions.[86] Using this method, grandfathering is less likely to look like the efficient choice. To understand why, consider the following example:

Say that the emission standard applicable to a new shoe factory will eliminate $60 worth of pollution-related harm through use of a technology that costs $40, generating potential net benefits of $20. Now say that installing that technology at an existing factory will yield the same benefit—$60—but at a cost of $65. Because the costs of regulating the existing factory outweigh the associated benefits, the existing factory will be grandfathered under a sequential approach.

But what if the market demand for shoes is sufficient to support only one shoe factory? No new factory will be constructed, the existing source will remain in operation, and the $20 in net benefits predicted to flow from the new-source standard will not be realized. Indeed, the standard could even yield negative benefits if it encourages the existing factory to stay in business longer than it otherwise would, delaying the construction of a more efficient replacement.

Now assume that a slightly less stringent emission standard could eliminate $50 worth of pollution at a cost of $35 to new sources and $45 to existing sources. If new-source standards are calibrated without regard to existing sources, this standard looks suboptimal because the $15 in potential net benefits is smaller than the $20 associated with the earlier, more stringent standard. But if we look at new- and existing-source standards together, the less stringent standard is the better choice: there is still only demand for one shoe factory, so again, no new factory will be constructed, and the new-source benefits will prove illusory. But this time, the existing factory will install pollution controls and generate $5 in net benefits by doing so. Thus, in this scenario, the joint optimization approach reveals that society as a whole will be better off if regulators opt for a less stringent standard and no grandfathering, rather than the stringent standard plus grandfathering that a sequential approach would suggest.

Admittedly, even with joint optimization, grandfathering may sometimes be the more efficient choice, such as when the existing sources in question have short, fixed lifespans and will thus be replaced by sources subject to the new-source standards in the near future.[87] This was not the case for power plants, however.

3. Political Pragmatism

Finally, in what is known as the "public choice" justification for grandfathering, some defend the practice as a necessary political evil that enables the passage of socially desirable legislation.[88] Rather than subject all sources to additional regulation, a law that includes grandfathering concentrates the burden of compliance on sources that have yet to be constructed. That result won't please everyone in the industrial community. It is not particularly desirable, for instance, for younger, growing companies that plan to open a large number of new facilities in the future. But grandfathering does appeal to mature players that have finished growing and are now more than happy to erect barriers to entry for potential competitors. With industrial opposition thus fractured, the legislation becomes easier to pass. And better a flawed law that includes grandfathering, the theory goes, than no law at all.[89]

The trouble with this logic is that when it comes to grandfathering, a flawed law is sometimes worse than no law. Indeed, it is possible for emissions to be higher under an environmental regulation that pairs a stringent new-source standard with an exemption for existing sources than they would have been in the absence of any regulation.[90] Think back to our earlier example in which the imposition of an environmental regulation for new sources ends up convincing a utility to continue running an old source it would otherwise have retired. Assume that the old plant emits 5 pounds of pollution per kilowatt-hour, while a new, unregulated plant would emit 3 pounds per kilowatt-hour. Meanwhile, assume that under the regulation, new plants can emit no more than 1 pound per kilowatt-hour.

With the new-source regulation in place, emissions will stay at 5 pounds per hour because the utility won't retire its old source. In the absence of regulation, meanwhile, emissions would be reduced to 3 pounds per hour because the utility would choose to build a newer, more efficient facility.[91] In other words, under the right circumstances, society can reap greater rewards from the unregulated status quo than from a new, nominally aggressive rule that includes grandfathering.

Furthermore, in the environmental context, the notion of grandfathering as a political necessity is belied by the fact that Congress managed to avoid the practice in a major environmental statute passed not long after the Clean Air Act: the Clean Water Act of 1972.[92] Like the Clean Air Act, the Clean Water Act imposed stringent federal standards on new industrial sources of pollution.[93] But unlike the Clean Air Act, it also imposed federal standards on existing sources.[94] Though less stringent than those imposed on new sources, these standards have been enormously successful, eliminating the vast majority of water pollution from industrial facilities.[95]

This is not to say, of course, that the framers of the Clean Water Act didn't make any undesirable compromises in the interest of political expediency. The statute's relatively lax treatment of so-called nonpoint sources of pollution—for example, fertilizer runoff from agricultural lands—has long been its Achilles heel.[96] Even so, if Congress in 1972 could pass the Clean Water Act without resorting to "bribing" opponents with a grandfathering clause, it's unclear why it wouldn't have been able to do the same for the Clean Air Act in 1970.

WHAT THE TRANSCRIPTS TELL US

We've now explored three reasons that legislators might theoretically have thought it wise to exempt existing sources from the Clean Air Act's performance standards: fairness, political pragmatism, and efficiency. We've also presented arguments against each. But whatever the merits of these potential justifications, did Congress actually have any of them in mind when it passed the Act? If not, why did legislators choose to grandfather?

Divining legislative intent is a notoriously tricky business.[97] Congress, after all, has hundreds of members, and different lawmakers can and frequently do have very different perspectives on the meaning of—or rationale behind—particular provisions in a bill.[98] Furthermore, the popularity of a given perspective is not always clear from the written record. The mere fact that a representative made an argument on the House floor, for example, doesn't convey whether his or her colleagues were persuaded by it. Nevertheless, congressional committee reports and hearing transcripts are often our best evidence of lawmakers' reasons for taking a particular course of action. Indeed, a 2013 survey of congressional staffs found that legislative history was "emphatically viewed" by almost all staffers, of both parties, as "the *most important* . . . interpretive tool" apart from the statutory text itself.[99]

In the case of the Clean Air Act's grandfathering, the relevant legislative history begins almost four years before the statute was passed. On January 30, 1967, President Lyndon Johnson proposed a bill called the Air Quality Act, which included a provision empowering the Secretary of Health, Education, and Welfare to establish national emission standards for major industrial sources of pollution that could "with reasonable effort and expenditures, be prevented or substantially reduced."[100] The provision made no distinction between new and existing sources.

In the months following the release of Johnson's proposal, Senator Muskie's Subcommittee on Air and Water Pollution held twenty-three days of hearings at which industry representatives consistently voiced vehement opposition to nationally uniform emission standards.[101] Utilities and manufacturers insisted that any emission standard imposed on an industrial source of pollution should be no more stringent than necessary to guarantee a safe concentration of total pollution in the ambient air. And because each community's preexisting air quality was different (due to "topographical, meteorological, and geographical particulars" as well as varying "degree[s] of urbanization and industrialization"), each would require different levels of emission control to achieve adequately clean air.[102] In other words, a city with a high number of industrial sources would likely require more stringent controls than a rural county with only a handful of such sources. Similarly, a region suffering from frequent temperature inversions that prevented the dispersion of pollution into the upper atmosphere would likely need more stringent emission standards than a region for which inversions were not a problem. As a result of all this variation, it was more sensible for emission standards to be set at the local, state, or regional level. The alternative—national emission standards set "without regard for a predetermined air quality objective"—would, industry claimed, be "illogical and wasteful," "arbitrary," and "inherently improper."[103]

Proponents of national emission standards, on the other hand, argued that geographically varied standards were unworkable. States with dirty air were unwilling to impose adequately tough standards due to fear that "strong regulations may cause them economic losses by making the operating costs of local industries higher than the costs of competitive industries in communities that do not have such strong regulations."[104] Only national standards could "prevent areas of low pollution concentration from gaining an unfair economic advantage."[105] Advocates for national standards also argued that the standards would help address interstate pollution by "prevent[ing] the possibility of emissions from low concentration areas contributing to the problems in areas of high pollution concentration."[106]

As the above excerpts suggest, early testimony and discussion focused on the all-or-nothing question of whether *any* sort of national emission standards were appropriate. On May 2, 1967, however, Senator Joseph Clark of Pennsylvania introduced a new idea, urging Muskie to adopt national emission standards but also suggesting that he consider exempting at least some existing sources from complying with them.

> SENATOR CLARK: Now, another approach, which in a sense is a bit pusillanimous but may be necessary, is to invoke what we call the grandfather clause, by which you permit certain installations to continue their present practices for a limited period of time but put the squeeze on them year after year by gradually increasing standards on a basis which is not unduly burdensome to them economically. In other words,

I don't think you can be 100-percent pure in this; there are too many vested interests which are not going to let you be. But you have got to get the job done, if not in my lifetime certainly in yours; otherwise, we are not going to leave our children the kind of a community that we really have an obligation to leave them.

SENATOR MUSKIE: With all due respect, I think your lifetime and mine may be largely coincidental.

SENATOR CLARK: This is possible.[107]

With his references to necessity, purity, and "vested interests," Clark here is making precisely the sort of public choice/political expediency pitch for grandfathering that we discussed above.

Muskie didn't acknowledge Clark's suggestion about grandfathering (at least, not on the record), but he seemed to internalize it all the same. Just over a week later, he began to publicly question witnesses about the differing costs of outfitting new and existing sources with pollution controls. Here's a colloquy he had with an executive vice president of Alcoa, the aluminum manufacturer, on May 10, 1967:

SENATOR MUSKIE: You point out, and I think rightly so, and other witnesses have, including the previous witnesses, that it is expensive to control the old established plants.

MR. HARRISON: It is, indeed.

SENATOR MUSKIE: Considering expenses then, should you not build new plants and install equipment as fast as possible whether or not the location at that particular time has an overall pollution problem?

MR. HARRISON: I would say, speaking only for Alcoa, Mr. Chairman, we would do so.

SENATOR MUSKIE: It sounds like a pretty good policy.[108]

A week later, Muskie asked similar questions of scientists from the National Center for Air Pollution Control, a forerunner of the EPA.

> SENATOR MUSKIE: Are there any figures to demonstrate the differential cost between installation of pollution control equipment in new plants as opposed to installation of equipment to accomplish a similar result in an existing plant? Do you have any such analysis dealing with any particular industry?
>
> I stipulate that this question is in the testimony by Alcoa last week in which they are putting in new equipment in all new plants where they are locating, but they have the real problem in existing plants.
>
> DR. LUDWIG: This is generally a recognized problem. . . .
>
> In the first place, you may not have the physical area to put a piece of control equipment, the roof is not designed strong enough to hold this massive piece of equipment that may be needed.
>
> I think the second point is that, if you are considering control equipment in a new plant, it can be engineered in with process changes.
>
> From this point of view you should be able to come up with a more economical solution by designing control as an integral part of the process than by looking at it as a piece of add-on equipment. You are dealing with essentially one process instead of two, and from this point of view you should be able to deal with it more economically.
>
> SENATOR MUSKIE: If the gap between the cost for a new plant and the cost for an old plant is too large, how would national emission standards apply in such a situation? Is it conceivable you would have a national emission standard applying only to new plants in a particular industry . . . ? What do you

envision is the possible policy of that kind of situation? The gap could be very great.

DR. MIDDLETON: You may wish to have different emission standards for new versus existing plants along the lines, policy wise, of changing standards for motor vehicles as improved technology occurs. It seems to me this is a collateral view.

. . .

MR. WILLIAMS: I don't think the gap would be great between old and new plants.

SENATOR MUSKIE: Have you had any orders of magnitude on this, Mr. Williams? It would seem to me when you are dealing with a steel plant, a pulp and paper plant, that the gap could be very great, indeed, but I don't know. I am simply guessing, and it seems to me we ought to have some idea as we contemplate the policy.[109]

Muskie, at this point, appears to be expressly contemplating the possibility of a bifurcated system of emission standards. What's more, he seems interested in grandfathering not for the public choice reasons cited by Clark but out of a concern for efficiency, a worry that forcing existing sources to meet the same standards as new sources will be more costly than it's worth.

Ultimately, Muskie and his colleagues in the 1967 Senate decided to punt on the question of national emission standards. Rather than revise President Johnson's proposed provision to apply only to new sources, they stripped it from the bill entirely. In justifying the decision, the committee report cited concern that national emission standards would eliminate some "essential," non-technological pollution control options, such as the relocation of a pollution source from a dense urban environment with poor air quality to a cleaner rural area where it could emit at the same rate without posing the same risk to human health.[110] Under a national emission standard, the source would have to achieve the same level of emission reduction regardless of its location—effectively ruling out relocation as a cost-effective control option. The committee report also noted that "[w]ise use of capital resources dictates that the first priority for the pollution control dollar is in areas where the problem is most critical" and that a system of "[n]ational emission standards would give equal priority to critical areas and areas where no problem presently exists."[111]

Even so, Congress didn't dismiss the idea of national emission standards entirely. Its revised version of the Air Quality Act, which President Johnson signed into law on November 21, 1967, instructed the Department of Health, Education, and Welfare to conduct a two-year study "of the concept [of national emission standards] and the full range of its implications."[112] The authorization for the study made no mention of distinguishing between new and existing sources. In the meantime, the federal role in controlling pollution from stationary sources would be limited to the development of "criteria of air quality necessary to protect public health and welfare," which were to reflect the latest scientific knowledge on the health and welfare effects of individual pollutants.[113] Based on these vaguely defined "criteria," each state was expected to determine its own ambient air quality standards and to establish a corresponding set of emission standards that would enable it to achieve those ambient goals.[114] But the Act provided no penalties for states that failed to meet these requirements.[115]

By the time the Department of Health, Education, and Welfare got around to releasing its "National Emission Standards Study" in April 1970, the Air Quality Act was widely viewed as a failure.[116] In two and a half years, only twenty-one state implementation plans had been submitted, and not one had received federal approval.[117] Indeed, the Department's study was released two months *after* President Nixon unveiled his proposed Clean Air Act of 1970 as a replacement for the 1967 Act. Unsurprisingly, the study endorsed a regulatory framework identical to that contained in Nixon's bill.[118]

Instead of letting each state pick its own ambient standards based on scientific guidance from the federal government, the Nixon Administration's proposal provided for the establishment of NAAQS, a single set of federally mandated ambient standards that would apply nationwide.[119] Furthermore, while each state would still be charged with developing a unique implementation plan for meeting the NAAQS, the federal government would now also directly regulate some stationary source categories through national emission standards. These included "major new sources" and all sources—existing *and* new—of "pollutants which are or may be extremely hazardous to public health."[120]

In justifying the decision to grandfather existing sources of nonhazardous pollutants, the Department of Health, Education, and Welfare's study did not cite concerns regarding the fairness of such regulation or the higher cost of retrofitting existing sources with pollution controls. Instead, it suggested that applying emission standards to all stationary sources "probably would result in a slowdown of State and local air pollution control activities," because state and local agencies would want to know what the federal standards required before adopting and enforcing any regulations of their own.[121] Meanwhile, "[s]elective application of national emission standards" only to major new sources and sources of extremely hazardous pollutants, the study concluded, "probably would not have such an effect."[122] The Department offered no explanation of why it believed this to be true.

Despite the Department's somewhat cryptic reasoning, over the next several months of House and Senate hearings, almost no one appears to have raised any serious objection to the exemption of existing sources of NAAQS pollutants from direct federal regulation. Industry representatives, for the most part, continued to argue against national emission standards of any kind—including for new sources—on the grounds that some regions could achieve or maintain a safe level of ambient pollution with less stringent emission standards than others.[123] Labor groups, meanwhile, praised the new-source standards as defense against the “the industrial blackmail to which workers are subjected by industries which threaten to leave or do leave states or areas with tough anti-pollution programs to those which do not.”[124] Environmental Action, one of the most prominent environmental organizations of the time, cautioned Congress not to dilute Nixon’s provisions regarding performance standards, which it vaguely claimed were “of dubious utility already,” but it did not argue that Congress should expand those provisions to cover more existing sources.[125]

The only speaker who did publicly argue in favor of expanding emission standards to encompass a broader set of stationary sources was Lee Iacocca, executive vice president of Ford Motor Co. Iacocca testified that “[c]lean air cannot be achieved if new plants are controlled while old plants are not.”[126] This comment, however, was buried in the middle of a vigorous attack on the Act’s provisions regarding motor vehicles, so it’s unsurprising that Congress didn’t pay much attention to it.

UNEXPECTED DEALS, UNEXPECTED DEVILS

What, if anything, can this somewhat meandering legislative history tell us about Congress’s reasons for grandfathering existing sources under the Clean Air Act? We can see that, while Congress’s decision to grandfather was a product of political compromise, it was not the sort of compromise described in the public-choice literature on grandfathering. The traditional public-choice story of grandfathering goes something like this: policymakers want to regulate all sources; industry objects; policymakers buy off some of the industry opposition by exempting existing sources from regulation. The history of the Clean Air Act reveals a much more complex series of negotiations.

The first round took place in 1967. One set of federal policymakers (the executive branch—led by President Johnson) wanted to directly regulate emissions from all major stationary sources, both new and existing, and industry strenuously objected. In response, another set of policymakers (the legislative branch—led, for this purpose, by Senator Muskie) appeared to flirt with the idea of limiting such direct regulation to new sources, due to concerns that regulating existing sources was politically impractical (as suggested by Senator Clark, who argued that legislative purity was unattainable and that some vested interests would need to be accommodated in order to pass a bill) and inefficient (as implied by Muskie, who focused on the higher cost of installing pollution control technologies on existing sources). In the end, though, Congress in 1967 decided to forgo federal emission standards altogether and instead embraced a system in which the federal government would loosely regulate the quality of the ambient air, and states would be left to control emissions from their individual sources as necessary to achieve the federal goals.

Why did Muskie and his colleagues choose this path? Some, most notably Ralph Nader, suggested that they were simply capitulating to industry's demands. The Nader Study Group's 1970 report noted that Muskie's final 1967 bill had borne a "striking resemblance . . . to the impressive body of industrial public relations literature that preceded it."[127] The report didn't accuse Muskie of out-and-out corruption, but speculated that as "an extremely astute politician who by temperament avoids conflict and unfavorable odds, [he] was influenced by a desire to get the bill through Congress with a minimum of acrimony" and therefore "took the path of least resistance," even though he knew it would result in a less effective bill.[128]

Muskie, of course, staunchly denied Nader's claims and argued that his subcommittee rejected emission standards "not for the dark, secret, conspiratorial reasons suggested by the Nader report," but because of a genuine concern that federal emission standards would not prove as effective as ambient standards in protecting public health.[129] The truth likely lies somewhere in between Nader's and Muskie's accounts. In a recent interview, Muskie's longtime chief of staff, Leon Billings, conceded that Muskie believed "health-based air quality standards were a more politically viable basis for making demands [on industry]."[130] Thus, it seems fair to say that Muskie's preference for a pollution-control scheme driven by health-based ambient standards rather than technology-based emission standards was at least partially a response to industry's clearly expressed opposition to the latter type of standards. But Billings also confirmed that the senator genuinely "did not believe that national emission standards would result in healthy air."[131]

And Muskie wasn't the only nonindustry figure who felt this way. At one of the 1967 hearings, a representative of the American Medical Association (AMA) agreed that a system of national emission standards for certain industries "would not accomplish its intended purpose" of protecting public health, because, unlike more localized standards, national standards could not be calibrated "according to the overall air pollution problems of the area in which the facility [was] located."[132] Whereas industry's fear was that national emission standards would lead to unnecessary *over*control of new sources in some areas, Muskie and the AMA seemed concerned that relying purely on national emission standards could result in *under*regulation of pollution in some of the dirtiest areas in the nation. What if installing state-of-the-art technology at the end of every industrial smokestack (and every vehicle tailpipe) still wasn't sufficient to produce healthy air in a particular city? Under a system of ambient standards, the local government would be forced to consider adopting more creative pollution-reduction strategies, such as land-use changes, investments in mass transit, fuel rationing, or the re-siting of some stationary sources. National emission standards, on the other hand, wouldn't encourage any of these changes.

Moving on to 1970, we encounter another unexpected political compromise. A new federal policymaker (the Nixon Administration) proposed an updated, more stringent system of ambient regulation that built on the structure of the 1967 Act, but paired this ambient framework with direct federal regulation (in the form of emission standards) for new stationary sources. And yet Muskie and his colleagues, who had previously rejected emission standards of any kind, did not object. Why not? Certainly they didn't stay silent to please industry. Industrial polluters, after all, would have preferred that emission standards be eliminated from the bill entirely, just as they had been in 1967. Instead, according to Billings, the New Source Performance Standards were seen almost entirely as a favor to labor unions.[133] Groups like the United Steelworkers of America and the AFL-CIO wanted assurance that efforts by Northern states to meet the NAAQS would not simply cause manufacturers to, in the words of the Steelworkers, "run away" to less polluted—and nonunionized—areas in the South where facilities could operate without installing any controls.[134] By imposing a uniform standard on all newly constructed sources, Congress ensured that a company could reap no regulatory benefit from closing down a facility in a highly polluted state and reopening in a cleaner one. In other words, if Congress was "paying off" opposition to the Clean Air Act by engaging in grandfathering, the intended beneficiary was labor, not capital.

MISSING THE MARK

In the *Poetics*, Aristotle's treatise on Greek tragedy, the famed philosopher argues that in a well-constructed tragedy, the hero's misfortune should be caused "not by wickedness, but by some *hamartia*."[135] The precise meaning of hamartia has long been a subject of debate among classical scholars. Some nineteenth- and early twentieth-century writers translated the term as "tragic flaw," reading Aristotle to require that a tragic hero's troubles stem from some defect in his or her own character—for example, Oedipus's temper, or Othello's pride.[136] But in more recent decades, scholars have rejected the moralizing implications of this interpretation. Pointing out that the most literal translation of hamartia is simply "to miss the mark"—as in archery—they argue that Aristotle meant only that a hero's downfall should result from some "great error," an "erroneous step, taken in ignorance . . . which leads eventually to the tragic catastrophe."[137] By this logic, Oedipus's hamartia is not his temper, but the fact that he doesn't know who his parents are (and thus can't realize that he has killed his father and married his mother).[138]

It is this latter conception of hamartia—a mistake born of ignorance, not moral weakness—that we find in the history of the Clean Air Act. Because whatever Congress's reasons for exempting existing sources, it seems clear that the legislators did not anticipate the negative consequences of their decision. More specifically, they did not appreciate the extent to which grandfathering would unnaturally extend the lives of the nation's oldest, dirtiest power plants. The hearing transcripts and committee reports on the Clean Air Act make no mention of the possibility of delayed plant retirement, and Thomas Jorling, who was Minority Counsel to the Senate Committee on Public Works at the time of the Act's passage, has suggested that "the replacement of existing plants within normal operating lifetimes with newer ones that were subject to [New Source Performance Standards] was implicit" for those working on the bill.[139]

Statements made in connection with later amendments to the Clean Air Act reinforce the idea that Congress assumed that old plants would retire on schedule, notwithstanding their grandfathered status. During a congressional hearing on the 1977 amendments, Senator Howard Baker of Tennessee predicted that most of the nation's 200 coal-fired power plants that were over twenty years of age at that time would be "phased out of operation in the next 5 to 20 years."[140] Similarly, during the Senate debate over the 1990 amendments to the Clean Air Act, Senator George R. Mitchell of Maine argued that when Congress passed the 1970 Act, "it was assumed that electrical utility units had an average lifetime of 30 years."[141]

Thus, while we have characterized grandfathering as the tragic flaw of the Clean Air Act, it doesn't appear to have resulted from any moral failing on the part of the lawmakers who crafted the statute. Instead, Senator Muskie and his colleagues seem not to have anticipated how severely an exemption for existing sources would undermine the goals of their groundbreaking law. On this point, they simply missed the mark.

4

Misadventures in Modification

Imagine a large wooden ship, in service for generations. As its planks decay, they are swapped out for new—but otherwise identical—timbers. Over time, every piece of the ship is replaced in this manner so that eventually not one of its original planks remains. Is it still the same ship? If not, when did it lose its identity? When the first plank was replaced? The last? At some point in between?

This ancient brainteaser, commonly known as the Ship of Theseus (after the mythical, Minotaur-slaying king of Athens), illustrates the classic philosophical problem of "Identity Through Time."[1] How much can an object change before it simply becomes something else? Philosophers have been debating that question for thousands of years. And so, since 1970, have the federal regulators charged with implementing the Clean Air Act.

As we explained in Chapter 3, the Clean Air Act authorized the EPA administrator to create performance standards only for "new" stationary sources of pollution.[2] But there was a twist: the statute defined a "new source" as "any stationary source, the construction *or modification* of which is commenced after the publication of [an applicable New Source Performance Standard]."[3] In other words, the Act included a mechanism—"modification"—by which a source's identity might change from "existing" to "new."

In theory, treating modified sources as "new" could have served as a de facto limit on the duration of grandfathering, preventing old plants from permanently avoiding compliance with federal performance standards. After all, no plant could keep running forever without requiring at least some upgrades.

But what sort of upgrades should qualify as a "modification" within the meaning of the Clean Air Act? For Congress and the EPA, answering this question proved every bit as difficult as determining whether it was the third, thirteenth, or thirtieth replacement plank that transformed the Ship of Theseus into a different vessel. As a result, many of the nation's power plants have managed to enjoy seemingly indefinite immunity from New Source Performance Standards, even after undertaking comprehensive renovations.

ALTERED STATES

Why did Congress decide to treat modified sources differently than other existing sources? There was very little discussion of the issue in the 1970 congressional hearings on the Clean Air Act, but we can surmise that legislators deemed it less burdensome for an existing plant to adopt state-of-the-art pollution controls when it was already going to the trouble and expense of other upgrades. This rationale finds support in the following colloquy between Senator Muskie and a representative of the pulp and paper industry during the 1967 hearings on the Air Quality Act:

> SENATOR MUSKIE: There is a difference in performance between the older mills and the newer ones. Now, how much of a problem would it be to require the older mills to meet at least the performance of the newer mills.
>
> DR. GEHM: I am afraid it would be extremely expensive because of the problems I have pointed out in my testimony. First, there is the large capital equipment of lesser efficiency in

the older mills. They have to be replaced entirely since they can't be readily revamped to reach anything like the efficiency of the new mills. . . .

SENATOR MUSKIE: While you are on this subject, you might also give us some idea of the degree to which you might improve performance in line with normal replacement of obsolescence; the equipment does wear out and have to be replaced. What are the prospects for upgrading its performance in the course of the process, and how much time would be involved?

DR. GEHM: That is a much easier question to answer because it is being done throughout the industry, old plants being refurbished and being rebuilt. Economically, it is sensible to employ the high efficiency equipment in such cases.[4]

Questioning a public relations manager from Bethlehem Steel Company later in the same hearing, Muskie all but expressly endorsed the idea of treating modified sources like new ones:

MR. BRANDT: I don't believe any new steelmaking plants have been built in the last 10 years.

SENATOR MUSKIE: Any modifications of the existing plants? . . . It would seem to me . . . that as you build new plants or replace old ones your policy ought to be building in every bit of technology that is available at any given time if you are really going to gear the future operations of that plant to the future of the area.[5]

Of course, Congress didn't end up adopting emission standards for any type of stationary source in 1967, but there's no reason to believe that Muskie's views on the wisdom of expecting modified sources to control their emissions had changed by 1970.

The notion that older facilities should sacrifice the benefits of grandfathering as a consequence of modification is hardly unique to the Clean Air Act. On the contrary, it is a relatively common feature in federal, state, and local laws. Under the Americans with Disabilities Act of 1990, for example, new public buildings are required to meet certain design standards to ensure their accessibility to those with disabilities.[6] Existing facilities are largely exempt from these requirements unless they undergo "alteration," in which case the altered portion must be made accessible to the "maximum extent feasible."[7] Similarly, the 2014 New York City Building Codes generally apply only to new construction, but expansion of an existing structure can sometimes result in the entire building being "made to comply with the [2014 Codes] as if it were a new building."[8]

Not just *any* modification will yield a new compliance obligation. Statutes typically require that the change in question be of a specific character or exceed a particular magnitude before grandfathering is sacrificed. An alteration renders a facility subject to accessibility obligations under the Americans with Disabilities Act only if it affects the "usability" of that facility.[9] An older building in New York City has to meet current construction codes only if it undertakes an expansion that more than doubles its original size.[10] These thresholds are lawmakers' answer to the "Identity Through Time" problem. They mark the boundary between mere change and reinvention.

The Clean Air Act, for its part, defines a "modification" as "any physical change in, or change in the method of operation of, a stationary source which increases the amount of any air pollutant emitted by such source or which results in the emission of any air pollutant not previously emitted."[11] In other words, New Source Performance Standards are triggered only by (1) physical or operational changes that (2) cause an increase in emissions.

At first glance, this seems like straightforward guidance. But upon further reflection, numerous questions arise. Consider a plant with a leaky pipe. If an owner patches the leak, has the plant truly undergone a "physical change"? Or has it merely been repaired and restored to its original state?

Now say that leaky pipe is a chronic problem. What if, after repeated patch attempts, the plant owner decides to swap out the entire pipe for a newer but otherwise identical replacement. Is *that* a physical change? Does it make a difference if the owner replaces more than one pipe? All of the pipes? Does it make a difference if the replacements happen all at once as opposed to one at a time? Over the course of a week as opposed to a decade?

Even if replacing the single leaky pipe does constitute a physical change under the Clean Air Act, will it result in increased emissions? Unless the leak somehow compromised the operating capacity of the plant, replacing the pipe won't affect the volume of pollution the plant emits *per hour*. Eliminating the need to periodically shut down the plant and patch the leak could, however, increase *its annual* emissions.

But not necessarily! It all depends on how we establish the "baseline"—that is, pre-change—level of emissions for the plant. If our baseline is the plant's emissions volume in the twelve months just prior to the replacement, we'll see an increase. If we instead look to the plant's emissions in its first year of operation, before the pipe degraded, we won't.

What is a change, and what is an increase? The EPA has spent forty-five years grappling with these questions. And more often than not, its interpretive choices—frequently made at the urging of trade associations—have served either to limit the number of activities that qualify as physical or operational changes or to reduce the likelihood that any activity that does qualify as a change will be found to increase a source's emissions.

SPARED CHANGES

In its first set of New Source Performance Standards, finalized in December 1971, the EPA took a narrow view of physical and operational change, declaring that four types of activities would not qualify as modifications under the Clean Air Act, regardless of their impact on a source's emissions.[12] First, "routine maintenance, repair, and replacement" would not be considered a physical change.[13] Additionally, none of the following would count as a "change in the method of operation": an increase in production rate, an increase in hours of operation, or the use of an alternative fuel or raw material.[14]

The EPA would later defend its exemptions as rooted in "common sense," noting that the statutory definition, standing alone, would "encompass the most mundane activities at an industrial facility (even the repair or replacement of a single leaky pipe, or a change in the way that pipe is utilized)."[15] In the agency's view, "Congress obviously did not intend to make every activity at a source subject to new source requirements."[16]

Fair enough, but Congress clearly intended for *some* activities to render sources subject to New Source Performance Standards, and the EPA provided no instructions on how to differentiate "routine" activities from exceptional ones. It drew no bright line between replacing one plant component and replacing all of them. Furthermore, while the regulations stated that the EPA would, upon a plant owner's request, "make a determination of whether actions taken or intended to be taken by such owner or operator constitute . . . modification," the owners were not *required* to consult with the agency before determining that a particular change qualified as routine.[17] Sources were, essentially, operating on the honor system. And with hundreds of millions of dollars in potential regulatory costs on the line, they had every incentive to behave dishonorably.

WHAT GOES UP . . . MIGHT NOT COUNT

In 1975, the EPA announced a set of additional "clarifications" to the regulatory definition of modification that further insulated existing sources from the threat of New Source Performance Standards.[18] Whereas the agency's initial set of exemptions had served to limit the universe of activities that qualified as physical or operational changes, the new rules aimed to reduce the likelihood that a given change would be found to increase a source's emissions. First, the agency distinguished between a "source" and a "facility," explaining that "'sources' are entire plants, while 'facilities' are identifiable pieces of process equipment or individual components which when taken together would comprise a source."[19] A single power plant (source), for instance, could contain several coal-fired, steam-generating boilers (facilities). The EPA's New Source Performance Standards applied to individual facilities, not entire sources, so if a utility decided to install an additional boiler at one of its existing plants, only that new boiler—the "affected facility"—would need to satisfy the agency's performance standards.[20] The old boilers—"existing facilities," in EPA parlance—could continue to emit at unregulated levels.

Building upon this source/facility distinction, the EPA adopted a "bubble concept," whereby a physical or operational change at a single facility would not be deemed a modification unless the emissions of the source as a whole (i.e., the aggregate emissions of *all* facilities at the source) increased as a result of the change.[21] In other words, even if a utility modified an individual boiler in a way that increased its emissions, the altered boiler would not have to meet New Source Performance Standards so long as the utility achieved offsetting reductions elsewhere at the plant—for example, by shutting down some other boiler.

Third, and perhaps most important, the EPA clarified that, when determining whether emissions had increased as a result of a physical or operational change, the agency would look to the source's *hourly* emission rate of a given pollutant, as opposed to its *annual* emissions of that pollutant.[22] This interpretation seriously undermined the ability of the modification rules to limit grandfathering, because a plant can undertake substantial upgrades that greatly extend its useful life without causing any increase in its *hourly* emissions. As a plant's equipment ages, its "availability"—the number of days it's able to operate each year—tends to decrease because it needs to go offline more often for both scheduled and emergency maintenance. Replacing or refurbishing major components allows a plant's owner to restore its availability and extend its useful life, but such activities, however extensive or costly, are far more likely to increase a plant's annual emissions than its hourly emissions.

The EPA tried to get at these "life extension" projects another way—by announcing that "reconstructing" (as opposed to merely modifying) a facility could trigger the application of New Source Performance Standards, even if the reconstruction didn't lead to an increase in the source's emission rate.[23] But a project qualified as a reconstruction under the EPA's rule only if it was at least half as costly as building a new facility from scratch,[24] and there was nothing to stop a plant owner from avoiding that 50 percent threshold by simply spreading the components of a reconstruction effort across multiple, cheaper phases. Furthermore, even if a single project did exceed the 50 percent threshold, New Source Performance Standards would apply only if EPA concluded that it was "technologically and economically feasible" for the facility to satisfy them.[25]

Not all of the 1975 "clarifications" survived judicial review. In *ASARCO, Inc. v. EPA*, the U.S. Court of Appeals for the District of Columbia Circuit struck down the "bubble concept" as inconsistent with the purpose of the Clean Air Act because its application "postpone[d] the time when the best technology must be employed" by existing sources (in other words, because it extended grandfathering beyond the limits envisioned by Congress).[26] In explaining its decision, the court emphasized that the bubble concept had not been the EPA's idea. Instead, the copper smelting industry had been pushing the agency to adopt the policy since 1972. Initially, the EPA had resisted, citing concerns that the bubble concept would "make emission standards extremely difficult to enforce" and "reward those operators who were presently using the fewest controls."[27] But after three years of steady pressure from the smelting industry and its allies in the Department of Commerce, the agency capitulated.[28] This would not, unfortunately, be the last time the EPA catered its modification rules to suit industry demands.

NEW LAYERS OF COMPLEXITY

In 1977, with large swaths of the nation still out of compliance with the NAAQS, Congress passed a set of extensive amendments to the Clean Air Act.[29] In addition to giving states more time to meet ambient standards, the amendments established a "New Source Review" program whereby all "major" new or modified sources—those that emitted either more than 100 or more than 250 tons per year of any pollutant, depending on the source type and location—were required to obtain preconstruction permits from the EPA or a qualified state agency.[30] Previously, states had had the option of incorporating permit programs into their state implementation plans, but they had not been required to do so.[31]

The requirements of the preconstruction permit depended on the source's location. In areas with better ambient air quality than the NAAQS, where the goal of the review process was to "prevent significant deterioration" of local air quality, major new or modified sources had to emit at a level commensurate with the "best available control technology."[32] In "nonattainment" areas—those with worse air quality than the NAAQS—any major new or modified source had to match the performance of the cleanest source of its type in the nation, a standard known as the "lowest achievable emission rate."[33] New or modified sources in nonattainment areas also had to obtain offsets from nearby existing sources to ensure that, despite their emissions, the area as a whole could continue to make "reasonable further progress" toward the NAAQS.[34] Whereas the EPA's New Source Performance Standards applied uniformly to all new or modified sources in a given category, both the "best available control technology" and "lowest achievable emission rate" standards were to be determined on a case-by-case basis.[35]

Congress relied on the exact same statutory definition of "modification" in the 1977 amendments that it had in the 1970 Act—a physical or operational change that increases a source's emissions.[36] The EPA was less consistent. Although it retained essentially the same parameters for determining whether a physical or operational change had occurred—such as exemptions for routine maintenance or an increase in operating hours unaccompanied by any physical changes[37]—it took a very different approach to the emissions-increase prong of the modification test. Whereas New Source Performance Standards applied whenever a change increased a source's hourly emissions by any amount, the EPA announced that New Source Review would apply only to "major" modifications, which the agency defined as those that increased a source's *annual* emissions by at least 100 or 250 tons per year.[38] Additionally, in areas that had achieved the NAAQS (but not in nonattainment areas), the EPA would take into account reductions achieved elsewhere at the source when determining whether an emissions increase had occurred.[39] In other words, the agency sought in its New Source

Review regulations to revive essentially the same "bubble concept" that the D.C. Circuit had rejected only months earlier in the context of New Source Performance Standards. And once again, the "bubbling" had not been the EPA's idea: its original New Source Review proposals had not allowed for intrasource offsets, and it admitted that they had been added to the final regulations to "accommodate industry's expressed concerns."[40]

Improbably, when environmental groups challenged the New Source Review regulations, the D.C. Circuit upheld the EPA's new version of the bubble concept, distinguishing its earlier *ASARCO* decision on a number of grounds and holding that the EPA could permissibly consider offsetting reductions at a source so long as they were "substantially contemporaneous" with the increase in question.[41] The court did, however, reject the EPA's attempt to limit New Source Review to modifications that increased emissions by more than 100 or 250 tons per year, noting that the statutory definition of modification was "nowhere limited to physical changes exceeding a certain magnitude."[42] By imposing such a threshold, the court reasoned, the EPA was giving some sources "a perpetual immunity" from the requirements of New Source Review and thus contravening Congress's intent to make the grandfathering of old sources only temporary.[43] If a change caused a net emissions increase, the EPA could exempt it from New Source Review only "on grounds of de minimis or administrative necessity."[44]

The EPA subsequently issued revised rules, which retained the phrase "major modification" but eliminated the blanket 100- and 250-ton thresholds and instead defined a major modification as any physical or operational change that would result in a "*significant* net emissions increase."[45] The agency then provided a variety of thresholds for "significance" that varied by pollutant and the NAAQS attainment status of the area in which the source was located.[46]

Below these thresholds, emissions increases would be considered de minimis and thus exempt from New Source Review.

In areas that had already met the NAAQS, the agency would take into account "contemporaneous" offsets elsewhere at the source when determining whether emissions had increased, with "contemporaneous" generously defined as anytime within five years of the change.[47] (The Reagan Administration later expanded the bubble concept to apply in nonattainment areas as well, a move that the Supreme Court upheld in the famous case of *Chevron U.S.A. Inc. v. Natural Resources Defense Council, Inc.*[48])

Adding to the complexity of this regulatory regime was the fact that New Source Review acted as a supplement to—not a replacement for—New Source Performance Standards. Thus, a source undertaking a physical or operational change might trigger one, both, or neither set of standards depending on the source's size, its category, the nature of the change being made, and, finally, how the change affected the source's emissions. If *hourly* emissions increased by *any* margin, New Source Performance Standards would apply. Meanwhile, if *net annual* emissions increased by a *significant* margin, New Source Review requirements would apply.

OLD PLANTS, NEW TRICKS

By the mid-1980s, it was public knowledge that the power sector was undertaking heroic efforts to extend the life of grandfathered generators. A 1985 report from the Congressional Research Service noted that, while power plants had traditionally been thought to have a useful life of thirty years,

> over the last five years, it has become clear that the actual lifespan of powerplants is not set, but relatively elastic. With

> new powerplants costing over $1000 a kilowatt to construct, utilities have powerful incentives to avoid construction and to rehabilitate older facilities instead. . . . With such rehabilitation estimated at about $500 a kilowatt . . . operating existing facilities for upwards of 60 years seems to be a developing trend.[49]

Despite the high costs of these life-extending overhauls, utilities were determined to shoehorn them into the routine maintenance exception to both New Source Performance Standards and New Source Review. The Edison Electric Institute, a trade association representing investor-owned utilities in the United States, advised its members to classify renovations as "upgraded maintenance programs" and to "downplay the life extension aspects . . . by referring to them as plant restoration projects."[50] It further suggested that utilities work through state regulators whenever possible and avoid going to the EPA with questions "because you won't like the answer."[51]

Edison Electric's "what the EPA doesn't know can't hurt us" approach was enabled by a Reagan Administration that had little interest in asking questions of regulated entities.[52] But in 1988, President Reagan's final year in office, the EPA was at last confronted with a violation too brazen to ignore.

The source in question was the Wisconsin Electric Power Company's (WEPCO) Port Washington plant in Milwaukee. Port Washington's five coal-fired units, each with a designed capacity of 80 megawatts, had come online between 1935 and 1950.[53] By 1984, all five units had degraded to such a degree that they posed "significant safety concerns."[54] As a result of the damage, the maximum generating capacity of four units had markedly declined, and the fifth had to be shut down altogether because the "possibility of catastrophic failure . . . was so great."[55]

WEPCO concluded that extensive renovations were necessary to keep the plant operational.[56] The changes it planned would allow the units, which were scheduled for retirement between 1992 and 1999, to operate at their designed capacity through 2010.[57]

As required by state law, the utility applied to its rate regulator, the Wisconsin Public Service Commission, for permission to undertake the upgrades.[58] The Commission consulted with the state's Department of Natural Resources to determine whether WEPCO needed to undergo New Source Review before commencing the renovations. The Department requested guidance from the regional EPA office, which referred the matter to EPA headquarters.[59]

Employing a five-factor test that weighed the "nature, extent, purpose, frequency, and cost" of the proposed work, the EPA concluded that the Port Washington renovations did not qualify for the routine maintenance exemption and instead constituted a physical change that would increase both hourly and annual emissions from the five units.[60]

In support of its determination, the EPA noted, among other things:

(1) the significance of the components being replaced;
(2) the time necessary to perform the work (4 years, with successive nine-month outages at each unit);
(3) the project's unprecedented nature (WEPCO had never before replaced these types of components at *any* of its coal-fired electric generating facilities); and, finally,
(4) its high cost (which, at $87.5 million, was about 15 percent of the cost of a brand new 400 megawatt plant).[61]

More generally, the agency found that:

> the work proposed at Port Washington is far from being a regular, customary, or standard undertaking for the purpose

> of maintaining the plant in its present condition. Rather, this is a highly unusual, if not unprecedented, and costly project. Its purpose is to completely rehabilitate aging power generating units whose capacity has significantly deteriorated over a period of years, thereby restoring their original capacity and substantially extending the period of their utilization as an alternative to retiring them as they approach the end of their useful physical and economic life.[62]

WEPCO appealed the EPA's decision to the U.S. Court of Appeals for the Seventh Circuit, arguing that its life-extension project did not fall within the statutory definition of modification because swapping out one piece of equipment with an essentially identical (if newer) replacement was not the sort of "basic or fundamental" alteration that Congress had in mind when it referred to a "physical change."[63] And even if the project did satisfy the statutory definition of modification, WEPCO maintained that it should nevertheless qualify for EPA's regulatory exemption for "routine maintenance."[64]

The court disagreed on both fronts. With respect to the statutory argument, it noted that the Clean Air Act quite clearly referred to "any" physical change as being sufficient to trigger the application of New Source Performance Standards.[65] Adopting WEPCO's cramped view of the word "change" would "open vistas of indefinite immunity" for existing plants and "might upset the economic-environmental balance [of the Clean Air Act] in unintended ways."[66] The court further held that the EPA had not abused its discretion in determining that WEPCO's project was far from routine.[67]

But while the Seventh Circuit agreed with the EPA's assessment that WEPCO's plan amounted to a physical change within the meaning of the Clean Air Act, it rejected some of the agency's assumptions regarding the effects of that change on the plant's emissions. First, the EPA had concluded that, as a result of the renovations, two of the Port Washington units would see their *hourly* emission rates increase and would thus be subject to New Source Performance Standards.[68] The Seventh Circuit took no issue with this finding.[69] The EPA had also concluded, however, that the renovations would increase the *annual* emissions of all five of the units by a significant margin and that, as a result, all five units would be subject to New Source Review and need to adopt the "best available control technology."[70] Here, the court disagreed.

To estimate the annual emissions increases, the EPA had compared the average of Port Washington's actual emissions in the two years prior to the renovation work to the plant's *potential* emissions in the year following the work. To calculate these potential emissions, the EPA assumed "round-the-clock operations (24 hours per day, 365 days per year), because WEPCO *could potentially* operate its facility continuously, despite the fact that WEPCO ha[d] never done so in the past."[71] The court found the agency lacked discretion "wholly to disregard past operating conditions at the plant" and needed to come up with a more realistic method for projecting future increases in annual emissions.[72] The EPA's finding that the renovations triggered New Source Review (as distinct from the application of New Source Performance Standards) was thus set aside.[73]

A FISHY FIX

Even though it managed to force two of the Port Washington units to comply with New Source Performance Standards, the EPA's loss on the question of whether the project would increase annual emissions was significant. WEPCO had allowed Port Washington's equipment to deteriorate to the point where it was both (1) capable of operating fewer days each year *and* (2) capable of burning less coal each hour. As a result, the challenged upgrades increased both annual and hourly emissions because the plant could now operate more days out of the year *and* at a higher capacity. But that was an unusual case: often, life-extension efforts enabled generating units to operate more frequently but did not affect their hourly capacity.[74] Thus, if EPA hoped to curb grandfathering, it had to find a new method of calculating annual emissions increases that would pass muster in court.

Utilities, on the other hand, wanted a method that would allow them to continue pursuing life-extension projects without triggering any new emission control obligations. Upon learning that the EPA had begun planning a revision of its New Source Review rules in response to the *WEPCO* decision, the head of Edison Electric wrote to a friend at the Department of Energy (DOE) requesting help in securing a "good WEPCO fix" and provided a wish list of suggested tweaks to the EPA's existing rules.[75] Two days later, an acting assistant secretary of the DOE sent a letter to the EPA insisting that it issue a "good and comprehensive WEPCO fix."[76] Complaining that the agency's current proposal was "not responsive to the needs of the electric utility industry," the DOE attached a draft rule of its own based on Edison Electric's suggestions.[77]

In 1992, the EPA finalized a new rule that amended the New Source Review regulations for power plants in a manner consistent with Edison Electric's suggestions.[78] Congressman Henry Waxman of California described the so-called "WEPCO Rule" as having the "fingerprints of . . . the Edison Electric Institute" all over it.[79] Most notably, the rule replaced the "actual-to-potential" emissions test that the EPA had unsuccessfully deployed in the *WEPCO* case with an "actual-to-future-actual" emissions test.[80] Whereas actual (pre-change) emissions had previously been determined by calculating average annual emissions during the two years immediately prior to a change (unless the source could demonstrate that those years were not representative of "normal operation"), a utility could now choose the average during any two consecutive years within the previous five.[81] Of course, allowing a plant to cherry-pick its highest-emitting years from the past half-decade as its baseline decreased the likelihood that a life-extension project would be found to cause a significant increase in emissions.

The new rule also gave utilities a great deal of flexibility when projecting a plant's "future actual" (post-change) emissions. These emissions could be projected to occur in any two-year period within ten years following the change that the source deemed representative.[82] Furthermore, in making this projection, the source could subtract any increases in utilization attributable to "system-wide demand growth" that "would have occurred and affected the unit's operations even in the absence of the physical or operation change."[83] Even worse, the plant was not bound to conform its future emissions to these projected levels.[84] As a result, utilities had a strong incentive to make overly conservative estimates of their post-change emissions, further reducing the chances that a project would be found to increase emissions and trigger New Source Review.

A NEW SHERIFF IN TOWN

Despite its success in influencing the WEPCO Rule, the utility industry continued to complain about the burdensome complexities and uncertainties of New Source Review.[85] As a result, in the early days of the Clinton Administration, the EPA convened an advisory committee of industry, environmental, and government stakeholders and made a series of unsuccessful attempts to revise and simplify the program.[86] In 1994, for instance, the EPA circulated an informal proposal to define routine maintenance as "minor maintenance or repair of parts or components and the replacement of minor parts or components with identical or functionally equivalent items," but the idea was scuttled by industry opponents that considered it too limiting.[87] The EPA tried a different proposal in 1996, but again the reforms went nowhere.[88] The assistant administrator charged with coordinating the task force would later describe the reform effort as doomed from the start because utilities and other industry participants had "no interest in any sort of workable reforms": "You were not going to reach agreement with some of these folks . . . because what they really wanted was to not have to do it."[89]

With prospective changes dead in the water, the Clinton EPA turned its attention to vigorous retrospective enforcement. Data the agency collected on the electric utility industry indicated that the sector's total fuel consumption and electric output had increased significantly during the 1980s and 1990s even as few new facilities were built and few existing facilities reported undergoing modifications.[90] The EPA responded by rolling out an aggressive and unprecedented investigation, sending more than 100 investigators to more than thirty plants to comb through records and interview employees.[91] Even applying the flexible standards of the WEPCO Rule, there was ample evidence of widespread flouting of the modification rules. The head of the enforcement division considered it "the most significant noncompliance pattern EPA had ever found."[92]

The EPA referred many of the cases to the Department of Justice, and in 1999 and 2000, the Department filed suit against nine power companies that together controlled well over a third of the nation's coal-fired generation capacity.[93] Collectively, the suits alleged that the companies had undertaken major modifications at almost three dozen plants without undergoing New Source Review.[94]

The utilities expressed outrage at the EPA's "frontal assault," which they saw as a "radical and retroactive reinterpretation of the New Source Review program."[95] But the records uncovered by the EPA suggested that power companies had been aware all along that their life-extension plans did not accord with the agency's view of routine maintenance. There was, for instance, the Edison Electric Institute's 1984 recommendation that its members refrain from asking the EPA to weigh in on whether planned renovations qualified as modifications for fear of their "not liking the answer."[96] Additionally, after the EPA made its initial determination that WEPCO's improvements at Port Washington were not eligible for the exemption, the Utility Air Regulatory Group (UARG), a trade association that was formed in 1977 for the express purpose of influencing Clean Air Act regulations, advised its members that to qualify as routine maintenance, a project needed to be "frequent, inexpensive, able to be accomplished at a scheduled outage, [not intended to] extend the normal economic life of the unit, [and] of standard industry design."[97]

Despite the weight of the evidence, only one of the accused utilities, Tampa Electric, settled the claims against it while Clinton was still in office.[98] The company agreed to pay a $3.5 million fine and to spend more than $1 billion on new pollution controls.[99] The other defendants held out in hopes that they would find a more sympathetic negotiating partner in a George W. Bush Administration.[100]

A SAFER HARBOR

The utilities had good reason for optimism. During the 2000 campaign, executives, employees, and political action committees from their industry had given almost $5 million to George W. Bush's campaign, the Republican National Committee, and the inaugural committee.[101] A full $2 million of that came from either the Edison Electric Institute or companies facing New Source Review enforcement actions.[102] Additionally, out of the only 200 or so "Pioneers" who raised more than $100,000 in individual donations for the campaign in 2000, three were senior executives of companies that were either in litigation regarding New Source Review violations or under investigation for violations, and six were lawyers or lobbyists for such companies.[103] Another was Thomas R. Kuhn, the president of the Edison Electric Institute and one of Bush's college classmates.[104] At one point during the campaign, Kuhn sent a memo to energy industry executives encouraging them to bundle their contributions to the campaign under a single tracking number to "ensure that our industry is credited."[105]

Utilities also engaged in more direct forms of lobbying. Between 1999 and 2002, Edison Electric spent over $49 million on advocacy related to New Source Review.[106] Additionally, six of the defendant companies in the Clinton cases formed a new advocacy organization, the Electric Reliability Coordinating Council, whose sole purpose was to lobby for New Source Review changes.[107] Between 2001 and 2011, the group spent over $8 million on these efforts.[108]

The investments paid off. Little over a week after taking office, Bush created the National Energy Policy Development Group, a task force led by Vice President Dick Cheney. Edison Electric and its research arm, the Electric Power Research Institute, had direct contact with the task force twenty-two times.[109] The Southern Company, a defendant in one of the Clinton enforcement actions, met with the task force seven times. Meanwhile, all nonindustry representatives put together had only twenty-nine interactions with the task force.[110] Overall, the task force's consultations with industry representatives outnumbered those with other groups 25 to 1.[111]

Among other things, the task force recommended that the President instruct the EPA to undertake an immediate ninety-day review of how New Source Review affected "investment in new utility and refinery generation capacity, energy efficiency, and environmental protection."[112] It also recommended that the Justice Department conduct a similar review of open enforcement actions to ensure that they were "consistent with the Clean Air Act and its regulations."[113]

Despite concern from environmental groups that President Bush's Attorney General, John Ashcroft, would use the task force report as an excuse to pull the plug on the Clinton enforcement actions entirely, the Justice Department concluded that the Clinton actions were "supported by a reasonable basis in fact and law" and did not represent a departure from the agency's earlier interpretations of the "routine maintenance" exemption.[114] But even if they couldn't drop the Clinton actions, Bush's newly installed leaders at the EPA showed little interest in bringing new ones. In a report responding to the Cheney task force's recommendations, the agency concluded that its current New Source Review regime "impeded . . . projects which would maintain and improve reliability, efficiency and safety of existing energy capacity" and should be reformed to provide greater clarity, particularly with regard to the proper scope of routine maintenance.[115]

Tasked with overhauling the program was Jeffrey Holmstead, a lawyer whom Bush had recently appointed as assistant administrator for the EPA's Office of Air and Radiation.[116] Prior to joining the Administration, Holmstead had worked as a lobbyist for the Alliance for Constructive Air Policy.[117] Thirteen of the Alliance's sixteen members were utilities, and four of those thirteen had been taken to court by the Clinton Administration for undertaking major modifications without permits.[118]

By far, the most dramatic of Holmstead's changes was the institution of the so-called "Safe Harbor Rule." Holmstead wanted to move away from *WEPCO*-style, case-by-case determinations of whether a particular project qualified as routine maintenance in favor of a bright-line rule that would exempt any "like-kind" replacement of components falling below a particular cost threshold. He asked Sylvia Lowrance, the EPA's deputy assistant administrator for enforcement, to suggest a percentage of a facility's value below which any renovation project could fairly be considered routine.[119]

Lowrance, who had supervised the Clinton-era investigations, concluded, based on years of data, that a plant could legitimately spend up to 0.75 percent of its total value on routine repairs.[120] Holmstead instead opted for a safe harbor of 20 percent, almost thirty times the limit suggested by Lowrance.[121] Furthermore, the new rule imposed no limit on the number of times a single facility could invoke the safe harbor, meaning that a plant could, in theory, replace itself entirely in five steps without ever triggering New Source Review.[122]

Virtually every illegal life-extension project challenged by the Clinton Administration would have been perfectly valid under the new rule.[123] The head of the Clean Air Trust, an environmental nonprofit co-founded by Senator Muskie, characterized the exemption as "such a huge loophole that only a moron would trip over it and become subject to [New Source Review] requirements."[124] The Natural Resources Defense Council called it "the most sweeping and aggressive attack that the Clean Air Act ha[d] faced in its thirty-year history."[125]

Environmental groups brought suit, arguing that the Safe Harbor Rule "flatly contradict[ed] the clear language of the Clean Air Act."[126] The D.C. Circuit agreed. In March 2006, a unanimous panel vacated the rule, finding (1) that Congress had unambiguously instructed the EPA to apply New Source Review to "any physical change that increases emissions"; (2) that the like-kind replacement of equipment fit within the common meaning of "physical change"; (3) that the EPA could exclude such changes from regulation only if they were trivial or de minimis; and, finally, (4) that the 20 percent rule would exempt changes that were far from trivial.[127]

Notwithstanding its loss in court, the Bush Administration continued to exercise its enforcement discretion as if the Safe Harbor Rule were still in effect. The Administration filed only one New Source Review enforcement action after 2006, and that case involved violations so egregious that they wouldn't have qualified for the safe harbor.[128]

CONSIDERING THE ALTERNATIVES

As the events chronicled above make clear, the treatment of modified sources as new failed to act as a meaningful check on the duration of grandfathering thanks largely to the political difficulties of implementation. Indeed, the EPA's repeated capitulation to trade associations on questions of statutory interpretation exposes an additional weakness in the "public choice" justification for grandfathering that was discussed in the last chapter. As a reminder, public choice theory suggests that grandfathering can ease the passage of important legislation by buying off some of the opposition. This may be true, but it overlooks the fact that grandfathering is not a one-time legislative gift but an ongoing regulatory benefit. Once grandfathered, lobbyists for old plants don't simply pack their bags and go. Instead, they work to preserve and enhance their new advantage. And if the grandfathering in question has a built-in sunset provision—like a requirement that modified sources be treated like new ones—those lobbyists will work just as hard to undermine the successful implementation of that provision as they would have worked to defeat the original legislation had it not grandfathered them. In other words, lawmakers have not *neutralized* the opposition by engaging in grandfathering; they've just shifted the opposition's harmful influence on policy to a later stage of decision making.[129]

And that is just what happened in the case of the Clean Air Act. Industry paid very little attention to the question of modified sources in the months leading up to the Act's passage: only the American Mining Congress specifically requested that the word "modification" be deleted from the Act's definition of "new source."[130] But once the Act was in effect, industry groups moved aggressively to shield changes at their facilities from EPA scrutiny, beginning with the smelters' aggressive push for the "bubble concept" in 1972.

Of course, political expediency is not the only justification for grandfathering. As we explored in the previous chapter, due to the differential pollution-control costs of new and existing sources, the temporary grandfathering of existing sources can sometimes be the most efficient regulatory choice. Given the political dynamics described above, though, how can a policymaker ensure that grandfathering intended to be temporary doesn't later become permanent?

It seems to us that the best way to set a time limit on grandfathering is to do just that: set a time limit on grandfathering. Rather than relying on a plant's decision to undergo modification as a proxy for the expiration of its economically useful life, Congress could instruct the EPA to determine that expiration date in advance and require the source either to meet any applicable New Source Performance Standards from that point forward or to shut down.

How would the EPA go about determining a facility's expected expiration date? One possibility is case-by-case assessment. For instance, if the unit is owned by a vertically integrated utility, an estimate of its useful life should be on file with the state public service commission, because the depreciation of a utility's assets factors into the rates it's allowed to charge its customers.[131] Alternatively, the EPA could make blanket determinations for all sources within a given category—for example, all coal-fired power plants would be assumed to have a useful life of thirty years.

Congress used a variation on this "expiration date" strategy in the Clean Water Act of 1972. While it didn't fully exempt any "point sources" of water pollution from federal effluent standards, it allowed old plants to increase the stringency of their water pollution controls in stages.[132] Existing sources were given until 1977 to install the "best *practicable* control technology," and until 1983 to upgrade to the "best available technology economically achievable" for their source category (a standard that was almost, but not quite, as stringent as that applicable to new sources).[133] The Clean Water Act also provided that any newly constructed point source that satisfied the Act's new-source standards at the time of its construction would be exempt from satisfying any more stringent existing-source standards for either ten years or until the source was fully depreciated, whichever time period was shorter.[134]

Setting a time limit on grandfathering doesn't eliminate the incentive of grandfathered sources to lobby regulators and legislators to delay the day of reckoning. But at least a decision to extend a compliance deadline is politically transparent. The same cannot be said for the thicket of routine maintenance exceptions, bubble concepts, significance thresholds, and lookback periods associated with the modification provisions of the Clean Air Act. Their dizzying complexity has made it much easier for regulated industries and regulators alike to obscure the real consequences of their policy positions. (HBO's John Oliver recently observed in the context of a different regulatory controversy that "[i]f you want to do something evil, put it inside something boring."[135] Surely the adoption of something called an "actual-to-future-actual emissions increase test" fits that bill.) As a result, while the EPA was only four years late in imposing stringent regulations on existing sources of water pollution, it is still struggling, forty-five years after the passage of the Clean Air Act, to control air pollution from such sources.[136]

5

Bad Neighbors

In Chapter 3, we examined how and why Congress decided to shield existing sources from the bulk of the EPA's performance standards for stationary sources. In Chapter 4, we showed how the duration of this grandfathering was extended by continued controversy over what qualified as a "modification" under the Act. What we haven't yet explored in depth is why grandfathering proved so detrimental to public health.

After all, even if existing sources weren't subject to federal performance standards, they were hardly exempt from *all* regulatory control. The Clean Air Act's most prominent element was a nationally uniform system of ambient air quality standards, the NAAQS, which were to be set at a level adequate to protect the public health.[1] Thus, lawmakers expected that any dangers posed by emissions from a state's existing sources would be addressed as part of the state's plan for achieving the NAAQS.[2]

Why didn't this happen? First, many states simply failed to meet the statutory deadline for complying with ambient standards. Indeed, significant swaths of the country are still out of compliance for certain pollutants.[3] (To be fair, the NAAQS have become more stringent over time because the Clean Air Act instructs the EPA to periodically reassess whether the standards are adequately protecting public health in light of current science.[4]) Second, the NAAQS system didn't adequately account for the interstate nature of air pollution, whereby emissions originating in one state can cause the bulk of their harm in another. As a result, some states managed to achieve the ambient standards while leaving their most-polluting sources completely unregulated—not because the sources didn't endanger public health but because their harms were felt in another jurisdiction. Had these sources been subject to direct federal regulation of their emissions of NAAQS pollutants like sulfur dioxide and nitrogen oxides, intransigent states would have had considerably less opportunity to skimp on pollution control at their neighbors' expense.

TALL ORDERS, TALLER STACKS

As we have emphasized in previous chapters, the Clean Air Act's air quality goals were aggressive, as was its timeline for achieving them. The Act gave the EPA just thirty days to propose "primary" and "secondary" NAAQS for a group of common pollutants that federal agencies had already identified as having adverse effects on public health and welfare.[5] Primary standards had to be sufficiently stringent to protect public health with an "adequate margin of safety."[6] Secondary standards had to be sufficiently stringent to protect public welfare, which encompassed nonhealth effects like damage to crops, wildlife, or property.[7]

By April 1971, the EPA had finalized NAAQS for six types of pollution: sulfur dioxide, nitrogen oxides, particulate matter, photochemical oxidants (now known as ozone), carbon monoxide, and hydrocarbons.[8] States then had just nine months to develop implementation plans that would allow them to achieve the primary standards "as expeditiously as practicable" but "in no case later than three years," and to achieve the secondary standards within a "reasonable time."[9] In May 1972, the EPA approved initial implementation plans for fifty states, four territories, and the District of Columbia.[10] And yet five years later, of the nation's 247 air quality control regions, 188 remained out of compliance with the NAAQS for particulate matter, 34 for sulfur dioxide, 70 for photochemical oxidants and carbon monoxide, and 15 for nitrogen oxides.[11] And those statistics overstate the success of the Act in those early years, because they obscure the fact that most of the areas that were in attainment in 1977 had been so since the day the NAAQS were set. For instance, of the 213 regions that met the sulfur dioxide standards in 1977, 146 had already met them in 1972.[12] Similarly, of the 232 regions in attainment for nitrogen oxides, 200 had already been in attainment in 1972.[13] What's more, nonattainment areas tended to have much larger populations than attainment areas. All but six of the nation's cities with populations greater than 200,000 were out of attainment for at least one pollutant in 1977.[14]

Why hadn't the state plans worked as expected? The answer depended, in part, on the pollutant. Carbon monoxide, for instance, was emitted primarily by mobile sources.[15] On top of the reductions in pollution from new motor vehicles required by federal emission standards, Congress expected states to reduce vehicular pollution through "transportation planning"—that is, by adopting policies to discourage driving.[16] But early experiments with gas rationing and urban parking fees provoked massive public opposition.[17]

More relevant for our purposes are the NAAQS pollutants generated primarily by stationary sources, such as sulfur dioxide—of which coal-fired power plants were by far the largest source.[18] The failure to adequately control SO_2 emissions was largely a result of states eschewing actual pollution controls in favor of so-called "dispersion enhancement techniques."[19] Dispersion enhancement operated not by reducing the total quantities of pollution emitted into the ambient air but by changing the conditions under which those quantities were emitted "in order to enhance their dispersion throughout the atmosphere."[20] The most popular and problematic of these strategies was the construction of taller smokestacks. In 1969, fewer than a dozen stacks in the nation were over 500 feet tall; a decade later, that number had climbed to 180—and all but 8 were attached to power plants.[21] Seventy-five of those 180 tall stacks were more than 700 feet tall; 35 were more than 800 feet tall. By comparison, the Empire State Building, then the world's tallest skyscraper, topped off at 1,250 feet.[22]

The logic behind tall stacks was simple: if NAAQS were concerned with the concentration of pollution at ground level, sources would release their emissions farther from the ground. The higher the stack, the more a state could allow the source to emit without risking violation of ambient standards. Georgia's state implementation plan, for instance, devised a formula under which a source's permissible level of SO_2 emissions was proportional to the cube of the stack height for stacks under 300 feet, and proportional to the square of the stack height for stacks over 300 feet.[23] Thus, a high enough stack would spare a source from having to reduce its emissions at all.[24] What's more, tall stacks were a relative bargain. Switching to low-sulfur coal or installing a scrubber was, by utility estimates, up to thirty times as expensive as simply increasing the height of a facility's stack.[25]

But solutions that sound too good to be true usually are. Although building a tall stack did reduce the concentration of pollution in the immediate vicinity of a source, emissions sent higher into the atmosphere didn't simply disappear. Instead, they ended up in other jurisdictions, carried hundreds of miles by prevailing winds and sometimes chemically transformed along the way into even more damaging forms of pollution.[26] We will explore the consequences of interstate emissions in greater detail later in this chapter. For now, it suffices to say that allowing upwind states to attain the NAAQS by building tall stacks made it considerably more difficult for their downwind neighbors to meet the ambient standards.

Despite protests from environmental advocates that dispersion enhancement was little more than an emissions shell game,[27] the EPA approved at least fifteen state implementation plans in the early 1970s that relied on tall stacks as a compliance strategy.[28] In 1974, however, the U.S. Court of Appeals for the Fifth Circuit ruled that a state could use dispersion enhancement to meet the NAAQS only if it had already exhausted more meaningful emission control techniques (like using scrubbers or switching to cleaner fuels).[29] Two other circuit courts followed suit, and, in 1976, EPA revised its state implementation plan guidelines to allow tall stacks only where the source in question "was already using the 'best available emissions control technology'" or "where use of technology would be economically unreasonable or technologically unsound."[30]

But tall stacks weren't the only reason the NAAQS didn't succeed in controlling emissions from existing sources. Another major problem was the failure of many states to *enforce* their implementation plans. A stringent emission limit didn't do much good if regulators were unwilling or unable to ensure that anyone followed it. Missouri's implementation plan, for instance, imposed tough SO_2 restrictions on existing sources in the St. Louis metropolitan area.[31] But shortly after the EPA administrator approved the plan, the state granted—and later renewed—one-year variances to all three of the city's coal-fired power plants.[32]

In other states, the enforcement problem stemmed from a lack of adequate resources. Illinois lacked the manpower to inspect most of its sources more than once a year.[33] In Massachusetts, a total of eight state employees were responsible for monitoring compliance at 10,000 regulated sources.[34] Without any hope of visiting all the sources, the engineers set inspection priorities based on citizen complaints about odors or simply by standing atop tall buildings in urban areas and looking for dark plumes of smoke, even though much of the NAAQS pollution emitted by stationary sources was invisible, odorless, or both.[35]

Finally, even when a source's noncompliance could be verified, some state regulators found their enforcement efforts stymied by political pressures. A Northeastern attorney general refused to prosecute violators without first checking with local elected officials.[36] A Southern state judge repeatedly delayed or failed to appear for hearings against a local polluter.[37]

The unsurprising result of all these barriers to enforcement was widespread noncompliance, particularly by coal-fired power plants. By 1977, the EPA reported to Congress that "as many as one-third of major coal-fired power plants [were] in violation of [state] emission limits."[38] According to the agency, some utilities appeared "to have spent more in defending their lack of progress or in attempting to have their emissions requirements changed than they had in controlling their sulfur dioxide emissions."[39]

In truth, choosing litigation over compliance was often a perfectly rational decision for a power plant owner. The Clean Air Act provided a very limited set of remedies for violations of state implementation plans or other statutory requirements: either a civil injunction or a criminal penalty in the form of a fine (up to $25,000 per day) or imprisonment (up to one year).[40] States and the EPA rarely pursued criminal charges due to both evidentiary hurdles (prosecutors had to show beyond a reasonable doubt that a polluter knowingly violated a statutory requirement) and political realities (courts were reluctant to find criminal liability in all but the most egregious cases).[41] Meanwhile, if a plant owner lost a civil suit for failing to meet a state standard, the most likely consequence was merely an order to comply with that standard at some future date.[42] Put another way, the "punishment" for missing a deadline was to be assigned a later deadline. Utilities thus had a strong incentive to vigorously defend their inaction—even if they didn't have a legal leg to stand on—as a delay tactic. Even the highest-priced law firm was a bargain compared to a scrubber.

THERE GOES THE NEIGHBORHOOD

When Congress amended the Clean Air Act in 1977, it made a number of changes designed to ensure better control of old plants under state implementation plans. On the enforcement side, it authorized the Department of Justice to pursue civil penalties of up to $25,000 a day for noncompliance with any emission standard, state or federal.[43] Unlike the criminal penalties available under the 1970 Act, these civil fines could be imposed without proving that the source in question knew it was violating a standard.[44] Furthermore, a civil case could be proved by a mere preponderance of the evidence (meaning it was more likely than not that a source had violated a standard), rather than the beyond-a-reasonable-doubt standard imposed in criminal cases. A civil case could also be tried by a judge rather than a jury.[45]

In a further effort to reduce the economic appeal of litigation and other delay tactics for old plants, the Act authorized both the EPA and states to assess a "noncompliance penalty" equal to the economic value of noncompliance for any source—meaning that authorities could force a plant to turn over any money it saved by refusing to comply with an emission standard.[46] Finally, Congress attempted to address political impediments to enforcement at the state level by requiring state permitting officials and air quality board members to disclose potential conflicts of interest.[47]

Of course, robust enforcement of state standards would do nothing to control an old plant's emissions if the state hadn't bothered to set any standards for that source in the first place. Accordingly, the 1977 amendments provided that state implementation plans for nonattainment areas had to require the areas' existing stationary sources to use "reasonably available control technology" to reduce their emissions.[48] Additionally, no new or modified source could begin operation in a nonattainment area without demonstrating that its contribution to the area's emissions would be more than offset by reductions at older plants in the region.[49]

These two provisions—the "reasonably available control technology" and offset requirements—marked Congress's first attempts to address directly the problem of uncontrolled emissions from old plants. But they were at best a partial fix, because they applied only to sources in nonattainment areas. In many cases, much of the pollution contributing to one state's environmental problems came from uncontrolled sources in a neighboring state that was not itself in violation of the NAAQS and thus had no obligation to control emissions from its existing sources.[50] As a result, a nonattainment area might find itself unable to achieve the NAAQS—even after installing reasonable controls at all of its own sources—due to the uncontrolled pollution of its neighbors.

Congress was certainly aware of the problem of interstate pollution in 1977, and it included two provisions in its new Clean Air Act amendments that were specifically designed to curtail transjurisdictional emissions. First, recognizing that many states were essentially "exporting" their pollution to other states with the help of tall stacks, legislators forbade the EPA administrator from crediting the dispersive effects of those stacks toward a state's NAAQS compliance.[51] This did not mean that states themselves were banned from constructing tall stacks (much less required to dismantle the ones they'd already built). It simply meant that when assessing the effectiveness of a state's implementation plan, the EPA had to model emissions as if all stacks in the state were of a height consistent with "good engineering practice," even if, in reality, some stacks were much taller.[52] Thus, the tall-stacks standard aimed to reduce interstate emissions indirectly. Presumably, if a state didn't get NAAQS compliance credit for its tall stacks, it would be forced to achieve actual emissions reductions at its existing sources, which would, in turn, reduce the volume of emissions it sent to other states.

The 1977 amendments also included a more explicit restriction on interstate emissions. In what became known as the Good Neighbor Provision, Congress required all state implementation plans to "prohibi[t] any stationary source within the State from emitting any air pollutant in amounts which [would] . . . prevent attainment or maintenance [of air quality standards] by any other State."[53] To ensure that this requirement was enforceable, Congress also gave any state or political subdivision the right to petition the EPA for a finding that a major source in another state was emitting pollution that prevented the petitioning state from meeting or maintaining the NAAQS.[54] If the EPA made such a finding, it was authorized to impose emission limitations on the offending source.[55]

Unfortunately, neither of the interstate provisions in the 1977 amendments proved particularly successful. The problem with the tall-stacks standard was that Congress largely left the question of what constituted "good engineering practice" up to the EPA. Although the statute instructed the agency to issue a definition of the phrase within six months,[56] the EPA took five years to do so, only to have parts of the interpretive rule struck down by the U.S. Court of Appeals for the District of Columbia Circuit as unjustifiably friendly to industry.[57] In 1985, the agency tried again, and once more, the D.C. Circuit vacated parts of the rule as inconsistent with Congress's instructions.[58] In the meantime, sources with tall stacks continued to evade meaningful limitations on their emissions.

The Good Neighbor Provision, too, was, undermined by the EPA's implementation decisions, as illustrated by the case of *Air*

Pollution Control District of Jefferson County, Kentucky v. EPA.[59] In 1979, portions of the populous Jefferson County, home to the city of Louisville, were in nonattainment for the SO_2 NAAQS, even though the county's power plants had already installed scrubbing devices that sharply reduced their emission rates.[60] These controls had cost the plants' operator, Louisville Gas & Electric, about $138 million.[61]

Meanwhile, just five miles across the Ohio River in rural Floyd County, Indiana, the Gallagher Station power plant emitted SO_2 at five times the rate of the Kentucky plants, having installed no emission controls whatsoever.[62] Gallagher's four coal-fired generating units had been built between 1958 and 1961 and were grandfathered out of compliance with the EPA's New Source Performance Standards.[63] Initially, this hadn't seemed of much consequence because Indiana's 1973 implementation plan for meeting the NAAQS required Gallagher and other coal-fired power plants to achieve an SO_2 emission limit of 1.2 pounds per million British thermal units of heat input—a standard that was identical to both the EPA's performance standard for new plants and Kentucky's standard for its own existing plants.[64] (A British thermal unit, or Btu, is the amount of heat needed to raise the temperature of a pound of water by one degree Fahrenheit.[65] Thus, when we describe a given quantity of fuel as equivalent to x Btus of heat input, we mean that, upon combustion, it will generate enough energy to heat x pounds of water by one degree.[66])

Unfortunately, Indiana soon realized that it wouldn't need to enforce a stringent performance standard at Gallagher to satisfy the SO_2 NAAQS within its borders, in large part because much of the pollution emitted from Gallagher's 550-foot stacks was blown east to Kentucky's Jefferson County.[67] In 1974, the state temporarily exempted Gallagher from the 1.2 pound standard, and in 1979, it scrapped the standard altogether, opting instead for an emission limit of 6.0 lbs/MMBtu, which wasn't really a limitation at all since Gallagher could satisfy the rate without adopting *any* pollution-control measures.[68]

Jefferson County, run at the time by none other than current Senate Majority Leader and antiregulatory crusader Mitch McConnell,[69] petitioned the EPA to find that Gallagher's SO_2 emissions violated the Good Neighbor Provision.[70] After delaying a decision for almost three years (despite a statutory requirement that it act within sixty days), the EPA denied the petition, concluding that (1) the Good Neighbor Provision applied where emissions from a source in one state "cause[d] or substantially contribute[d] to" nonattainment of the NAAQS in another state; (2) Gallagher contributed only 3 percent of the SO_2 emissions in the portions of Jefferson County that exceeded the NAAQS; and (3) a 3 percent contribution was not "substantial."[71]

In the ensuing litigation, Jefferson County challenged the EPA's findings on a number of grounds. For one, the county disagreed with the agency's estimate of the volume of Jefferson County pollution that could be traced back to Gallagher.[72] It was impossible to physically measure Gallagher's contribution to Jefferson County's SO_2 levels. Pollution molecules don't carry passports, and the SO_2 emitted by the Indiana plant was physically indistinguishable from that emitted by Kentucky's own sources. As a result, the EPA relied on air quality modeling to generate an estimate of Gallagher's contribution.[73] The results of such modeling depended on a variety of assumptions regarding factors like the velocity of a plant's emissions and the likely meteorological conditions at the time of emission.[74] And although the EPA's model estimated that only 3 percent of the SO_2 in Jefferson County's nonattainment areas originated at Gallagher, the county's model suggested that Gallagher's emissions *alone* were sufficient to violate the SO_2 NAAQS in parts of Jefferson County, without taking into account any of the county's own emissions.[75] In the absence of more detailed statutory guidance, however, the U.S. Court of Appeals for the Sixth Circuit found that the EPA's "choice of modeling factors was neither arbitrary nor capricious" and deferred to the agency's estimate.[76]

Jefferson County also objected to the EPA's contention that a plant's contribution to another state's nonattainment had to be "substantial" to violate the Good Neighbor Provision.[77] In the county's view, the plain language of the Good Neighbor Provision forbade states from emitting pollution in *any* amount that would prevent attainment in another state.[78] Again, the court sided with the EPA, noting that, while the Good Neighbor Provision itself did not mention a threshold for agency intervention, a related section of the statute did: all nearby states were entitled to notice of any proposed new or modified sources that might "*significantly contribute* to levels of air pollution in excess of the national ambient air quality standards in any air quality control region outside the State in which such source intend[ed]to locate . . . ."[79] The court reasoned that since the purpose of the notice requirement was "to enable affected states to take action" under the petition provision of the law, it was logical to infer that the notice and petition provisions shared a common trigger: both were activated only by "significant" interstate emissions.[80]

Finally, Jefferson County pointed out that, even if one accepted the validity of the EPA's model showing that Gallagher contributed only 3 percent of SO_2 pollution in the portions of Jefferson County that exceeded the NAAQS, the same model also found that Gallagher contributed far larger percentages of the SO_2 pollution in portions of the county that were in compliance with the NAAQS.[81] Indeed, in certain parts of the county, the EPA found that Gallagher contributed pollution equal to 34.5 percent of the primary NAAQS for SO_2 (the limit for avoiding health effects) and 47 percent of the secondary NAAQS (the limit for avoiding welfare effects).[82]

The county emphasized the inequity of the situation, arguing that Kentucky's state implementation plan had been "designed to create a margin of clean air in Jefferson County" that "would allow future industrial growth . . . without the NAAQS being violated" and that this margin for growth had "been stolen by Gallagher to the economic disadvantage of Jefferson County."[83] In other words, the city of Louisville would have a very hard time opening new sources and expanding its economy not because its own plants were insufficiently controlled to ensure clean air but because Indiana's plant was unfairly hogging the region's limited capacity to safely accommodate air pollution.

After first receiving Jefferson County's petition in 1979, the Carter Administration's EPA had expressed support for this "margin of growth" argument. In a June 1980 announcement that solicited comments on the petition, the agency remarked that it considered "the degree of protection afforded by the interstate pollution provisions [to include] not only protection against NAAQS violations, but also protection against unreasonable interference with a maintenance program or margin for growth in the [state implementation plan]."[84] But by the time the EPA rejected Jefferson County's petition in February 1982, under the Reagan Administration, it had changed its tune. The agency now argued that the Good Neighbor Provision was concerned only with states' ability to satisfy *national* ambient standards, not the sort of "individually tailored" local goal for air quality implied by Jefferson County's "margin for growth."[85] By this logic, Gallagher could have been responsible for literally 100 percent of the pollution in parts of Jefferson County, and the Clean Air Act would have nothing to say about it so long as those parts of the county didn't violate the NAAQS.

The Sixth Circuit declined to find that the agency's new, cramped reading of the Good Neighbor Provision was an unreasonable interpretation of the provision's relatively vague language, but it did express sympathy for Jefferson County's predicament:

> In a most practical sense, Jefferson County's concerns are understandable. There would appear to be a patent unfairness in an Agency policy which would tolerate so much higher a level of SO_2 emissions in one area than in another, especially given the high costs which Jefferson County has already incurred to reduce its own pollution. Nevertheless, we believe that the construction placed upon the statute by the EPA appears to be literally correct, even though arguably at odds with the important policy values represented by the 1977 amendments.[86]

The notion that the EPA's interpretation of the Good Neighbor Provision, while technically permissible, was undermining Congress's legislative goals became something of a running theme in court decisions during the 1980s. Despite numerous petitions from downwind states, the EPA did not once exercise its authority under the Good Neighbor Provision between 1977 and 1998.[87] And while reviewing judges expressed concern about the health and environmental consequences of the agency's inaction, they were unwilling to substitute their own nonexpert judgment for that of the agency in an area of such scientific complexity.[88]

The decisions required were undoubtedly complex. Indeed, from a modeling perspective, Jefferson County's was one of the simpler cases that the EPA and the courts faced. For one thing, it involved the same pollutant—sulfur dioxide—on both sides of the state line. In *Connecticut v. EPA*, on the other hand, Connecticut argued that emissions of SO_2 from two oil-fired plants on Long Island—Port Jefferson and Northport—would prevent attainment of the NAAQS for *particulate matter* in Connecticut.[89]

Like Gallagher's, both Northport's and Port Jefferson's generating units had been constructed prior to 1971 and were thus exempt from the EPA's New Source Performance Standards.[90] And like Gallagher, the plants had originally been subject to a state emission limit every bit as strict as the federal standards for new sources: New York's initial implementation plan required them to burn oil containing 1 percent sulfur or less, which resulted in emissions below the federal limit of 1.2 lbs/MMBtu of heat input.[91] But in 1976, the state received the EPA's permission to temporarily impose a "special limitation" on the plants that allowed them to burn oil containing up to 2.8 percent sulfur.[92] When the EPA approved a three-year renewal of that higher limit in 1980, Connecticut objected.[93]

The U.S. Court of Appeals for the Second Circuit did not dispute that sulfur dioxide gradually reacted with other elements in the atmosphere to form sulfate particles.[94] Nor did the judges seem to doubt that high concentrations of suspended sulfates posed "severe health risks" when inhaled, including "higher mortality rates, aggravation of heart and lung disease in the elderly, aggravation of asthma, excess risk of acute lower respiratory disease in children and excess risk of bronchitis."[95] But the EPA argued that its models were incapable of estimating the percentage of Connecticut's particulate matter that could fairly be attributed to New York's SO_2 emissions, and the court declined to force the EPA "to consider an effect it cannot measure."[96] As in the *Jefferson County* decision, the court was careful to note that its holding was not intended to "commend or even condone" the EPA's decision, but merely to confirm that the EPA's action was neither irrational nor blatantly inconsistent with its statutory responsibilities.[97]

Another simplifying factor in the *Jefferson County* case was the fact that the upwind source and the downwind nonattainment area were only a few miles apart. In *New York v. EPA*, by contrast, the offending source was almost 600 miles from the petitioning state.[98] New York challenged the EPA's approval of a new SO_2 emission limit for the enormous Kingston plant in Tennessee, arguing that the agency erred by modeling only the short-range effects of the increased SO_2 emissions and making no effort to assess how the change might affect efforts to attain both the SO_2 and particulate matter NAAQS in distant states like New York.[99]

Like the plants in the previous examples, Kingston—which was operated by the Tennessee Valley Authority, a unique, federally chartered utility—was grandfathered out of federal performance standards but had initially been subjected to an equally stringent state emission standard.[100] Rather than install a scrubber or use lower-sulfur coal, however, Kingston had built a pair of 1,000-foot stacks that brought the surrounding county into attainment with the SO_2 NAAQS by sending the plant's pollution farther afield.[101] And in 1979, Tennessee had successfully applied to the EPA for permission to revise its implementation plan to more than double the facility's emission limit to 2.8 lbs/MMBtu.[102]

The EPA could not deny that it was possible for pollution emitted in Tennessee to wind up in New York. On the contrary, a 1983 report published by the agency had concluded that, under the right meteorological conditions, emissions from a Midwestern smokestack could travel more than 1,000 kilometers (or 620 miles) in just two days.[103] But the agency did deny that it could accurately estimate *how much* Tennessee pollution would reach the Empire State.[104] The EPA's preferred models estimated effects only up to a distance of 50 kilometers, and it argued it had no obligation to employ newer, untested methods.[105] As in the *Jefferson County* and *Connecticut* cases, the reviewing court deferred to the agency's modeling expertise.[106]

In July 1988, a panel of the D.C. Circuit that included future Supreme Court Justice Ruth Bader Ginsburg affirmed the EPA's rejection of yet another set of Good Neighbor petitions from Maine, New York, and Pennsylvania.[107] Ginsburg joined her colleagues in finding that the EPA had acted within its statutory discretion in denying the petitions, but she wrote a separate concurrence to acknowledge a simple truth:

> The EPA has taken *no* action against sources of interstate air pollution . . . in the decade-plus since [the Good Neighbor Provision and petition provision] were enacted. Congress, when it is so minded, is fully capable of instructing the EPA to address particular matters promptly. . . . Congress did not supply such direction in this instance; instead, it allowed and has left unchecked the EPA's current approach to interstate air pollution. The judiciary, therefore, is not the proper place in which to urge alteration of the Agency's course.[108]

In other words, the Reagan EPA had rendered the Good Neighbor Provision a dead letter, and there was nothing the courts could do about it. Interstate pollution required a political solution, not a judicial one.

As luck would have it, a political solution was already in the offing. Less than a month after the publication of Ginsburg's concurrence, George Herbert Walker Bush, Reagan's Vice President, won the 1988 Republican nomination for President. Two weeks later, he stood before a crowd on the Michigan shore of Lake Erie and made a surprising announcement for a man who had made his fortune in the West Texas oil business and spent his vice presidential years as the chair of Reagan's Task Force for Regulatory Relief: "I," the future President declared, "am an environmentalist."[109]

Bush's interest in strengthening environmental protections was, by all accounts, sincere, but that doesn't mean there weren't elements of Nixonian political calculation in his pledge to be the

"Environmental President."[110] As the twentieth anniversary of Earth Day approached, public interest in environmental issues had been reignited by extensive media coverage of the Exxon-Valdez oil tanker spill in Alaska and by an unusually hot, smog-filled summer.[111] According to *National Journal*'s Richard Cohen, the Bush team believed that an environmental focus would appeal to the suburban, moderate voters whose support Bush needed to win key Electoral College victories in California and New Jersey.[112] And so, like Nixon before him, Bush set out to position himself as greener than his liberal rival, the popular Massachusetts governor Michael Dukakis. In what was viewed as one of the most influential ads of the campaign season, Bush blasted Dukakis for his failure to clean the fetid Boston Harbor during a decade as the state's leader.[113]

But Bush also needed to maintain his conservative bona fides. Thus, while he proudly branded himself an environmentalist in that August 1988 speech in Michigan, he was also quick to clarify that an interest in clean air and water was "not inconsistent with being a businessman," nor "with being a conservative."[114] "In fact," he asserted, "it is an essential part of the thinking that should guide either one."[115]

To prove the compatibility of environmental conservation and economic conservatism, Bush and his team set to work on a plan that would harness the power of the free market—Reagan-era conservatives' most revered institution—to address a seemingly intractable environmental problem: acid rain.

WHO WILL STOP THE RAIN?

The problem of acid rain hadn't been on Congress's radar screen when the Clean Air Act was passed in 1970. The results of the first U.S. study on the phenomenon weren't published until 1974, in the prestigious journal *Science*.[116] The researchers found that the acidity of rain in the eastern United States and Europe had increased to 100 to 1,000 times its normal levels over the course of just two decades.[117] Whereas rain historically had the pH of a potato, a spring shower was now typically as acidic as a tomato.[118] In some cases, it was equivalent to pure lemon juice.[119]

What was driving this change? As discussed earlier, sulfur dioxide emissions from coal-fired power plants are gradually transformed in the atmosphere into sulfate particles.[120] Through a similar process, nitrogen oxides can become nitrates.[121] When suspended in the ambient air, these sulfates and nitrates contribute to particulate pollution, which is dangerous to human health.[122] But they can also combine with moisture to become sulfuric and nitric acid, which then falls to earth in the form of acid rain (a catch-all term that actually encompasses not just rain but also snow, fog, mist, and what is known as "dry deposition").[123]

This acidic precipitation has myriad environmental consequences. It stunts forest growth.[124] It strips paint from cars and erodes the stone facades of historic buildings and monuments.[125] Perhaps most dramatically, it compromises the ability of freshwater lakes and rivers to support life.[126]

By the 1980s, it was clear to policymakers that acid rain was a major policy concern. It was equally clear that a decade of federal and state regulation under the Clean Air Act had done little to alleviate the problem. Why? Because the pollution that caused it was emitted primarily by older power plants that had been grandfathered out of the Act's strict New Source Performance Standards. President Carter's EPA administrator, Douglas Costle, told the Senate as much in a 1980 hearing:

> [W]e have set a very stringent standard for new coal-fired plants, so that we have in effect capped that problem. The acid

rain problem is not a function of new plants. It is a function of the existing plants which we are not controlling as tightly.[127]

Five years later, a thorough report from the Congressional Research Service (CRS) delivered a similar message: "Any adverse effects now being experienced from acid precipitation are the result primarily of emissions from sources that do not meet current New Source Performance Standards."[128] Coal-fired power plants, the CRS report noted, were responsible for almost two-thirds of the nation's SO_2 pollution, and 90 percent of that two-thirds came from grandfathered plants.[129] In some cases, these plants emitted pollution at a rate more than six times the limit for new sources.[130]

Because they were largely exempt from direct federal regulation, "any controls imposed on these older plants," the CRS report observed, would have to be required by state implementation plans, "as States found additional reductions necessary to meet NAAQS."[131] But, in the view of the report's authors, the NAAQS system was not well suited to the acid-rain problem, for three reasons.

First, any ambient standard for sulfates that was targeted specifically at eliminating acid rain would need to be a "secondary" rather than a "primary" NAAQS, because the best-understood effects of acid rain were harmful to the public welfare, not the public health.[132] And while primary NAAQS theoretically had to be satisfied within three years of their promulgation, there was no statutory deadline for attaining secondary NAAQS; a state simply had to achieve them within "a reasonable time." Given that when the report was published in 1985, many urban areas were still out of attainment with primary NAAQS that had been set in the 1970s, the prospects for attaining a new secondary NAAQS looked grim.[133]

Second, the NAAQS had proven useful in alleviating only local pollution problems, whereas acid rain was a regional problem.[134] Although its effects were largely suffered in the

Northeast—particularly in New York's Adirondack Mountains, where more than 200 lakes were devoid of fish by 1983—the emissions that caused it were mostly generated elsewhere.[135] Indeed, EPA Administrator Costle estimated in 1980 that 60 percent of the acid rain-causing pollution in New York and New Jersey was attributable to out-of-state sources.[136]

Looking at the emission statistics for various states, it's not hard to see why. Consider that, in 1985, New York was responsible for 397,000 tons of SO_2 emissions, compared to Ohio's 2.3 million tons, Indiana's 1.5 million tons, and West Virginia's 1 million tons.[137] On a per capita basis, the disparity was even more striking: New York emitted 44.6 pounds per resident, while West Virginia emitted 1,029.5 pounds, Indiana emitted 550.9 pounds, and Ohio emitted 425.6 pounds.[138]

But the problem was not simply that existing power plants in the Midwest and Appalachia had higher aggregate or per capita emissions of SO_2 than their Northeastern counterparts. This, after all, could suggest merely that those states had a greater demand for electricity due to a higher concentration of heavy industry.[139] No, the problem was that the plants had much higher *rates* of emission—meaning that they emitted more pollution for each kilowatt-hour they generated—because they had adopted few, if any, emissions controls. Of the large coal plants that emitted SO_2 at the highest rates in 1980, all but two of the top sixty were located in the Midwest or Appalachia.[140] Forty-five of these were located in just four states: Missouri, Ohio, Indiana, and Wisconsin.[141] Meanwhile, only one was located in the Northeast—in Pennsylvania.[142]

Thus, even if the EPA set a secondary NAAQS for sulfates, the only way a state like New York could meet it at a reasonable cost would be to get plants in states like Ohio to reduce their SO_2 emissions. And that, of course, would require invocation of the Good Neighbor Provision, something that no state had successfully convinced the EPA to do for *any* interstate pollution problem. Indeed, the CRS report noted that the Reagan EPA's Assistant Administrator for Air and Radiation had already explicitly stated that the agency had no intention of using the Good Neighbor Provision to address acid rain.[143]

Third, and most important, the CRS report concluded that a NAAQS was a poor tool for controlling acid rain because "the NAAQS address concentrations of pollution, but not total loadings."[144] In other words, a sulfate NAAQS would focus on how much sulfate was present in the ambient air at any given moment, but the negative impacts of acid rain were a product of total emissions over time: in 1984, an international task force found that negative ecological effects in freshwater lakes could be observed once the total amount of sulfate deposition reached 27 pounds per acre per year.[145]

Ultimately, the CRS concluded, "[a]ny commitment to abate acid precipitation would seem to require amending the [Clean Air Act] in some way, whether to force action on a sulfate standard or to require emission rollbacks from existing sources."[146] Industry groups like the National Coal Association disagreed. They had spent the early 1980s arguing to Congress that new legislation extending emission standards to existing plants was unnecessary because SO_2 emissions would eventually decline on their own as older plants were retired and replaced with newer plants that were subject to New Source Performance Standards.[147] Similarly, the Electric Power Research Institute—the research arm of the Edison Electric Institute—estimated that, thanks to plant retirements, New Source Performance Standards alone would, by 2015, achieve the same level of reduction as a program that applied to both new and existing sources.[148]

The CRS didn't buy it. Its 1985 report noted that the Electric Power Research Institute's optimistic estimate assumed "a life-span of about 40 years for existing uncontrolled facilities," ignoring the increasing popularity of "life extension" projects that allowed plants to operate for decades longer than originally planned (a trend that Edison Electric itself was explicitly encouraging, as we discussed in Chapter 4).[149] In other words, utility advocates were ignoring the "old plant effect" created by the Clean Air Act's grandfathering scheme—the powerful incentive for grandfathered plants to operate longer than they otherwise would in order to avoid the expense of complying with the Act's standards for new sources. If one assumed an average life of sixty years for existing plants, the CRS found, SO_2 emissions wouldn't begin to decline until at least 2010.[150]

TO MARKET, TO MARKET

Dozens of acid rain bills were proposed in the 1980s, mostly by representatives of Northeastern and Western states.[151] Most of these failed proposals sought, essentially, to extend the 1.2 lbs/MMBtu SO_2 standard that already applied to new plants to existing plants as well.[152] By contrast, President Bush's proposal, which became the centerpiece of the 1990 amendments to the Clean Air Act, didn't impose a reduction requirement on any particular plant or group of plants. Instead, it set a national cap on SO_2 emissions and relied on an emission trading market to allocate reductions among plants.[153] These reductions were to occur in two phases, the first beginning in 1995 and the second beginning in 2000.[154] In the first phase, only the 110 largest, most highly polluting plants would be subject to the cap. Each would be given emission allowances equivalent to its average annual heat input between 1985 and 1987, multiplied by a benchmark emission rate of 2.5 lbs/MMBtu.[155] In the second phase, the cap would be expanded to cover virtually all fossil fuel-fired plants, and the benchmark emission rate would be tightened to 1.2 lbs/MMBtu.[156] Ultimately, the program sought to reduce sulfur dioxide emissions by about 10 million tons below 1980 levels—a 50 percent reduction.[157]

If a source emitted more tons than it was allocated, either because it generated more electricity than it had in the mid-1980s or because it emitted at a higher rate than the benchmark, it had essentially two options. It could (1) reduce its emissions, whether by switching to lower-sulfur coal or installing a scrubber, or (2) purchase additional allowances from another plant or from the EPA at auction. Similarly, if a source emitted fewer tons than it was allocated, it could sell its excess allowances. Presumably, sources that could reduce their emissions relatively cheaply would become net sellers of allowances, while sources that faced higher-than-average retrofit costs would become net purchasers. In this way, the reduction burden would be efficiently allocated, and total compliance costs would be minimized.[158]

The basic formula described above—whereby plants were allocated allowances based on historical heat input multiplied by a benchmark emission rate—imposed the highest costs on Midwestern and Appalachian states, because their plants' emission rates were much more likely to be significantly above the benchmark.[159] Thus, these plants would either have to buy a large number of additional allowances or significantly reduce their emissions. Either option would be expensive.

Unsurprisingly, politicians from these highly polluting states argued that clean-up costs should be shared more broadly. But their neighbors were largely unmoved.[160] After all, the cleaner states' own plants would face fewer costs under the trading scheme primarily because they had *already* invested large sums in pollution control. "It's hard to see why consumers in states that have already done their part should be paying a second time for those who have dragged their feet on environmental protection," observed the governor of Minnesota.[161]

Nevertheless, during the final days of negotiation, Midwestern legislators managed to shoehorn some relatively modest cost-sharing provisions into the bill. Most notably, coal-burning plants in Ohio, Indiana, and Illinois were allocated 200,000 "bonus" allowances per year during Phase I.[162] Over the course of five years, this subsidy was worth $200 million.[163]

In October 1990, with the trading program's fiercest opponents at least somewhat mollified, the Clean Air Act Amendments of 1990 passed both houses of Congress with overwhelming bipartisan support.[164] The vote was 401–25 in the House and 89–10 in the Senate.[165] President Bush signed the amendments into law on November 15, 1990, just over a month shy of the Clean Air Act of 1970's twentieth anniversary.[166]

Congress's confidence in President Bush's plan turned out to be well placed. Not only did the Acid Rain Trading Program achieve substantial reductions in SO_2 emissions, but it also did so at a much lower cost than even the program's advocates expected. During the legislative debate, most analysts predicted allowance prices of about $250 to $350 per ton in Phase I and $500 to $700 in Phase II.[167] Some industry groups estimated that prices would climb to $1,000 per ton or higher.[168] In reality, allowances prices stayed in the $100 to $200 range during Phase I and then hovered around $200 for much of Phase II (until reduction targets were tightened in connection with a later policy, the Clean Air Interstate Rule, which will be discussed below).[169]

Sulfur dioxide reductions were cheaper than expected for two reasons. First and most important was a large drop in the cost of rail freight. The nation's lowest-sulfur coal comes from the Powder River Basin in northeastern Wyoming.[170] This coal is not only cleaner but also cheaper to mine than the high-sulfur varieties found in the Midwest and Appalachia.[171] But for most of the twentieth century, it was very expensive to transport Wyoming coal to end users in the Eastern half of the country. Indeed, for Midwestern users, transportation could account for more than two-thirds of the delivered cost of Powder River Basin coal.[172] As a result, most of the coal-fired power plants in the Midwest chose to burn the dirtier coal mined closer to home.[173]

Up until the mid-1970s, rates for freight rail transport were set by the Interstate Commerce Commission.[174] But legislative reforms in 1976 and 1980 gave rail companies the freedom to set their own rates and to negotiate contracts with large-volume shippers, like coal companies.[175] Between 1979 and 1993, the average cost of shipping Wyoming coal to the Midwest plunged by more than 50 percent.[176] As a result, by the time acid-rain trading began in 1995, it was much cheaper for Midwestern plants to switch to low-sulfur coal than economists had predicted when the program was first proposed.

The other factor that drove down compliance costs was technological innovation. Under newfound regulatory pressure, plants found cheaper ways to convert their boilers to burn lower-sulfur fuel and cheaper ways to operate scrubbers.[177] Ultimately, the marginal cost of operating a scrubber was 40 percent lower than expected.[178]

THE SINCEREST FORM OF FLATTERY

The Acid Rain Trading Program was such a success that the EPA began to look to trading as a means of addressing other problems caused by air pollution. Nonattainment of the NAAQS was still a major concern for the agency, particularly with respect to ground-level ozone.[179] And, once again, grandfathered power plants were a major culprit.

Many people think of ozone as a good thing, and it is true that the ozone produced naturally in the stratosphere (between 6 and 30 miles above ground level) shields life on earth from the sun's harmful ultraviolet rays.[180] But when produced at lower altitudes, ozone can cause or worsen a variety of serious respiratory problems.[181]

This dangerous ground-level ozone, the primary ingredient in urban smog, is formed by a reaction between nitrogen oxides, sunlight, and volatile organic compounds (also known as hydrocarbons).[182] Power plants are the nation's second-largest source of nitrogen oxides, and, at the end of the twentieth century, many plants still lacked state-of-the-art NO_x controls.[183] More specifically, a report from the Government Accountability Office (GAO) found that, as of 2000, 73 percent of power plants constructed prior to the passage of the Clean Air Act emitted NO_x at a level above the standard applicable to new sources.[184] The GAO further found that reducing the emissions of these plants to a level consistent with that of new sources would cut the power sector's total NO_x emissions by almost 30 percent.[185]

By the late 1990s, a group of twelve Northeastern states between Maine and the District of Columbia had already made substantial reductions in their NO_x emissions through a voluntary regional trading program.[186] But even these steep cuts had proven insufficient to bring the region's cities into attainment, because, as with acid rain, much of the pollution contributing to the Northeast's ozone problem originated in the Midwest and Appalachia, whose plants had adopted far fewer controls.[187] A 1997 analysis by the Congressional Budget Office found that achieving additional NO_x reductions in Connecticut, Massachusetts, and Rhode Island—all of which contained nonattainment regions—would cost an average of $7,900 a ton.[188] Meanwhile, reductions in Ohio, West Virginia, and Indiana could be had for the relative bargain of $785 a ton.[189]

In August 1997, eight Northeastern states petitioned the EPA to use its power under the Good Neighbor Provision to reign in the out-of-state emissions that were preventing them from attaining the ozone NAAQS.[190] This time, remarkably, the agency took action.

The agency had not abandoned the "significant contribution" test upheld in *Jefferson County*. On the contrary, the 1990 amendments had actually codified that phrase into the language of the Good Neighbor Provision itself.[191] But it was still up to the agency to determine when a contribution qualified as significant; the statute provided no definition.[192]

In what became known as the "NO_x SIP Call," the EPA acknowledged that, because ozone was a secondary pollutant formed from the reaction of nitrogen oxides with other airborne pollutants, it was "not possible to determine the downwind impact [of] each individual source in an upwind state."[193] But rather than using this complexity to justify inaction, as the Reagan Administration had done, the EPA decided to look to the "collective contribution" of all sources in the upwind state.[194] First, it identified twenty-two upwind states that it considered "significant contributors" to nonattainment in downwind jurisdictions based on the magnitude and frequency of their border-crossing emissions.[195] Next, it assigned each state an emission budget that reflected the reductions the state could achieve using "highly cost effective controls," which the EPA defined as those that could be implemented for less than $2,000 per ton.[196] States had discretion to satisfy their budgets by whatever means they preferred, including by participating in an interstate emission trading program like the one the EPA had already established for SO_2.[197]

Coal interests and upwind states challenged the NO_x SIP Call in the D.C. Circuit, arguing that the Clean Air Act did not permit the EPA to consider the cost of reduction when determining what portion of a state's emissions "contribute[d] significantly" to nonattainment in another state.[198] But the court deferred to the EPA's interpretation, determining that the agency could consider costs because "the term 'significant' does not in itself convey a thought that significance should be measured in only one dimension—here, in the petitioners' view, health alone."[199]

In 2005, with more than 100 areas still out of attainment for ozone, the EPA, now under the administration of George W. Bush, expanded the NO_x trading program to cover five additional states *and* an additional pollutant, fine particulate matter, for which almost forty areas were out of attainment.[200] Like the NO_x SIP Call, the Clean Air Interstate Rule first identified states that it deemed "significant contributors" to at least one other state's nonattainment by virtue of the magnitude and frequency of their interstate emissions.[201] As with the earlier rule, these states were then assigned emission budgets that reflected the reductions they could achieve using "highly cost-effective" emission controls.[202] And, as before, states were given the option to participate in an EPA-managed cap-and-trade program as an alternative to imposing individual controls on their sources.[203] The EPA estimated that the rule would, by 2015, reduce the number of ozone nonattainment areas in the United States from 108 to 6 and the number of particulate matter nonattainment areas from 36 to 14.[204]

Another suit was brought in the D.C. Circuit, and this time, the court sided with the challengers, notwithstanding the similarities between the challenged regulation and the NO_x SIP Call it had upheld eight years earlier.[205] Among other things, a majority of the judges found that, by allowing for unfettered interstate trading, the rule did not "actually require elimination of emissions from sources that contribute significantly and interfere with maintenance in downwind nonattainment areas."[206] Theoretically, under a trading scheme, sources in one state could purchase enough allowances to cover all of their current emissions, resulting in no change in their contribution to nonattainment in other states.[207] In the court's view, the Good Neighbor Provision did not permit such an outcome.

Initially, the circuit court vacated the Clean Air Interstate Rule entirely.[208] But when that threw existing emission trading markets into chaos, it decided to leave the regulation in place while a replacement was fashioned.[209] That task would ultimately fall to the Obama Administration, as will be discussed in Chapter 7.

GRANDFATHERING'S GRIM TOLL

The full costs of grandfathering are impossible to tally. We will never know exactly what would have happened had Congress chosen to impose some sort of federal performance standards on existing sources of NAAQS pollutants like SO_2 and NO_x. (The results would depend, for one thing, on the stringency of those existing-source standards relative to the new-source standards.)

That said, the EPA's estimates of the benefits of the Acid Rain Trading Program, the NO_x SIP Call, and the Clean Air Interstate Rule offer some insight into the damage caused by exempting older sources, because all three of these programs were efforts to solve interstate pollution problems that likely wouldn't have existed—or, at least, wouldn't have persisted for so long—if not for grandfathering.

In 2005, an EPA study estimated that by the time the program was fully implemented in 2010, the Acid Rain Trading Program would prevent close to 18,000 deaths each year.[210] As of 2008, the NO_x SIP Call was projected to prevent 1,800 deaths annually.[211] And, finally, the EPA projected that the further cuts mandated by the Clean Air Interstate Rule would prevent 17,000 additional deaths per year from 2015 onward.[212]

If these partial antidotes to grandfathering could save more than 35,000 lives a year, consider how many hundreds of thousands more would have been spared if grandfathered plants had been subject to federal regulation even a decade sooner.

6

A Warming World

In the preceding chapters, we've focused largely on what is often called "traditional pollution": soot and smog and their precursors, sulfur dioxide and nitrogen oxides. But power plants are also the nation's largest source of a very different sort of pollutant: carbon dioxide.[1] Unlike traditional pollution, atmospheric CO_2 does not pose a threat to public health through inhalation.[2] As every schoolchild learns, humans exhale CO_2 during normal respiration, and plants absorb it as part of the photosynthesis that fuels their growth.[3]

Carbon dioxide does, however, act as a "greenhouse gas." Like the glass of a greenhouse, molecules of CO_2 let sunlight pass through to warm the earth but then trap some of the heat that radiates back from the planet's surface.[4] Up to a point, this heat-trapping effect is beneficial; without it, the earth would be too cold to support life.[5] But when humans burn fossil fuels, carbon that has been sequestered underground for millions of years is rapidly released in the form of CO_2, and the natural carbon cycle is altered.

As the concentration of CO_2 in the atmosphere increases, the greenhouse effect becomes stronger, and the earth's surface temperature rises.[6] Over time, warming driven by ever-increasing industrial emissions of CO_2 is expected to have serious, possibly devastating consequences for all corners of human society.[7] (There are other greenhouse gases, like methane, but CO_2 is by far the most common, accounting for more than 75 percent of global greenhouse gas emissions and almost 85 percent of U.S. emissions.[8])

And yet, when President Obama took office in 2009, almost forty years after the U.S. Congress passed a piece of legislation designed to eliminate *all* air pollution that posed a threat to public health and welfare, emissions of carbon dioxide were still entirely unregulated at the federal level. As the President observed in his first Earth Day address on April 22, 2009: "[W]e place limits on pollutants like sulfur dioxide and nitrogen dioxide and other harmful emissions. But we haven't placed any limits on carbon dioxide and other greenhouse gases. It's what's called the carbon loophole."[9]

In this chapter, we explore the origins of that "carbon loophole" and the ways in which its pernicious effects have been exacerbated and extended by the Clean Air Act's grandfathering of existing sources. We find that, in the absence of grandfathering, the electricity sector's CO_2 emissions would be substantially lower because a greater number of pre-1980 plants would have been retired and replaced by new plants that, although not legally required to emit CO_2 at lower rates, would have done so anyway. We also find that grandfathering contributed to the failure of proposed cap-and-trade legislation for greenhouse gases in 2009, because public and political support for the bill was undermined by excessive concessions to old coal plants that, but for grandfathering, would no longer have been operating.

THE CARBON LOOPHOLE: A HISTORY

The basic mechanics of the greenhouse effect have been understood since 1859, when a British scientist named John Tyndall performed a series of experiments demonstrating the capacity of CO_2 (then known as carbonic acid) and certain other gases to absorb heat.[10] Just shy of forty years later, a pair of Swedish scientists, Arvid Högbom and Svante Arrhenius, became the first to speculate that emissions of CO_2 caused by burning fossil fuels might strengthen this greenhouse effect (and thus increase global average temperatures) by increasing the concentration of CO_2 in the atmosphere.[11]

But the technology necessary to test this theory—namely, instruments capable of measuring the level of CO_2 in the atmosphere—wouldn't arrive until the late 1950s. In 1958, an American chemist named Charles Keeling began to take continuous CO_2 measurements from an observatory atop the Mauna Loa volcano in Hawaii.[12] Plotted on a graph, these data points formed what would eventually be known as the "Keeling Curve," an upwardly sloping line that has continued its climb for almost six decades now—rising from 315 parts per million in 1958 to just over 400 parts per million in 2014.[13] (Meanwhile, the preindustrial concentration of CO_2 is believed to have been about 275 parts per million.[14])

By 1965, Keeling had accumulated enough data for President Lyndon Johnson's Science Advisory Committee to cite his findings in a report to the President as showing "clearly and conclusively" that the carbon dioxide content of the atmosphere was rising.[15] In the Committee's view, industrial society was conducting "a vast geophysical experiment" with little understanding of the potential consequences:

> Within a few generations, [humankind] is burning the fossil fuels that slowly accumulated in the earth over the past 500 million years. The CO_2 produced by this combustion is being injected into the atmosphere; about half of it remains there.[16]

The Committee projected a 25 percent increase in CO_2 levels by the year 2100 and advised that such an increase "may be sufficient to produce measurable and perhaps marked changes in climate."[17] But in the absence of more sophisticated atmospheric modeling techniques, it was "impossible to predict these effects quantitatively."[18]

A year later, a report from the House of Representatives' Subcommittee on Science, Research, and Development offered a similar assessment of the state of climate science: "The net result is that we do know the carbon dioxide concentration has increased and is increasing. Once again, we do not know what this means or what to do about it if action is called for."[19] Presciently, the House report noted that if the harm of carbon dioxide emissions became clearer, the long-term desirability of coal as a fuel source would decrease:

> The present investment in coal-fired electric generating plants, and the realistic cost differential between this and other energy sources, precludes any rapid demise of the coal industry. Further elucidation of the threat from carbon dioxide might alter this picture.[20]

But clarity on carbon was slow in coming.

Leon Billings, Senator Muskie's longtime chief of staff, has written that he does "not recall any talk about global warming" when the Clean Air Act was passed, in 1970. Instead, "the issue was barely on anyone's radar screen."[21] Consistent with Billings' recollection, transcripts of the congressional hearings on the Clean Air Act reveal that the potential for CO_2-induced warming was mentioned only a handful of times during the proceedings. What's more, the few witnesses who did raise the issue expressed uncertainty about the extent to which the greenhouse effect of CO_2 emissions would be offset by the cooling properties of particulate pollution.[22] (Whereas ambient CO_2 keeps solar-generated heat *in* the atmosphere, particulate matter can, by blocking incoming sunlight, keep heat *out*, a phenomenon known as "solar dimming."[23])

At a time when Americans were still dying somewhat regularly in acute, inversion-related pollution episodes, it is unsurprising that legislators were more concerned with the known harms of sulfur dioxide and carbon monoxide than the uncertain, seemingly distant threat of climate change. But the Clean Air Act's architects also recognized that the scientific community's understanding of air pollution was constantly evolving and that their statute would need to be flexible enough to deal with as-yet-unrecognized sources of harm. Accordingly, instead of providing the EPA with an exhaustive list of pollutants to regulate, Congress required the agency to regulate any air pollutant that endangered the public health or welfare.[24] Initially, the Act's guidance on what qualified as an "air pollutant" was unhelpfully tautological: "The term 'air pollutant' means an air pollution agent or combination of such agents."[25] But when Congress amended the Act in 1977, it made clear that the term "air pollutant" encompassed "any physical, chemical, biological, radioactive . . . substance or matter which is emitted into or otherwise enters the ambient air."[26]

By the late 1970s, most scientists were confident that any cooling attributable to particulate pollution, which remains in the atmosphere for a few weeks at most, would be outweighed by warming linked to CO_2 emissions, whose greenhouse effects are felt for a century or more.[27] Testifying at a June 1977 hearing of the House Subcommittee on the Environment and the Atmosphere, Dr. Alvin Weinberg of the Institute for Energy Analysis predicted that the projected doubling of global CO_2 emissions by 2025 could lead to a two-degree Celsius increase in global average temperature.[28] Another testifying scientist, David Gates of the University of Michigan, predicted a three- to five-degree Celsius increase by the end of the twenty-second century and warned that the ecological effects of such a climatic shift could include coastal flooding, the shifting of viable agricultural land toward the north and south poles, and large-scale migration of fish populations.[29]

Generally, the hearing witnesses agreed that man-made climate change was not yet well enough understood to justify immediate mitigation efforts.[30] They did, however, emphasize that "significant research" needed to be undertaken "over the next ten years in order to get the answers regarding its seriousness."[31]

A 1977 report of the National Academy of Sciences similarly acknowledged the "profound uncertainties regarding the carbon cycle, climate, and their interdependence" but warned policymakers against using these uncertainties to justify complacency:

> Unfortunately, it will take a millennium for the effects of a century of use of fossil fuel to dissipate. If the decision is postponed until the impact of man-made climate changes has been felt, then, for all practical purposes, the die will already have been cast.[32]

As a result, the authors of the report encouraged policymakers to feel "a lively sense of urgency in getting on with the work of illuminating the issues that have been identified and resolving the scientific uncertainties that remain."[33] More specifically, they recommended implementation of a "worldwide comprehensive research program," which would include "studies of the carbon cycle, climate, future population changes, and energy demands and ways to mitigate the effects of climatic change on world food production."[34]

Congress responded by enacting the National Climate Program Act in 1978, which instructed President Carter to create a National Climate Program Office that would coordinate climate-related research among a wide variety of agencies and other government entities, including EPA, NASA, the National Science Foundation, and the Departments of Agriculture, Energy, and State.[35] Though it was repeatedly targeted for cuts by the Reagan Administration,[36] government research into the causes and likely effects of climate change continued through the 1980s, and, by June 1988, NASA scientist James Hansen was ready to testify before the Senate Energy and Natural Resources Committee that he was 99 percent certain "the greenhouse effect has been detected and it is changing our climate now."[37] Based on temperatures recorded for the first five months of the year, Hansen predicted that 1988 would turn out to be the warmest year in recorded history.[38] (He was right, and that 1988 record has since been broken many times over.[39])

Also in 1988, the World Meteorological Organization and the United Nations Environment Program created the Intergovernmental Panel on Climate Change (IPCC) "to provide internationally co-ordinated scientific assessments of the magnitude, timing and potential environmental and socio-economic impact of climate change and realistic response strategies."[40] The IPCC's First Assessment, released in 1990, expressed certainty that "emissions resulting from human activities [were] substantially increasing the atmospheric concentrations" of carbon dioxide and other greenhouse gases and that "the increases [would] enhance the greenhouse effect, resulting on average in an additional warming of the Earth's surface."[41] The IPCC further concluded that, because carbon dioxide and some of its peers were "long-lived gases," their atmospheric concentrations would be slow to decline in response to emission reductions. In fact, the IPCC "calculated with confidence" that simply stabilizing CO_2 concentration at 1990 levels would require an immediate 60 percent reduction in global emissions. If emissions instead continued on their current trajectory, the IPCC predicted a three-degree Celsius increase in global average temperatures by 2100 and a corresponding 2-foot rise in average sea levels, with substantial regional variation in both figures.[42]

The IPCC's finding spurred the United Nations to action. At the 1992 Earth Summit in Rio de Janeiro, 154 countries, including the United States, signed the United Nations Framework Convention on Climate Change (UNFCCC), which aimed to stabilize atmospheric greenhouse gas concentrations "at a level that would prevent dangerous anthropogenic interference with the climate system."[43] The UNFCCC stated that developed countries should "take the lead" in addressing climate change (because, historically, their emissions had been much greater),[44] but, largely because of opposition from the United States, the treaty did not include binding reduction targets.[45] Instead, developed countries made a voluntary pledge to stabilize greenhouse gas emissions at 1990 levels by the year 2000.[46] President George H.W. Bush signed the UNFCCC on behalf of the United States, and the Senate unanimously ratified it.[47] But the Bush Administration showed little appetite for major domestic policy change aimed at reducing emissions, focusing instead on modest, mostly voluntary energy conservation programs.[48]

Bill Clinton entered office in 1993 with decidedly more aggressive plans, proposing a "Btu tax" on all energy sources other than wind, solar, and geothermal power.[49] But when that initiative proved enormously unpopular, the Administration retrenched and ended up releasing a "Climate Change Action Plan" that was essentially a more expansive version of the Bush strategy: an assortment of small programs, most of them voluntary and focused on energy conservation.[50] Environmental groups were underwhelmed.[51]

In 1995, the IPCC released its Second Assessment Report, which concluded that global surface temperatures had already increased between 0.3 and 0.6 degrees Celsius since the late nineteenth century and that the "balance of evidence . . . suggest[ed] a discernible human influence on global climate."[52] In other words, the world was getting warmer, and man-made emissions were at least partially responsible. The report further projected that, in the absence of mitigation efforts, temperatures would increase another 2 degrees Celsius (3.6 degrees Fahrenheit) by 2100.[53]

As for the consequences of this warming, the IPCC estimated that sea level would rise 50 centimeters by 2100 (on top of a 10 to 25 centimeter rise that had already occurred in the past century) due to thermal expansion of the oceans (the volume of water increases slightly as it warms) and to the melting of glaciers and ice sheets.[54] It also predicted more severe droughts and floods in some parts of the world and noted the possibility of "more extreme rainfall events."[55]

The following year, having already concluded that the voluntary commitments made in Rio were inadequate, the parties to the UNFCCC met in Kyoto, Japan, to negotiate a set of binding reduction targets.[56] The resulting Kyoto Protocol provided an individualized greenhouse gas emission target for each developed country, with the goal of reducing overall emissions from these countries to 5 percent below 1990 levels by 2012.[57] Vice President Al Gore was instrumental in brokering the agreement, and he committed the United States to reducing its emissions to 7 percent below 1990 levels.[58] But several months prior to the negotiations, the U.S. Senate had passed a unanimous resolution warning that it wouldn't ratify any treaty that included binding reduction commitments for the United States and other developed nations if the agreement didn't also require reductions from developing countries within the same compliance period.[59] Thus, when Gore signed the final draft of the protocol in November 1998, he noted that the act imposed "no obligations on the United States" in the absence of Senate ratification and that it would not be submitted to the Senate "without the meaningful participation of key developing countries in efforts to address climate change."[60]

By 2000, U.S. greenhouse gas emissions were 14 percent *above* 1990 levels.[61] Clinton left office having never submitted the Kyoto Protocol for Senate ratification.[62] Not long after his inauguration, President George W. Bush declared that his administration would not support the treaty.[63]

With no chance of ratifying Kyoto and equally grim prospects for the passage of any domestic climate legislation, environmental groups turned to the air-pollution law that was already on the books. In October 1999, shortly before Bush took office, nineteen environmental organizations filed a petition demanding that the EPA regulate greenhouse gas emissions from motor vehicles under the Clean Air Act.[64] As support for their position, the groups cited a 1998 memo from the EPA's then general counsel, Jonathan Cannon, to Administrator Carol Browner. Cannon had concluded that, as a "physical [and] chemical substance . . . which is emitted . . . into the ambient air," carbon dioxide satisfied the Act's definition of "air pollutant" and was thus susceptible to regulation by the EPA, *if* the administrator found that CO_2 emissions were "reasonably anticipated to cause or contribute to adverse effects on public health, welfare, or the environment."[65]

Agencies rarely respond to petitions with anything resembling alacrity, and the EPA waited more than three years to issue a formal denial.[66] The agency—now led by Bush appointee and former New Jersey governor Christine Todd Whitman—justified its decision on two alternative grounds. First, the EPA claimed that it could not grant the petition because greenhouse gases didn't qualify as air pollutants within the meaning of the Clean Air Act.[67] In connection with this point, the EPA noted that its new general counsel, Robert Fabricant, disagreed with Cannon's earlier findings and had explicitly withdrawn the Cannon memo "as no longer expressing the views of EPA's General Counsel."[68] Second, the agency argued that, even if it did have statutory authority to regulate the greenhouse gas emissions of motor vehicles, it should not do so in light of a variety of policy considerations, such as lingering gaps in the scientific understanding of climate change; the desirability of a comprehensive, international solution to the problem as compared to piecemeal domestic actions; and the possibility that greenhouse gas emissions standards for motor vehicles would encroach on the Department of Transportation's authority to establish fuel economy standards.[69]

A lengthy court battle ensued, and, in 2007, a five-Justice majority of the Supreme Court roundly rejected the EPA's reasoning. In *Massachusetts v. EPA,* the Court, like Cannon, found that greenhouse gases fit within the statutory definition of "air pollutant" and that, as a result, the EPA could decline to regulate motor vehicles' emissions of such gases "only if it determine[d] that greenhouse gases do not contribute to climate change or if it provide[d] some reasonable explanation as to why it [could not or would not] exercise its discretion to determine whether they do."[70] In the majority's view, the "policy judgments" offered by the EPA in its petition denial had "nothing to do with whether greenhouse gas emissions contribute to climate change and [did] not amount to a reasoned justification for declining to form a scientific judgment."[71] The Court further cautioned the EPA that it could not "avoid its statutory obligation by noting the uncertainty surrounding various features of climate change and concluding that it would therefore be better not to regulate at this time."[72] Uncertainty could justify inaction only "if it [was] so profound that it preclude[d] EPA from making a reasoned judgment" as to whether greenhouse gas emissions from motor vehicles could "reasonably be anticipated to endanger public health or welfare."[73]

But by this point, the weight of the scientific evidence for human-caused climate change made it essentially impossible for a rational policymaker to find profound uncertainty as to whether greenhouse gas emissions posed a threat to human health. The Fourth Assessment Report of the IPCC, released the same year as the Court's decision in *Massachusetts v. EPA*, cited "unequivocal" evidence that the world's climate was warming and concluded, with greater than 90 percent confidence, that the majority of warming since the mid-twentieth century was due to increases in greenhouse gas emissions associated with human activities.[74] President Bush's EPA administrator, Stephen Johnson, echoed these conclusions in a draft "endangerment finding" for greenhouse gases that he prepared in December 2007.[75] Johnson's draft also noted that, as a result of warming over the course of the coming century, the United States was expected to suffer a host of ill effects, including "an increase in the intensity of precipitation events and the risk of flooding"; an intensification of the "magnitude, frequency, and duration" of severe heat waves, "with likely increases in mortality and morbidity"; increased ozone pollution, "with associated risks in respiratory infection, aggravation of asthma, and potentially premature death in people with heart and lung disease"; "a change in the range of vector-borne diseases"; and "a likely trend toward more intense hurricanes . . . and other extreme weather events."[76] Accordingly, Johnson proposed to find that elevated atmospheric concentrations of greenhouse gases were "reasonably anticipated to endanger public welfare."[77]

But, even after its loss at the Supreme Court, the Bush Administration was determined to avoid making such a finding. Only minutes after one of Johnson's deputies emailed the draft to the White House's Office of Information and Regulatory Affairs (OIRA) for review, White House officials called to demand that he recall the message.[78] The deputy refused, and OIRA, in turn, refused to open the email, taking the position that the ninety-day review period for agency regulations was triggered when the email containing a draft regulation was opened, not when it was received.[79]

Six months later, the EPA released a far milder document that reviewed the legal and economic implications of regulating greenhouse gases under the Clean Air Act without actually reaching any conclusion about the dangers they posed.[80] It thus fell to Obama's EPA administrator, Lisa Jackson, to propose an actual endangerment finding, which she did on April 17, 2009.[81]

BETWEEN A CAP AND A HARD PLACE

Five days later, when President Obama gave his Earth Day address in Newtown, Iowa, he explained that, one way or another, the carbon loophole was finally about to close: "[T]here is no question that we have to regulate carbon pollution in some way; the only question is how we do it."[82] With Administrator Jackson's endangerment finding in motion, regulation under the Clean Air Act was imminent, but Obama had a different plan in mind:

> We'd set a cap, a ceiling, on all the carbon dioxide and other greenhouse gases that our economy is allowed to produce in total, combining the emissions from cars and trucks, coal-fired power plants, energy-intensive industries, all sources.
>
> And by setting an overall cap, carbon pollution becomes like a commodity. It places a value on a limited resource, and that is the ability to pollute. And to determine that value, just like any other traded commodity, we'd create a market where companies could buy and sell the right to produce a certain amount of carbon pollution. And in this way, every company can determine for itself whether it makes sense to spend the

> money to become cleaner or more efficient, or to spend the money on a certain amount of allowable pollution.
>
> Over time, as the cap on greenhouse gases is lowered, the commodity becomes scarcer—and the price goes up. And year by year, companies and consumers would have greater incentive to invest in clean energy and energy efficiency as the price of the status quo became more expensive.
>
> What this does is it makes wind power more economical, makes solar power more economical. Clean energy all becomes more economical. And by closing the carbon loophole through this kind of market-based cap, we can address in a systematic way all the facets of the energy crisis: We lower our dependence on foreign oil, we reduce our use of fossil fuels, we promote new industries right here in America. We set up the right incentives so that everybody is moving in the same direction towards energy independence.[83]

The substance of Obama's proposal was hardly novel. Emission trading had been a favored environmental policy tool since the success of the Acid Rain Trading Program in the 1990s, and it made particular sense in the context of a global pollutant like carbon dioxide. (A ton of CO_2 has the same impact on the global climate whether it is emitted in New York, New Mexico, or New Zealand.[84] Thus, a unit of emission reduction that occurs in one jurisdiction is effectively interchangeable with one that occurs hundreds or even thousands of miles away.) Obama's Republican rival for the presidency in 2008, Senator John McCain, had recognized as much all the way back in 2003, when he cosponsored the Senate's first (unsuccessful) carbon trading bill with Democrat Joe Lieberman.[85]

But while President Obama was not the first American politician to propose a nationwide cap-and-trade plan for carbon, he seemed likely to be the first to succeed in getting the policy enacted.

Cap-and-trade had gained a great deal of momentum since that first McCain-Lieberman bill was voted down in 2003. In 2008, ten Northeastern states had begun trading carbon allowances as part of the Regional Greenhouse Gas Initiative, which aimed to cut emissions from the region's electricity sector 10 percent by 2019.[86] Meanwhile, California was gearing up to launch an even more ambitious, economy-wide trading program pursuant to its Global Warming Solutions Act of 2006, which committed the state to reducing its greenhouse gas emissions to 1990 levels by 2020.[87]

And at the federal level, the Supreme Court's decision in *Massachusetts v. EPA* had made clear that the status quo was no longer an option. Faced with the potential for less flexible, costlier regulation under the Clean Air Act, some major emitters, including oil companies and utilities, decided they were better off playing an active role in shaping new climate legislation than refusing to negotiate altogether. On January 15, 2009, five days before Obama was inaugurated, the U.S. Climate Action Partnership (USCAP), a coalition of major environmental groups and Fortune 500 corporations—including utilities and oil companies—released a "Blueprint for Legislative Action" laying out their preferred framework for a cap-and-trade bill.[88]

With some of the nation's largest polluters and its most influential environmental groups agreeing on the basic framework of a bill, and sympathetic Democrats in control of the White House and both chambers of Congress, the passage of cap-and-trade seemed not just possible, but probable.[89]

LET'S MAKE A DEAL

The USCAP blueprint was a relatively detailed document. It included, for instance, specific recommendations for long-term emission reduction targets, proposing to cut U.S. emissions 14 to 20 percent below 2005 levels by 2020, 42 percent by 2030, and 80 percent by 2050.[90] But on one topic, the document was conspicuously vague: it declined to say exactly how carbon allowances—the new "commodity" that the President described in his Earth Day speech—should be allocated.[91] And this question of distribution was far from inconsequential. On the contrary, it would prove to be the most controversial aspect of cap-and-trade, one that ultimately scuttled any chance of enacting the legislation.

There are essentially two methods of distributing allowances in a trading program: auctioning them to the highest bidder or freely allocating them to existing firms.[92] Distribution choices do not affect the environmental benefits of the trading scheme—emission reductions are entirely a function of the cap—but they do determine who bears the cost of those reductions.[93] Under an auction system, each polluter must buy an allowance for each unit of pollution it emits. Thus, all polluters bear costs in direct proportion to their share of overall emissions. Those who pollute the most pay the most.

With free allocation, this isn't necessarily the case—it all depends on how the allowances are divvied up. Consider the utility sector. If allowances are allocated in proportion to historical *generation volume*—in other words, if each plant gets a set number of carbon allowances for each megawatt-hour it generated in the baseline year—plants that pollute at high rates will face greater abatement burdens (expressed as percentages of their current emissions) than cleaner plants, just as they would in an auction system. But if allowances are instead allocated in proportion to plants' historical *emission volume*, clean and dirty plants will have identical abatement burdens (again, relative to their current emissions).

To understand why, imagine a cap-and-trade scheme that is limited to just two plants. Last year, these plants collectively emitted 45 tons of pollutant *x*, with Plant A emitting 15 tons and Plant B emitting 30 tons. Furthermore, each plant generated 5 megawatt-hours of electricity. Thus, Plant A's emission rate was 3 tons per megawatt-hour, while Plant B's was twice as high at 6 tons per megawatt-hour.

Now, imagine that this year, the plants are required to reduce total emissions of pollutant *x* by a third, with emissions capped at 30 tons. If the thirty allowances are freely allocated based on last year's generation volume, each plant will receive half (fifteen allowances), because each plant generated half of last year's electricity. Assuming that both plants generate the same 5 megawatt-hours this year, Plant A will face no abatement cost, as it has enough allowances to cover its emissions. Plant B, on the other hand, is 15 units short. It will either have to reduce its own emission rate by 50 percent or pay Plant A to reduce its emissions and sell Plant B its spare allowances.

But what if allowances are instead allocated based on historical emissions? Plant A will receive only ten allowances, because it was responsible for one-third of last year's total emissions, while Plant B will receive twenty, because it emitted two-thirds of last year's total. Now *both* plants will need to reduce their emissions rate by one-third or purchase an equivalent number of allowances from the other. This is, of course, a better deal for dirty Plant B, which would otherwise need to reduce/purchase 50 percent of its emissions, but it is less desirable for clean Plant A, which would otherwise have no reduction/purchase obligation. Thus, the financial "winners" and "losers" in any cap-and-trade scheme are determined almost entirely by the manner in which emission allowances were allocated.

In the case of a national trading program for carbon dioxide, policymakers had to determine how to allocate allowances not just *within* industries but also *across* them. The utility sector may have been the nation's largest source of CO_2, but it was hardly the only one. How should allowances be split between power plants and the oil companies that provided gasoline for motor vehicles? What about steel plants and aluminum smelters?

The member companies of USCAP were not prepared to answer these questions with any specificity when they released their cap-and-trade blueprint in January 2009. Thus, while the proposal urged that allowances be freely allocated in the early years of the cap-and-trade program—with auctioning phased in over time in order to "buffer" the program's "economic impacts on energy consumers and businesses"[94]—it didn't spell out exactly how those free allowances should be divided. Instead, USCAP kept its recommendations fuzzy—suggesting, for example, that manufacturers of energy-intensive commodities subject to foreign competition should receive an "adequate amount of allowances," and that efforts to reduce public infrastructure's vulnerability to climate change should receive "sufficient allowance value."[95]

President Obama, meanwhile, had campaigned on the idea that 100 percent of allowances should be auctioned from the start, with the resulting billions of dollars in annual revenue being either invested in renewable energy development or returned to lower- and middle-income Americans in the form of a tax cut that would offset any increases in their energy costs.[96] But the Democratic legislators charged with shepherding such a bill through the House, Representatives Henry Waxman of California and Ed Markey of Massachusetts, had other plans. To pass the House Energy and Commerce Committee, the bill would need the support of Representative Rick Boucher.[97] And Boucher, a Democrat from Virginia coal country with strong ties to the utility industry, would never agree to an all-auction scheme.[98] One of Boucher's largest campaign contributors, Duke Energy, which generated 70 percent of its electricity from coal and was the nation's third-largest emitter of CO_2, had already spoken out against the President's auction proposal, telling the *New York Times* that it amounted to a "coal state stickup" that would disproportionately drive up electricity rates in coal-dependent states like Indiana and Kentucky, because the dirty plants in those states would need to buy more allowances than plants in states that relied on a cleaner energy mix.[99] (The company's spokesman neglected to mention that even if the 40 percent increase he predicted did occur, electricity rates in Indiana and Kentucky would still be well below those in the Northeast.[100])

After six weeks of negotiation with Boucher (and, through him, Duke Energy's CEO, Jim Rogers), Waxman and Markey emerged with a bill that would reduce emissions 17 percent below 2005 levels by 2020, 42 percent by 2030, and 84 percent by 2050—right in line with USCAP's goals—but that also included what the journalist Eric Pooley described as a "breathtaking set of concessions for coal."[101] The bill freely allocated 85 percent of allowances in the early years of the trading program, though that percentage was set to decline every few years.[102] By far the largest share of allowances—35 percent—would be allocated to the electric sector, an amount that represented 90 percent of its current emissions.[103] Thus, by 2020, the electric sector as a whole would need to achieve only a 10 percent reduction in its carbon emissions or to purchase an equivalent number of additional allowances from other industries subject to the cap. (The sector was also free, of course, to reduce its emissions by *more* than 10 percent and sell its extra allowances to other industries.)

Pursuant to an allocation formula devised by the Edison Electric Institute, most of the utility sector's allowances would be divided among individual utilities based 50 percent on their historic share of electricity sales and 50 percent on their historic share of carbon emissions.[104] This was a compromise between Edison Electric's lower-emitting members on the coasts, whose gas-heavy fleets would have reaped a windfall in a formula based purely on past electricity sales, and its higher-emitting, coal-dependent members in the Midwest and South, which wanted a formula based purely on historical emissions.[105] But the end result was that utilities with coal-heavy fleets would receive more allowances per unit of electricity sold than their cleaner peers.

In addition to its coal-friendly allocation scheme, the Waxman-Markey bill provided a host of other "goodies" for coal interests, including $10 billion for research into carbon capture-and-storage technology and $181 billion of bonus allowances for utilities that successfully implemented such technology.[106]

Coddling coal may have won the approval of Congressman Boucher and Duke Energy's Rogers, but it earned the ire of a number of environmental groups, as well as disdain from news outlets like the *New York Times,* which described the bill as "fat with compromises, carve-outs, concessions and out-and-out gifts," with the biggest prizes going to utilities "which wanted assurances that they could continue to operate and build coal-burning power plants without shouldering new costs."[107] The *Washington Post* editorial board observed that while cap-and-trade "was supposed to allow Congress to avoid picking winners and losers in the fight against climate change," Waxman-Markey would "devote $60 billion to making sure clean coal isn't a loser."[108]

Brent Blackwelder, president of Friends of the Earth, argued that the bill was more certain to benefit Wall Street than to reduce pollution.[109] Even congressional Republicans criticized the bill as too friendly to industry, claiming that it would enrich "several big corporations at the expense of American consumers, their jobs, their livelihoods, and their futures."[110]

Perhaps most important, the bill provoked outrage from the oil industry, which had been allocated only 2 percent of total allowances despite producing almost a quarter of the nation's CO_2 emissions.[111] In protest, the oil company members of USCAP withdrew from the coalition, and the American Petroleum Institute began an aggressive (and effective) public relations campaign against the bill, hosting a series of rallies across the country at which industry employees urged legislators to "pass on $4 gas."[112]

Ultimately, Waxman and Markey had found themselves victim to a catch-22. They needed the support of coal-dependent utilities to pass the legislation, but the compromises necessary to win that support—essentially, a further extension of grandfathering—made the result unpalatable to everyone else. Their bill squeaked out of the House on June 29, 2009, by a vote of 219–212, but its Senate counterpart never even came to a vote.[113] By March 2010, the *New York Times* was ready to declare cap-and-trade dead.[114]

WHAT'S GRANDFATHERING GOT TO DO WITH IT?

What, one might wonder, does any of this have to do with grandfathering? This book, after all, is primarily concerned with the ways in which our nation's efforts to reduce air pollution have been undermined by the Clean Air Act's pairing of stringent performance standards for new sources with *no* performance standards for existing sources. And, as the above chronology makes clear, the U.S. government has historically declined to regulate carbon dioxide emissions from *any* sources, new or old. Whereas newly constructed power plants have been required to control their sulfur dioxide emissions since 1971 and to control their nitrogen oxides emissions since 1978, they have, until recently, had no obligation to reduce their CO_2 emissions.[115] Nonetheless, grandfathering has affected greenhouse gas emissions in two indirect but significant ways. Both are consequences of the "old plant effect" we described in Chapter 3, whereby utilities have delayed retiring old plants in order to avoid building replacements that must comply with expensive new-source standards for sulfur dioxide and nitrogen oxides emissions.

First, because older plants tend to emit CO_2 at higher rates than new ones, grandfathering-induced retirement delays have kept the electric sector's greenhouse gas emissions higher than they otherwise would be. Second, by keeping old coal plants in operation longer than originally planned, grandfathering gave rise to the excessive allowance demands from coal-dependent utilities that undermined support for cap-and-trade legislation in 2009.

1. Higher Emissions

Even though they are not subject to legal restrictions on their CO_2 emissions, new plants tend to emit less of the gas than their predecessors. For one, they are much more likely to burn natural gas, which produces half as much carbon dioxide per unit of electricity as coal: on average, coal plants operating in 2010 emitted 2,160 pounds of CO_2 per megawatt-hour generated, while gas plants emitted 980 pounds.[116] Since 1980, less than 20 percent of new generating capacity in the United States has been coal-fired, while more than 55 percent has been gas-fired.[117] (Another 20 percent has come from energy sources that produce *no* carbon emissions, like nuclear, hydroelectric, wind, and solar energy.[118]) And the preference for gas has become even stronger since 1990: less than 10 percent of capacity additions since 1990 have been coal-fired, while close to 80 percent have been gas-fired.[119]

Even the small fraction of newer plants that *do* rely on coal as a fuel source tend to produce less CO_2 than their older counterparts because they are more efficient, requiring less fuel (and thus emitting less pollution) for each unit of electricity they generate. This is the case for two reasons. First, plants generally lose efficiency after about twenty-five years of service due to wear and tear on various components, so, even if an old plant were to be replaced with one of the exact same design, the replacement would emit less pollution.[120] Second, the technology used in newer coal plants tends to be inherently more efficient than the systems used in older plants.[121] As a result, while older coal plants in the United States often emit over 2,500 pounds of carbon dioxide per megawatt-hour—indeed, the dirtiest as of 2006 emitted at the astounding rate of 3,600 pounds per megawatt-hour—the emission rate of a brand new coal plant is a comparatively modest 1,450 to 1,800 pounds per megawatt-hour, depending on the combustion technology used.[122]

Given the tendency of new plants to burn cleaner fuel and use more efficient combustion technology, we can assume that whenever an old plant is retired and replaced, total carbon emissions from the electric sector decline. Thus, by encouraging older plants to delay retirement, grandfathering has kept the sector's greenhouse gas emissions higher than they would otherwise be.

2. Undermining of Waxman-Markey

As of 2010, just over 36 percent of the nation's coal-fired generating capacity had been constructed prior to 1971, when the EPA promulgated the first set of New Source Performance Standards for SO_2. Another 25 percent of current coal capacity had been constructed before 1978, when the EPA increased the stringency of the SO_2 standards and added NO_x standards. Given that these plants were expected to operate for only thirty years, this means that some 61 percent of the nation's coal-fired generation capacity was already overdue for retirement by the time Waxman-Markey was negotiated in 2009.[123] In other words, many of the coal-fired power plants the bill took such pains to protect with generous allowance allocations and other subsidies wouldn't have still been operating but for the effects of grandfathering. Indeed, a 2010 study estimated that if all existing plants had been required to satisfy New Source Performance Standards in 1985—in other words, if the Clean Air Act's grandfathering had been subject to a fifteen-year time limit—an additional 350 coal-fired generating units would have been retired and replaced with lower-emitting, gas-fired units by 1995.[124]

Consider the portfolio of Duke Energy, whose CEO, Jim Rogers, played a key role in negotiating the cap-and-trade bill's many concessions to coal-fired power producers.[125] As of 2007, Duke's six highest-emitting power plants, both in terms of CO_2 emission rate and total CO_2 emissions, all contained pre-1971 grandfathered generating units.[126]

Had Duke's plants and others like them retired on schedule in the 1990s and 2000s, they would almost certainly have been replaced by sources that emitted less CO_2, thanks to the use of either cleaner fuel or more efficient coal-combustion technology. Indeed, the average emission rate of plants constructed in the 1990s (1,454 pounds per megawatt-hour) is 33 percent lower than that of plants constructed thirty years earlier, in the 1960s (2,098 pounds per megawatt-hour), and the average rate of plants constructed in the 2000s (1,016 pounds per megawatt-hour) is 51 percent lower than that of plants constructed in the 1970s.[127]

Thus, in the absence of grandfathering, two things would likely have been true when Waxman-Markey was negotiated in 2009. First, with a higher proportion of low-emitting, gas-fired plants in the national energy mix, the utility sector as a whole would have had far lower total emissions and presumably would have demanded significantly fewer allowances as a condition of supporting cap-and-trade, perhaps freeing some up for allocation to other industries, like the disgruntled oil sector. Second, with the nation's oldest, highest-emitting coal plants already retired, there would have been fewer utilities with a vested interest in preserving such facilities' regulatory advantage over newer, cleaner plants.

In that alternate reality, would cap-and-trade have become law? It's impossible to know, of course. Certainly the legacy of grandfathering wasn't the only obstacle that Waxman-Markey faced. For one, the ongoing financial crisis had left the American public wary of embracing market-based solutions to any problem.[128] For another, the White House took a regrettably hands-off approach to the legislation, instead focusing its resources on moving healthcare reform through Congress.[129]

But it is undeniable that criticism from environmental groups, the media, Republican legislators, and the oil industry over what was perceived as excessive pandering to utilities—particularly coal-dependent utilities—played a large role in souring public and political opinion of the bill. And it does seem likely that, in a world without grandfathering, the bill's sponsors wouldn't have felt so pressured to make such dramatic concessions.

7

Hope for Redemption

The Walter C. Beckjord Generating Station sits on the banks of the Ohio River, less than twenty miles southeast of Cincinnati, in Clermont County, Ohio.[1] Beckjord offers a near-perfect case study of the costs of grandfathering. Construction of the plant was announced in November 1948, and its first 100-megawatt coal unit was operational by June 1952.[2] Five additional units came online between 1953 and 1969.[3]

Because the units were constructed prior to 1971, all were exempt from the EPA's New Source Performance Standards. For most of the 1970s, they also managed to avoid complying with any emission limitation under Ohio's implementation plan for meeting the sulfur dioxide NAAQS, even though Ohio's original plan, approved by the EPA in 1972, would have subjected Beckjord to a state emission standard—1.6 pounds of SO_2 per million Btus of heat input—that was only 33 percent less stringent than the federal new-source standard of 1.2 lbs/MMBtu.[4]

In 1973, Ohio utilities convinced the U.S. Court of Appeals for the Sixth Circuit to invalidate the Ohio plan on procedural grounds.[5] The court ordered the EPA to hold an additional hearing at which regulated plants could voice their objections, but before the agency could oblige, the governor of Ohio withdrew the plan from consideration.[6] A year later, Ohio submitted a far less stringent proposal that would have allowed Beckjord to continue emitting at its uncontrolled level: 4.8 lbs/MMBtu.[7] But that plan, too, was struck down on procedural grounds, this time by a state environmental review board.[8]

In 1976, after Ohio failed to offer any replacement for its second proposal, the EPA stepped in with a federal plan that would limit Beckjord's emissions to 2.02 lbs/MMBtu.[9] (This, according to the latest EPA computer modeling, was the level necessary for Ohio to attain the sulfur dioxide NAAQS.[10]) After yet more litigation by Ohio utilities—including Beckjord's owner, Cincinnati Gas & Electric—the bulk of the federal plan was upheld in 1978.[11] (In rejecting the utilities' challenge, the Sixth Circuit noted that Ohio was the only state in the country that still lacked an enforceable SO_2 implementation plan.[12])

Even under the federal plan, which Beckjord satisfied by burning low-sulfur coal at some of its units, the plant was allowed to emit 70 percent more pollution per megawatt-hour than a new source could.[13] And the performance gap between Beckjord and new sources grew even wider in 1978, when the EPA revised its New Source Performance Standards to require all new plants to scrub their uncontrolled emissions by either 70 or 90 percent, depending on the sulfur content of the coal being burned.[14] While the nominal emission ceiling remained 1.2 lbs/MMBtu under this 1978 standard, the percentage reduction requirement yielded much lower emission rates in all plants except those burning very high sulfur coal.[15]

Over the course of the next three decades, Beckjord managed time and again to avoid making further reductions in its emissions of SO_2 or any other pollutant. For example, in a 1981 petition alleging violations of the Good Neighbor Provision, New York listed Beckjord as one of the out-of-state plants whose emissions formed sulfates that prevented New York from attaining the particulate matter NAAQS and contributed to acid rain in the state.[16] But, after three years of delay, the EPA denied the petition, finding, among other things, that acid rain was outside the purview of the Good Neighbor Provision and that Midwestern states' contribution to particulate pollution in New York (an estimated 4 to 6 percent of the total concentration) could not be deemed significant.[17]

In 1999, the Clinton Administration sued Beckjord's then owner, Cinergy, for undertaking major modifications at the plant in the late 1980s and early 1990s without undergoing New Source Review.[18] The updates in question cost almost $20 million per unit (compared to a typical annual maintenance budget of $2 to $3 million per unit), took more than three months to complete, involved the replacement of more than forty separate components, were designed to restore the units to their original operating capacity and efficiency, and added more than twenty years to their projected lifespans.[19] Nonetheless, Cinergy denied that the projects could properly be characterized as modifications under the Clean Air Act.[20]

In December 2000, just weeks before President Clinton left office, Cinergy tentatively agreed to settle the case and reduce its SO_2 and NO_x emissions at Beckjord and other plants by two-thirds.[21] But after the George W. Bush Administration took office and announced its plans to overhaul the rules governing New Source Review, Cinergy backed out of the deal.[22] The case dragged on for another seven years, and, in 2008, a jury sided with Beckjord (now owned by Duke Energy).[23] Once again, the plant was spared the responsibility of controlling its emissions.

By this point, Beckjord had been operating for more than fifty-five years and was ranked as one of the "Top 50 Dirtiest Power Plants in the United States" by the Environmental Integrity Project.[24] Meanwhile, a 2010 report from the Clean Air Task Force estimated that Beckjord's pollution was responsible for 141 deaths, 102 hospitalizations, and 217 heart attacks *each year.*[25]

In the wake of its New Source Review victory, Beckjord seemed destined to continue emitting pollution at staggering rates for at least another decade. But only three years later, in July 2011, Duke announced that Beckjord's coal-fired units would be permanently retired in 2014.[26] In an ironic twist, the plant is now being repurposed as a battery-based energy storage facility, enabling increased use of wind and solar power in the region.[27] (One weakness of renewable energy is its inability to be dispatched "on demand." After all, the wind doesn't always blow, and the sun doesn't always shine. But a battery facility can store excess power generated during the sunniest or windiest portion of the day and release it when needed.[28])

And Beckjord was hardly the only grandfathered power plant to announce its retirement in recent years. Indeed, as of August 2014, utilities planned to shutter a full 80 percent of their pre-1970 units by 2025.[29] In 2012 alone, about 10.2 GW of coal capacity retired—just over 3 percent of the U.S. total.[30] The retiring units had an average age of 51 years.[31]

To what can we credit this rash of retirements by plants that only recently seemed likely to operate indefinitely? Prices and policies. By "prices," we mean sustained low prices for natural gas that have made gas-fired plants cheaper to operate. And by "policies," we mean three recent rulemakings of the Obama Administration that have made coal-fired generators more expensive to operate. These twin forces have fueled an unprecedented "dash to gas" by the utility sector that has the potential to end the harmful legacy of grandfathering once and for all.

THE DASH TO GAS

When we first discussed grandfathering's "old plant effect" in Chapter 3, we suggested that in the wake of the EPA's 1971 New Source Performance Standards for SO_2, utilities constructing new plants had two options: they could burn high-sulfur, Eastern coal and use a multimillion-dollar scrubber to remove pollution from the stack *after* combustion, or they could burn low-sulfur, Western coal, which, for plants in the eastern half of the country, was very expensive to transport. And after the EPA updated its standards in 1978, a scrubber became mandatory regardless of the type of coal burned.

But what if the plant didn't burn coal at all? There was no scrubber requirement for plants powered by natural gas, which releases only trace amounts of SO_2 upon combustion (not to mention considerably smaller quantities of NO_x and CO_2).[32] Why, then, didn't utilities respond to the EPA's restrictions on new-source emissions by building gas plants?

The trouble wasn't that utilities didn't know how to use the cleaner fuel. Gas-fired generating units date back to at least the 1940s, and, by 1970, gas had a 30 percent share of the electricity market, just over half that of coal.[33] Instead, the problem was one of supply. When the Clean Air Act was passed, gas simply wasn't plentiful enough to replace coal as the electric sector's fuel of choice.

This was largely a result of the artificial suppression of the interstate gas supply by government price controls.[34] Like coal, natural gas is a fossil fuel—formed, in this case, from the ancient remains of microscopic, ocean-dwelling plants and animals.[35] But unlike coal, gas is, well, a gas (or, more accurately, a mixture of gases), which makes it tricky to transport.[36] Thus, although the nation's first commercial gas well was drilled in 1821, widespread distribution of the fuel became possible only after a complex network of interstate pipeline was constructed beginning in the 1920s.[37] Because this infrastructure was quite expensive to build, many areas were served by a single distributor.[38] Concerned that pipeline owners would exploit these natural monopolies to exact unfair prices, Congress passed the Natural Gas Act of 1938, which gave the Federal Power

Commission authority to set "just and reasonable rates" for the interstate transmission and sale of gas.[39]

At first, the Federal Power Commission controlled only the price at which gas was sold *by* interstate pipeline owners to local distribution companies. In 1954, however, the Supreme Court held that the Commission also had the power to set the "wellhead rate"—that is, the price at which gas was sold *to* interstate pipeline owners by individual gas producers.[40] The goal of the Natural Gas Act, the Court reasoned, was "the protection of consumers," and the wellhead rate had "a direct and substantial effect on the price paid by the ultimate consumers."[41] For the next twenty years, the Federal Power Commission kept wellhead rates essentially flat, even as demand increased.[42]

At the time, most gas was produced as a byproduct of oil wells, and artificially low prices gave producers little incentive to develop new, independent gas resources.[43] As a result, when U.S. oil production peaked in 1970, gas production stalled as well, and pipeline companies were left unable to meet customer demand. Between 1970 and 1976, gas curtailments—interruptions in service due to inadequate supply—became twenty times more common.[44] Frustrated industrial and residential consumers looked to more reliable sources of energy, and natural gas consumption fell by 10 percent between 1972 and 1979, even as the nation's overall energy demand increased.[45] In the electric sector, the market share of gas declined from 30 percent to 20 percent during the 1970s, while coal's share rose from 56 percent to 66 percent.[46]

Recognizing that the nation's recurrent gas shortages were at least partially attributable to federal price regulation, Congress passed the Natural Gas Policy Act of 1978, which provided for a gradual phasing out of wellhead price controls.[47] Unfortunately, legislators also mistakenly assumed that even after price ceilings were removed, gas production would continue to decline in tandem with oil production.[48] In the interest of "national energy security," they resolved to discourage the use of gas for economically essential activities like electricity generation.[49] The resulting Powerplant and Industrial Fuel Use Act of 1978 restricted the construction of new gas-fired power plants and encouraged utilities to instead embrace nuclear and coal-fired power.[50] In other words, promptly after abandoning a policy that artificially suppressed the gas *supply*, the United States set to work artificially suppressing gas *demand*. As a result, natural gas use declined another 15 percent between 1979 and 1986, while total energy use fell only 3.5 percent.[51]

The gas industry's fortunes finally changed when Congress repealed the ban on new gas-fired plants in 1987.[52] The deregulation of many states' electricity markets toward the end of the decade proved another boon for gas producers.[53] The independent generating companies that popped up to compete with vertically integrated utilities favored gas because gas-fired plants were much cheaper to construct (even if the fuel itself remained more expensive than coal).[54] By the turn of the century, almost all new power plants under construction were designed to burn gas.[55]

But for their first decade or so in service, many of these new gas plants were underused. In 2009, gas-fired plants represented 41 percent of total U.S. generating capacity but produced only 30 percent of the nation's electricity.[56] Coal-fired plants, meanwhile, represented only 30 percent of capacity but generated 44 percent of electricity.[57]

To see why, it's useful to understand the basics of electricity dispatch. Demand for electricity varies by time of day—people tend to use more power in the post-work evening hours, when their lights and gadgets are on—and time of year—people tend to use more power in the summer, when their air conditioners are running.[58] As a result, not all plants on the grid need to be generating power at all times. Instead, electricity markets operate on the principle of "economic dispatch."[59] Essentially, the plants with the lowest operating costs are turned on first, to service the minimum level of demand that's always present in the system (also known as "base load"), and the plants with higher operating costs are brought into play only when needed to service excess demand (also known as "peak load").[60]

Until quite recently, coal-fired plants were typically run almost continuously, while gas plants were saved for periods of high demand—mostly because coal was considerably cheaper than gas.[61] But between 2008 and 2013, the price of natural gas declined by more than 50 percent, thanks in large part to a dramatic increase in the supply of "shale gas," which is found in fine-grained, largely impermeable rock formations.[62] While shale gas was traditionally considered impractical to extract, recent advances in horizontal drilling and hydraulic fracturing technologies have enabled explosive growth in its production.[63] (Hydraulic fracturing involves the pumping of large volumes of water, sand, and chemical additives into a well at high pressure.[64] The fluid mixture creates tiny cracks in the surrounding rock, through which gas can flow back out into the well.[65]) Whereas, in 2007, shale gas represented 8 percent of U.S. gas production, that figure had climbed to 40 percent by 2013.[66] During the same period, total U.S. gas production increased by almost a third.[67]

With shale production continuing to climb and gas prices staying relatively low, utilities have begun to fire up their gas plants more and more often and, consequently, dispatch their coal plants less.[68] Indeed, in April 2015, gas overtook coal as the top source of U.S. electricity for the first time in history, generating 31 percent of the nation's power to coal's 30 percent.[69] In the same month just four years earlier, coal had supplied 44 percent of electricity while gas generated 22 percent.[70] As coal plants become less economic to operate relative to gas, they also become more likely to be retired altogether.[71]

THE ROLE OF REGULATION

At the same time that new gas plants are becoming cheaper to operate, old coal plants are becoming more expensive to run. Why? Here, we return at last to the regulations of the Obama Administration that we introduced at the start of this book—the three major fronts of the President's supposed "war on coal." They are, in increasing order of importance, the Cross-State Air Pollution Rule (also known as the Transport Rule), the Mercury and Air Toxics Standards (MATS), and the Clean Power Plan. All three rules are issued under the authority of the Clean Air Act, and all three, by imposing additional pollution-reduction obligations on grandfathered plants, increase the cost of operating such facilities.

Transport Rule

The Transport Rule is the EPA's latest attempt to implement the Clean Air Act's Good Neighbor Provision by eliminating interstate pollution (mostly from the Midwest and Appalachia) that "significantly contributes" to nonattainment of the NAAQS for ozone and particulate matter (mostly in the Northeast).[72] Like its predecessors, the NO_x SIP Call and the Clean Air Interstate Rule, the Transport Rule employed a two-step analysis to set state reduction targets—with the first step focused entirely on air quality impacts and the second taking into account compliance costs. First, the EPA identified all upwind states that contributed at least 1 percent of the maximum permissible concentration of either ozone or particulate matter in at least one downwind state that was out of attainment.[73] For each of the twenty-seven states whose contribution exceeded this threshold, the EPA then determined an emission budget based on the volume of reduction available at $500 per ton.[74]

As in the two prior rules, regulated sources were permitted to engage in emission trading.[75] But, mindful of the U.S. Court of Appeals for the D.C. Circuit's invalidation of the Clean Air Interstate Rule—and the court's disapproval of the idea that a state could satisfy its budget entirely by purchasing credits from out-of-state sources and thus not reduce its own emissions at all—the EPA limited the extent to which sources could trade across state lines.[76] Instead, the agency required that each state meet its budget primarily through reductions within its own borders.[77]

Notwithstanding this and other compromises designed to satisfy the court, the D.C. Circuit struck down the Transport Rule in 2011, objecting to, among other things, the agency's setting state reduction obligations based, in part, on the costs of the reductions rather than air quality impacts alone.[78] But the agency petitioned for Supreme Court review, and, in April 2014, the Court upheld the Transport Rule on a 6–2 vote. (Justice Alito was recused.)[79] The rule finally took effect on January 1, 2015—three years behind schedule.[80] It will eventually reduce SO_2 emissions from covered sources by 73 percent below their 2005 levels and their NO_x emissions by 54 percent below their 2005 levels.[81] In so doing, the EPA estimates that the rule will prevent 13,000 to 24,000 premature deaths annually, along with 15,000 nonfatal heart attacks, 19,000 hospital visits, and 400,000 asthma attacks.[82]

Mercury and Air Toxics Standards

The Obama Administration's next major Clean Air Act rule, MATS, targets power plants' emissions of heavy metals like mercury, arsenic, and nickel, as well as "acid gases" like hydrochloric and hydrofluoric acid.[83] Unlike the Transport Rule, which established statewide SO_2 and NO_x budgets, MATS imposes emission standards directly on 1,400 existing coal- and oil-fired generating units at 600 different power plants.[84]

How did the EPA get around the Clean Air Act's grandfathering and directly regulate emissions from these plants? As we mentioned back in Chapter 3, the 1970 Act carved out a separate regulatory framework, known as Section 112, for "hazardous air pollutants"—essentially, toxic substances that could cause serious health problems even when not highly concentrated in the ambient air. For these pollutants, Congress empowered the EPA to set national emission standards for both new and existing sources that "provided an ample margin of safety to protect the public health."[85]

But the EPA showed little interest in using its Section 112 powers during the first two decades of Clean Air Act implementation. Between 1970 and 1990, the agency classified only seven toxic pollutants as hazardous, leaving hundreds of others unaddressed.[86]

Exasperated with the EPA's inaction, Congress eliminated a great deal of the agency's discretion in this area in the 1990 amendments.[87] In particular, lawmakers took it upon themselves to classify 189 pollutants as hazardous and provided strict timetables for the EPA's regulation of major sources of those pollutants.[88]

The 1990 amendments also explicitly required the EPA to take action with respect to power plants. First, the agency was tasked with performing a study of "the hazards to public health reasonably anticipated to occur" as a result of the emission of hazardous air pollutants from power plants, and with reporting the results of this study to Congress within three years.[89] The EPA was then required to regulate the plants if, after considering the results of its study, it found that such regulation was "appropriate and necessary."[90]

Despite the three-year statutory deadline, the EPA did not complete the required study until 1998 (and only after environmental groups sued to force the agency's hand).[91] In the study, the EPA concluded that although power plants emit a number of hazardous air pollutants, mercury was "of greatest concern" because it is "highly toxic, persistent, and bioaccumulates in food chains."[92] As the agency explained, when airborne mercury settles in bodies of water, it can change into methylmercury, which then accumulates in fish that live in the polluted water. Humans who eat this contaminated fish risk neurological damage. And because developing fetuses are especially vulnerable to the effects of mercury exposure, the EPA was particularly concerned with the consumption of contaminated fish by women of childbearing age.[93]

Even though power plants were the largest source of mercury in the United States, it took the EPA an additional two years to conclude, in the waning days of the Clinton Administration, that regulating plants' mercury emissions under Section 112 was "appropriate and necessary" because the emissions "present[ed] significant hazards to public health and the environment."[94] And almost five more years passed before George W. Bush's EPA took the next step of setting binding limits on those emissions.[95]

But instead of regulating mercury under Section 112, the Bush Administration decided to do so under Section 111(d), a more flexible provision of the Clean Air Act that applies to nonhazardous pollutants.[96] The resulting "Clean Air Mercury Rule" was struck down by the D.C. Circuit, which found that the EPA had not properly withdrawn its earlier conclusion that regulating the mercury emissions of power plants under Section 112 was "appropriate and necessary."[97]

And so, three years later, the Obama Administration promulgated MATS under Section 112.[98] Once it's fully implemented, the rule is expected to cut mercury emissions from coal- and oil-fired power plants by 90 percent and "acid gas" emissions by 88 percent.[99] (Natural gas plants, which produce negligible amounts of hazardous pollution, are unaffected by the rule.[100]) Because many plants will achieve the necessary reductions in their toxic emissions by installing scrubbers, MATS will have the "co-benefit" of reducing the power sector's sulfur dioxide emissions by an additional 41 percent beyond the level required by the Transport Rule.[101] The EPA estimates that these reductions alone will prevent up to an additional 11,000 premature deaths each year, along with 4,700 heart attacks and 130,000 asthma attacks.[102]

Clean Power Plan

The third major Clean Air Act rule, the Clean Power Plan, targets existing power plants' greenhouse gas emissions.[103] Like MATS, the Clean Power Plan is promulgated under a section of the Clean Air Act that has been around since 1970 but that the EPA has used only rarely: Section 111(d) (the same provision the George W. Bush Administration attempted to use to regulate mercury).[104] Senator Muskie and his colleagues intended Section 111(d) to play a gap-filling role, covering existing sources' emissions of air pollutants that were neither subject to a NAAQS nor regulated as hazardous.[105] Greenhouse gases fall in this narrow category.

As already discussed in Chapter 6, the Obama Administration's first EPA administrator, Lisa Jackson, made an official endangerment finding for greenhouse gases under the Clean Air Act in December 2009.[106] Jackson subsequently set limits on the emission of such gases from automobiles in May 2010.[107]

About six months after finalizing emission standards for motor vehicles, the EPA settled a suit brought by a group of states and environmental organizations that sought to force the agency to impose similar limits on the greenhouse gas emissions of power plants.[108] Pursuant to the settlement, the EPA was required to promulgate greenhouse gas emission standards for both new power plants, under Section 111(b) of the Clean Air Act, and existing plants, under Section 111(d), by May 2012, but that deadline came and went without action.[109] The EPA proposed standards for new plants in March 2012 but never finalized them.[110] Then, in June 2013, President Obama unveiled his "Climate Action Plan," a set of executive actions designed to reduce U.S. greenhouse gas emissions to 17 percent below 2005 levels by 2020 and thus fulfill a pledge the President had made at the United Nations' Copenhagen Summit in 2009.[111] In service of that goal, Obama established new deadlines for the EPA to propose greenhouse gas limits for power plants.[112] The EPA subsequently finalized rules governing CO_2 emissions from both new and existing plants in August 2015.[113]

The new-source rule imposes a CO_2 emission limit of 1,400 lbs/megawatt-hour on newly constructed coal-fired generating units and 1,000 lbs/megawatt-hour on newly constructed gas-fired units.[114] But the EPA expects these standards to have a negligible impact on the electric sector's total CO_2 emissions.[115] For one thing, the gas limit can be satisfied by using highly efficient "combined-cycle" combustion technology, which utilities are expected to choose for new units even in the absence of a rule.[116] And although meeting the coal standard would require the use of partial carbon capture and storage technology, the requirement is largely irrelevant because utilities weren't planning to build any new coal units anyway.[117] For these reasons, the EPA projects that the new-source rule will have no costs and no benefits.[118]

The existing-source rule, by contrast, is expected to have quite a substantial effect on total emissions and to generate tens of billions of dollars in climate and health benefits.[119] Commonly known as the Clean Power Plan, the rule calculates a set of emission targets for each state by estimating the reductions the state could reasonably achieve through three strategies: (1) improving the efficiency of existing coal-fired plants; (2) substituting increased electricity generation from existing, lower-emitting gas plants for generation from existing, higher-emitting coal plants; and (3) substituting increased generation from new zero-emitting renewable sources (like wind and solar installations) for generation from existing coal plants.[120] Each state is assigned both a rate-based goal (pounds of CO_2 emitted per megawatt-hour generated) and a mass-based goal (pounds of CO_2 emitted per year) and can choose to comply with either.[121]

In total, the EPA estimates that the Clean Power Plan will cut the power sector's carbon dioxide emissions to 32 percent below 2005 levels by 2030, yielding $20 billion in climate-related benefits each year from that point forward. Furthermore, as with MATS, the EPA expects the rule to produce massive "co-benefits" in the form of particulate matter reductions that will prevent up to 3,600 premature deaths, 1,700 heart attacks, and 90,000 asthma attacks annually.[122]

Three things to note about these rules:

1. If not for grandfathering, we probably wouldn't need them

In the absence of grandfathering, the Transport Rule, MATS, and the Clean Power Plan likely wouldn't be necessary, at least not at their present stringency. The Transport Rule, after all, is an effort to tackle an interstate pollution problem that wouldn't exist if old power plants in the Midwest and Appalachia were subject to the same federal performance standards as new plants. Furthermore, while the EPA has never before regulated mercury or other toxic emissions from any power plants, new or old, some of the control technologies that will be used to comply with MATS are the same ones that new plants install to satisfy New Source Performance Standards for NAAQS pollutants—such as scrubbers (typically used to reduce SO_2, but here used to reduce mercury) and selective catalytic reduction systems (typically used to reduce NO_x, but here used to reduce mercury).[123] Thus, if all existing plants were already compliant with the New Source Performance Standards for NAAQS pollutants, they would also be compliant with MATS.[124]

Finally, as discussed in Chapter 6, CO_2 emissions from the electric sector would be much lower, due to earlier retirements of coal plants and increased reliance on gas-fired capacity, if the Clean Air Act had subjected existing plants to the same SO_2 and NO_x standards as new ones. As a result, we can assume that but for grandfathering, at least some portion of the 32 percent emission cut contemplated by the Clean Power Plan would already have been achieved. Furthermore, as was also explained in Chapter 6, grandfathered plants played a key role in derailing the 2009 effort to pass a comprehensive cap-and-trade bill for greenhouse gases. Had that bill or a similar proposal successfully become law, regulation of power plants' carbon emissions under the Clean Air Act wouldn't be necessary.

2. Of the three, the Clean Power Plan is the most important

While all three rules will have a significant impact on grandfathered plants, the most consequential by far is the Clean Power Plan. In 2011, when it finalized the Transport Rule, the EPA estimated that 4.8 gigawatts of coal-fired generating capacity would become ripe for closure as a result of the rule.[125] In 2012, when it finalized MATS, the agency estimated that the rule would render an additional 4.7 gigawatts of coal capacity uneconomic to operate.[126] And in 2015, when it finalized the Clean Power Plan, the EPA estimated that the rule would prompt 27 to 38 gigawatts to retire.[127] In other words, the projected impact of the Clean Power Plan was at least five times that of each of the earlier two rules.

Analyses by the Bipartisan Policy Center also suggest that the Clean Power Plan will drive far more retirements than the other two rules. In 2012, the Center estimated that MATS and the Transport Rule would collectively lead 16 gigawatts of coal capacity to retire, and, in 2015, it estimated that the Clean Power Plan—in its June 2014 draft form—would push between 32 and 39 gigawatts of coal capacity over the economic edge.[128]

3. Even without them, a lot of coal plants would still be retiring

The 27 to 38 gigawatts of coal-plant closures that the EPA expects the Clean Power Plan to spur (between 9 and 13 percent of the nation's total coal capacity) are *in addition to* 70 gigawatts (around 25 percent of the nation's total coal capacity) that the agency predicts will retire by 2030 even if the rule doesn't take effect.[129] This "base case" figure does include the effects of MATS and the Transport Rule,[130] but even if we subtract the approximately 10 gigawatts of retirements that the EPA's earlier analyses attributed to those rules, we're still left with 60 gigawatts of expected retirements that appear primarily driven by market forces—that is, low gas prices. Thus, it seems that more than half of expected coal retirements would still be projected to occur even in the absence of *all three* of the Obama Administration's "regulatory assaults" on existing coal plants.

BUMPS IN THE ROAD AHEAD

In its 1985 report on acid rain, the Congressional Research Service predicted that, by the year 2000, gas-fired electricity generation would be phased out completely.[131] In reality, gas had a 14 percent market share in 2000.[132] Predictions about energy markets are often wrong.

Thus, while it is certainly heartening to hear that 80 percent of pre-1970 plants are expected to retire in the next decade, it is also important to recognize that the end of grandfathering is hardly assured.[133] Much could go awry between now and 2025.

For one thing, while some analysts expect gas prices to stay low for years to come, there are no guarantees.[134] And even a relatively small shift in price can have a marked impact on the electric sector. The Bipartisan Policy Center's analysis of the June 2014 draft version of the Clean Power Plan, for example, found that if gas prices were 11 to 15 percent higher than expected from 2020 to 2030, gas's projected share of the electricity market under the plan would decline by 13 percent, while coal's share would increase by 6 percent.[135]

On the regulatory front, both MATS and the Clean Power Plan remain vulnerable to legal challenges. Indeed, the EPA has already suffered a high-profile loss on MATS. In May 2015, the Supreme Court ruled that the agency improperly failed to consider the cost of regulation when determining whether it was "appropriate and necessary" to regulate power plants' mercury emissions—a finding that, as mentioned earlier in this chapter, was first made by the Clinton Administration in 2000.[136] The EPA did, in fact, conduct an extensive cost-benefit analysis of the rule and found that the benefits outweighed the cost by a factor of at least three.[137] However, it waited to perform this analysis until the *second* stage of rule making, when it determined how stringent to make the regulation.[138] A majority of the Justices found that the agency was also required to consider compliance costs at the first stage, when it determined whether it was "appropriate and necessary" to regulate mercury emissions at all.[139]

The Supreme Court did not, however, strike MATS down. It simply remanded the case to the D.C. Circuit with the instruction that the EPA "must consider cost . . . before deciding whether regulation is appropriate and necessary."[140] Given that the EPA has already concluded that the benefits of MATS greatly outweigh its costs, the D.C. Circuit is likely to leave the rule in place while the EPA makes the necessary revisions to its "appropriate and necessary" determination. But it's certainly possible that the judges will instead vacate the rule and force the EPA to start the regulatory process—one that has already taken fifteen years—all over again.

The Clean Power Plan, meanwhile, has already withstood several lawsuits filed by states and mining companies, all of which have been dismissed as premature.[141] Traditionally, the federal courts will not entertain a challenge to an agency action until it is final.[142] And although the EPA released a copy of the final Clean Power Plan online on August 3, 2015, the rule will not be considered *truly* final for litigation purposes until it is published in the Federal Register.[143] Once that happens, probably in late October 2015, its opponents will undoubtedly renew their claims.

Outside the courts, the Clean Power Plan faces a number of political hurdles. At the federal level, the Republican chairman of the Senate's Environment and Public Works Committee, James Inhofe, has pledged to use every tool available to try to block the rule.[144] Republicans in the House have attempted to hold the EPA's entire budget hostage, stuffing appropriations bills for the agency with "policy riders" that would prohibit it from finalizing or implementing the plan.[145]

Meanwhile, Senate Majority Leader Mitch McConnell has taken the fight to the states, urging their leaders to refuse to design plans to implement the rule once it is finalized.[146] In April 2015, Oklahoma's governor became the first to commit her state's environmental agency to such inaction.[147]

The EPA does have authority to impose federal implementation plans in states that fail to design their own.[148] However, given the timing of the rule—state plans are due in the fall of 2016, but states can easily get two-year extensions[149]—the task of issuing any federal plans will likely fall to the next presidential administration. And if that administration is Republican, it is almost certain to drag its feet. Environmental groups might sue to force action, but that could take years.

To be sure, the progress the Obama Administration has made toward cleaning up or retiring grandfathered plants could not, at this point, be undone completely. For one thing, the Supreme Court has already upheld the Transport Rule. And while MATS remains in legal limbo, the vast majority of plants subject to the rule have already come into compliance, meaning they have already either retired, converted to gas, or installed the necessary emission controls.[150] Even if the D.C. Circuit does vacate the rule, plants that have already closed up shop almost certainly won't come back into service. Nor will plants that have already invested in scrubbers and other pollution control technologies dismantle their expensive new equipment, although some might decide not to use it.

But the most significant of the three rules, the Clean Power Plan, has not yet taken effect, and it remains vulnerable to both legal and political attacks. If it fails, a significant number of grandfathered plants may live to pollute another day—or decade.

Conclusion: A Farewell to Harms

In December 2014, mining companies and coal-dependent utilities gained an unlikely new ally in Harvard law professor Laurence Tribe. Tribe—a liberal icon who previously served as one of Al Gore's lawyers in *Bush v. Gore,* the Supreme Court case that decided the 2000 election, and as Barack Obama's constitutional law professor at Harvard—has been retained by Peabody Energy, the world's largest private-sector coal company, to advocate on its behalf in administrative and legal proceedings on the proposed Clean Power Plan.[1]

In comments to the EPA on the proposed rule, Tribe argued that "coal has been a bedrock component of our economy and energy policy for decades," and that by "manifestly proceed[ing] on the opposite premise," the Clean Power Plan "represents a dramatic change in directions from previous Democratic and Republican administrations."[2] But as this book has made clear, that's simply not true. Instead, every administration for the past twenty-five years has supported policies designed to reduce pollution from our nation's aging coal-fired power plants.

First, George H.W. Bush championed the 1990 amendments to the Clean Air Act, which created the Acid Rain Trading Program to reduce interstate emissions of sulfur dioxide, primarily from grandfathered coal plants in the Midwest. Those amendments also prodded the EPA into action on coal plants' emissions of toxic pollutants, setting a deadline for it to undertake a study on whether such regulation was "appropriate and necessary."

Building on the success of the acid-rain initiative, the Clinton Administration developed the NO_x SIP Call, which sought to tackle a different interstate pollution problem linked to grandfathered coal plants: excessive concentrations of ground-level ozone. The Administration then took even more direct aim at grandfathered plants through its aggressive enforcement initiative, going after utilities that had undertaken major modifications without complying with the standards applicable to new sources.

The Clinton EPA also moved the ball forward on toxics, concluding that it *was* "appropriate and necessary" to regulate mercury emissions from existing coal plants. Finally, the agency's general counsel under President Clinton, Jonathan Cannon, became the first to conclude formally that greenhouse gas emissions from power plants and other sources were susceptible to regulation under the Clean Air Act.

The record of George W. Bush's Administration was somewhat mixed. On the one hand, its Clean Air Interstate Rule built on prior efforts to tackle interstate pollution through emission trading. The Administration also attempted to regulate power plants' toxic emissions by promulgating the Clean Air Mercury Rule.

On the other hand, the Bush Administration took aggressive action to undermine the New Source Review rules on modification and failed to follow through on the Clinton enforcement initiative. Additionally, despite a Supreme Court ruling that essentially made the regulation of greenhouse gases under the Clean Air Act mandatory, the Administration steadfastly refused to take action, going so far as to suppress its own EPA administrator's endangerment finding.

The Obama Administration, for the most part, picked up where its predecessors left off. Indeed, of the three major regulations that opponents have characterized as a "war on coal," not one was entirely discretionary. The Transport Rule, for instance, was a necessary replacement for the Clean Air Interstate Rule, which had been struck down by the D.C. Circuit and left in place only to give the EPA time to fashion a substitute.

Obama's Mercury and Air Toxics Standards, too, were crafted to replace a Bush-era rule the D.C. Circuit had vacated, the Clean Air Mercury Rule. Indeed, given that the Clinton Administration had already made the "appropriate and necessary" finding for mercury, the only way the Obama Administration could have avoided issuing its own rule would be to conclude "that emissions from no source in the category . . . exceed a level which is adequate to protect public health with an ample margin of safety and [that] no adverse environmental effect will result from emissions from any source."[3] Making such a determination was essentially impossible given the EPA's previous findings that power plants were the largest source of mercury pollution in the country and that such pollution was a threat to public health and the environment.[4]

The regulation of power plants' greenhouse gas emissions under the Clean Power Plan was similarly preordained. After the Supreme Court's decision in *Massachusetts v. EPA,* the agency could decline to regulate greenhouse gas emissions from motor vehicles only by making one of two scientifically insupportable findings: (1) that greenhouse gases did not contribute to climate change, or (2) that the uncertainty surrounding climate change was so "profound" that the EPA could not make a "reasoned judgment" as to whether greenhouse gases contributed to climate change.[5] Given the existence of what Administrator Lisa Jackson would later describe as "decades of sound, peer-reviewed, extensively evaluated scientific data" linking greenhouse gas emissions to climate change, the agency could not defensibly reach either of those conclusions.[6]

And once the agency took steps to regulate greenhouse gas emissions from cars and trucks, it didn't have a persuasive defense against a lawsuit seeking to compel it to do the same for power plants. As an earlier Congressional Research Service report had noted, the statutory triggers for regulating emissions from motor vehicles under Section 202(a) of the Clean Air Act and those from "stationary sources" under Section 111 were almost identical.[7] In other words, having already found that greenhouse gas emissions from cars and trucks contributed to dangerous climate change, the agency was going to have a pretty difficult time convincing a court that emissions from power plants didn't pose a similar danger to public health and welfare, especially considering that power plants were (and still are) the largest source of carbon dioxide in the United States.

In emphasizing the pre-Obama roots of the Transport Rule, MATS, and the Clean Power Plan, we do not seek to discount the essential role President Obama has played—and continues to play—in implementing the three rules. Even though the EPA had preexisting statutory and/or judicial obligations to promulgate each, a different White House might have tried to delay the day of reckoning—as the Clinton Administration did with the "appropriate and necessary" finding for power plants' mercury emissions, and as the Bush Administration did with the endangerment finding for motor vehicles' greenhouse gas emissions. It is to the President's credit that, under his watch, the EPA has embraced rather than evaded its legal responsibilities.

What we do want to emphasize, however, is that those legal responsibilities were not *created* by President Obama. Instead, they are the product of a multidecade, iterative process of legislation, regulation, and adjudication that bears the fingerprints of multiple presidential administrations of both parties. The Transport Rule, MATS, and the Clean Power Plan may be components of a larger struggle, but that struggle is not an unprecedented, unilateral, and ideological "war on coal."

In 1906, Edith Wharton's tragic novel *The House of Mirth* was adapted for the stage and flopped. Wharton's friend William Dean Howells, editor of the *Atlantic Monthly,* attributed the failure to American tastes: "Yes, what the American public always wants," he remarked, "is a tragedy with a happy ending."[8] Howells did not, of course, intend this quip as a compliment, but the notion of a happily ending tragedy is not as outlandish as one might think. Aristotle himself maintained in the *Poetics* that the best tragic plot featured a hero who realized the cause of his misfortune in time to avert a final catastrophe.[9]

With any luck, the saga of grandfathering will turn out to be just this sort of tragedy. Forty-five years ago, Congress passed the Clean Air Act, a hugely progressive law that contained a terrible flaw: the grandfathering of existing sources, most notably coal-fired power plants. This flaw made it all but impossible for the Act to fulfill its central promise of safe, clean air for all Americans.

But by the late 1980s, policymakers in Washington had realized their mistake and began an earnest, bipartisan effort to correct it. Progress has been slow but relatively steady, with each successive administration taking steps to further the cause. And now, almost three decades later, an end to the harmful legacy of grandfathering is finally within the nation's grasp.

It is, unfortunately, too late to avert all of grandfathering's tragic consequences. We cannot restore the lives lost to excessive interstate pollution over the years. Nor can we rid our atmosphere of the greenhouse gases that would never have been emitted if aging, inefficient coal plants had shut down on schedule—at least, not with current technology. But with most grandfathered plants finally set to retire within the next decade, and the rest required to install scrubbers and other emissions controls, we do have an opportunity to prevent further harm and to give this story the happy, thoroughly American ending it deserves.

ACKNOWLEDGMENTS

Throughout the process of writing this book, our colleagues at the Institute for Policy Integrity were a consistent source of advice and good cheer. Particular thanks are due to Denise Grab, Austen Hartwell, Jayni Hein, Phoebe Hinton, Jason Schwartz, and Derek Sylvan.

We are very grateful to Michael Livermore and Albert Podell for their detailed and insightful editorial comments.

Struggling for Air builds on Richard Revesz's previous scholarship on grandfathering and the Clean Air Act. In particular, Chapters 3 and 4 draw from Jonathan Remy Nash & Richard L. Revesz, "Grandfathering and Environmental Regulation: The Law and Economics of New Source Review," 101 *Northwestern University Law Review* 1677 (2007), and Richard L. Revesz & Allison Westfahl Kong, "Regulatory Change and Optimal Transition Relief," 105 *Northwestern University Law Review* 1581 (2011). Special thanks are due to those collaborators. Additionally, Chapter 5 draws from Richard L. Revesz, "Federalism and Interstate Environmental Externalities," 144 *University of Pennsylvania Law Review* 2341 (1996).

This book also benefited greatly from the excellent research assistance of many students at the New York University School of Law, particularly Taylor Andrews, Paul Balik, Peter Black, Will Clark, Otis Comorau, Patrick Corrigan, Elspeth Hans Faiman, Ann Jaworski, LeeAnn Kim, Zachary Kolodin, Julianne Marley, Dorna Mohaghegh, Stefanie Neale, Amy Nemetz, Brian Perbix, Ross Peyser, Jay Rodriguez, Yael Tzipori, Jessica Wilkins, and Patrice Wylly. We are also grateful to the students in Revesz's 2014–15 reading group on greenhouse gas regulation (Harry Black, Isabelle Foley, Corey Hansen, Alaina Heine,

Julia Kantor, Sarah Krame, Kartik Mandiraju, Julia Quigley, Zak Randell, and Alexander Walker), who discussed a draft and provided valuable feedback.

Finally, thanks to the team at Oxford University Press—including David McBride, Kathleen Weaver, Molly Morrison, and Cassie Tuttle—for guiding us so ably through a speedy production process, and to two anonymous referees for excellent suggestions.

NOTES

Prologue

1. Phil Kerpen, Opinion, *Obama Declares a War on Coal*, FoxNews.com, June 25, 2013, http://www.foxnews.com/opinion/2013/06/25/obama-declares-war-on-coal.
2. Phil Kerpen, Opinion, *Obama's War on Coal Hits Your Electric Bill*, FoxNews.com, May 22, 2012, http://www.foxnews.com/opinion/2012/05/22/obamas-war-on-coal-hits-your-electric-bill.
3. Jonathan S. Tobin, *The Casualties of Obama's War on Coal*, Commentary, May 27, 2012, http://www.commentarymagazine.com/2014/05/27/the-casualties-of-obamas-war-on-coal-china-kentucky-senate-race.
4. Travis H. Brown, Opinion, *The War on Coal Is a War Against American Jobs*, Forbes, June 6, 2014, http://www.forbes.com/sites/travisbrown/2014/06/06/the-war-on-coal-is-a-war-against-american-jobs.
5. Federal Implementation Plans: Interstate Transport of Fine Particulate Matter and Ozone and Correction of SIP Approvals, Final Rule, 76 Fed. Reg. 48,208 (Aug. 8, 2011).
6. National Emission Standards for Hazardous Air Pollutants from Coal- and Oil-Fired Electric Utility Steam Generating Units and Standards of Performance for Fossil-Fuel-Fired Electric Utility, Industrial-Commercial-Institutional, and Small Industrial-Commercial-Institutional Steam Generating Units, 77 Fed. Reg. 9304 (Feb. 16, 2012).
7. Carbon Pollution Emission Guidelines for Existing Stationary Sources: Electric Utility Generating Units (Aug. 3, 2014), http://www2.epa.gov/cleanpowerplan/clean-power-plan-final-rule (not published in Federal Register as of this writing).

8. Dave Gilson, *109 Things Obama Has Declared War On*, Mother Jones, Feb. 8, 2012, http://www.motherjones.com/mixed-media/2012/02/obama-war-xmas-christians-cheerios.
9. Nick Wing, *Joe Manchin Shoots Cap-and-Trade Bill With Rifle in New Ad*, Huffington Post, May 25, 2011, http://www.huffingtonpost.com/2010/10/11/joe-manchin-ad-dead-aim_n_758457.html.
10. Kerpen, *Obama's War on Coal Hits Your Electric Bill*, *supra* note 2.

Chapter 1

1. *Encyclopedic Entry: Coal*, Nat'l Geographic, http://education.nationalgeographic.com/education/encyclopedia/coal/?ar_a=1 (last visited June 11, 2015).
2. *Id.*
3. *Id.*
4. Union of Concerned Scientists, How Coal Works, http://www.ucsusa.org/clean_energy/coalvswind/brief_coal.html#.VXoasVxVikp (last visited June 11, 2015).
5. *Encyclopedic Entry: Coal*, *supra* note 1.
6. How Coal Works, *supra* note 4.
7. *Encyclopedic Entry: Coal*, *supra* note 1.
8. In 2013, total U.S. underground mine production was 341,685,000 tons of coal, and surface mine production was 641,191,000 tons. U.S. Energy Info. Admin., Annual Coal Report 2013, at 8 (2015), *available at* http://www.eia.gov/coal/annual/pdf/acr.pdf.
9. Mine Safety & Health Admin., Table 1: Number of Operator Injuries, Injury-Incidence Rates, Average Number of Employees, Employee Hours, and Production by Type of Coal Mined and Work Location, Jan.–Dec. 2013, http://www.msha.gov/STATS/PART50/WQ/2013/table1.pdf (last visited Sept. 9, 2015).
10. U.S. Energy Info. Admin., Where the United States Gets Its Coal, http://www.eia.gov/energyexplained/index.cfm?page=coal_where (last updated Mar. 30, 2015).
11. U.S. Energy Info. Admin., DOE/EIA-0035(2015/07), Monthly Energy Review: July 2015, at 94–95 (2015), *available at* http://www.eia.gov/totalenergy/data/monthly/archive/00351507.pdf.
12. How Coal Works, *supra* note 4.
13. Tom Zeller, Jr. & Stefan Milkowski, *Burning Coal at Home Is Making a Comeback*, N.Y. Times, Dec. 8, 2008, http://www.nytimes.com/2008/12/27/business/27coal.html.

14. *Pearl Street: The Birthplace of the Electric Age*, ConEdison, http://www.coned.com/pearlstreet125/ (last visited June 11, 2015) (describing history of Pearl Street generating station); U.S. Energy Info. Admin., Competition Among Fuels for Power Generation Driven by Changes in Fuel Prices (July 13, 2012), http://www.eia.gov/todayinenergy/detail.cfm?id=7090 (showing change in coal's market share from 1950 to 2012).
15. Reid Wilson, *The States That Will Be Hit Hardest by the EPA's Coal Regulations, in One Map*, Wash. Post, June 2, 2014, http://www.washingtonpost.com/blogs/govbeat/wp/2014/06/02/the-states-that-will-be-hit-hardest-by-the-epas-coal-regulations-in-one-map/.
16. *How Do Coal-Fired Plants Work?*, Duke Energy, https://www.duke-energy.com/about-energy/generating-electricity/coal-fired-how.asp (last visited June 10, 2015).
17. *Id.*
18. *Id.*
19. *Id.*
20. *Id.*
21. Michelle Nijhuis, *Can Coal Ever Be Clean?*, Nat'l Geographic, Apr. 2014, http://ngm.nationalgeographic.com/2014/04/coal/nijhuis-text.
22. GreenPeace, Mining Impacts (Apr. 15, 2010), http://www.greenpeace.org/international/en/campaigns/climate-change/coal/Mining-impacts/.
23. Ctrs. for Disease Control & Prevention, Workplace Safety & Health Topics: Coal Mining-Related Respiratory Diseases, http://www.cdc.gov/niosh/topics/surveillance/ords/CoalMining RelatedRespiratoryDiseases.html (last updated Aug. 8, 2012).
24. Union of Concerned Scientists, Environmental Impacts of Coal Power: Air Pollution, http://www.ucsusa.org/clean_energy/coalvswind/c02c.html#.VbJLjs7qup0 (last visited July 24, 2015).
25. National Park Service, Sulfur Dioxide Effects on Health, http://www.nature.nps.gov/air/AQBasics/understand_so2.cfm (last updated Jan. 10, 2013).
26. EPA, Sulfur Dioxide: Health, http://www.epa.gov/oaqps001/sulfurdioxide/health.html (last updated Mar. 25, 2015).
27. *Id.*
28. EPA, Acid Rain: What Is Acid Rain?, http://www.epa.gov/acidrain/what/index.html (last updated Dec. 4, 2012).
29. Union of Concerned Scientists, How Coal Works, http://www.ucsusa.org/clean_energy/coalvswind/brief_coal.html#.VXoasVxVikp (last visited June 11, 2015).
30. EPA, Nitrogen Dioxide, http://www.epa.gov/airquality/nitrogenoxides/index.html (last updated Aug. 15, 2014).

31. EPA, NITROGEN DIOXIDE: HEALTH, http://www.epa.gov/airquality/nitrogenoxides/health.html (last updated Aug. 15, 2014).
32. *Id.*; WHAT IS ACID RAIN?, *supra* note 28.
33. *Id.*
34. EPA, MERCURY: BASIC INFORMATION, http://www.epa.gov/mercury/about.htm (last updated Dec. 29, 2014).
35. *Id.*
36. *Id.*
37. *Id.*
38. EPA, CLIMATE CHANGE: BASIC INFORMATION, http://www.epa.gov/climatechange/basics/ (last updated July 21, 2015).
39. Endangerment and Cause or Contribute Findings for Greenhouse Gases Under Section 202(a) of the Clean Air Act, 74 Fed. Reg. 66,496, 66,532, 66,498, 66,524 (Dec. 15, 2009).

Chapter 2

1. H. Comm. on Energy & Commerce, *E&C Members Rally Support to Stop the War on Coal*, YOUTUBE (Sept. 20, 2012), https://www.youtube.com/watch?v=JMvgaeS1zLM&feature=g-upl.
2. Press Release, H. Comm. on Energy & Commerce, House to Battle Obama's War on Coal Next Week (Sept. 13, 2012), *available at* http://energycommerce.house.gov/press-release/house-battle-obamas-war-coal-next-week.
3. H. Comm. on Energy & Commerce, *E&C Members Rally Support to Stop the War on Coal*, *supra* note 1.
4. Kate Sheppard, *House Passes Extra-Terrible Pro-Coal Bill Before Heading Home*, MOTHER JONES, Sept. 21, 2012, http://www.motherjones.com/blue-marble/2012/09/house-passes-extra-terrible-pro-coal-heading-home.
5. Press Release, H. Comm. on Energy & Commerce, *supra* note 2.
6. Pete Kasperowicz & Ben Geman, *House Approves "Stop the War on Coal" Bill in Last Act Before November Election*, THE HILL, Sept. 21, 2012, http://thehill.com/blogs/floor-action/house/250957-house-approves-coal-deregulation-bill-in-last-act-before-election.
7. Sheppard, *supra* note 4.
8. Pete Altman, *Obama Is Not the Spokesperson-In-Chief for Clean Coal*, SWITCHBOARD: NATURAL RES. DEF. COUNCIL STAFF BLOG (Feb. 5, 2009), http://switchboard.nrdc.org/blogs/paltman/obama_is_not_the_spokespersoni.html.
9. AMERICAN COALITION FOR CLEAN COAL ELECTRICITY, WHO WE ARE, http://americaspower.org./who-we-are (last visited Oct. 13, 2014).

10. American Coalition for Clean Coal Electricity, *Barack Obama Supports Developing Clean Coal Technology*, YouTube (Dec. 12, 2008), https://www.youtube.com/watch?v=GehK7Q_QxPc.
11. *Id.*
12. *Id.*
13. Anne C. Mulkern, *A "Propaganda War" Over "Clean Coal,"* N.Y. Times, Apr. 20, 2009, http://www.nytimes.com/gwire/2009/04/20/20greenwire-propaganda-war-over-coal-escalates-ahead-of-hi-10594.html.
14. Debra McCown, *Biden: "It's Nice To Be Back in Coal Country,"* Bristol Herald Courier (Va.), Sept. 21, 2008, http://www.heraldcourier.com/news/biden-it-s-nice-to-be-back-in-coal-country/article_c4a6a834-1c5a-5eaf-a227-faa42d4954b0.html.
15. Mannix Porterfield, *Rahall Sees Obama as Dedicated to Ending War in Iraq*, The Register-Herald (Beckley, W. Va.), Aug. 27, 2008, http://www.register-herald.com/news/local_news/rahall-sees-obama-as-dedicated-to-ending-war-in-iraq/article_25026b75-c35c-5a52-b744-94df4951226d.html.
16. *See* Alec MacGillis & Steven Mufson, *Coal Fuels a Debate Over Obama*, Wash. Post, June 24, 2007, http://www.washingtonpost.com/wp-dyn/content/article/2007/06/23/AR2007062301424.html.
17. Caleb Hale, *Defending Coal Throughout Illinois: Durbin and Obama Say Bush Administration Seems to Be Favoring Western Coal Over Midwest and East Supplies*, The Southern, Apr. 15, 2004, http://thesouthern.com/news/defending-coal-throughout-illinois-durbin-and-obama-say-bush-administration/article_07807e38-2a94-5441-92ed-465dc249.
18. *See* David Biello, *Can Captured Carbon Save Coal-Fired Power?*, Sci. Am., May 17, 2009, http://www.nature.com/scientificamerican/journal/v19/n2s/full/scientificamericanearth0609-52.html.
19. Alec MacGillis, *Obama's Dirty, Coal-Loving Past*, New Republic, May 29, 2014, http://www.newrepublic.com/article/117951/obamas-dirty-coal-loving-past.
20. *See* John M. Broder, *Obama Affirms Climate Change Goals*, N.Y. Times, Nov. 18, 2008, http://www.nytimes.com/2008/11/19/us/politics/19climate.html.
21. EPA, Clean Energy: Natural Gas, http://www.epa.gov/cleanenergy/energy-and-you/affect/natural-gas.html (last updated Sept. 25, 2013).
22. *See* Ralph R. Reiland, *Obama's Energy-Draining Policies*, Pittsburgh Trib. Rev., Mar. 29. 2009, http://triblive.com/x/pittsburghtrib/opinion/columnists/reiland/s_614884.html#axzz3fJHvfUxl.
23. Steve Bennish, *President Obama's Emissions Plan Could Hurt Ohio; Area Energy Producers Say Rules Could Force Electric Rates to Rise 40 Percent*, Dayton Daily News (Ohio), Mar. 16, 2009, at A4.

24. Tom Troy, *Latta Likens Climate Bill to War on Ohio*, The Blade (Toledo, Ohio), May 22, 2009, http://www.toledoblade.com/State/2009/05/22/Latta-likens-climate-bill-to-war-on-Ohio.html.
25. Editorial, *Between a Rock and a Hard Place; West Virginians Expect Their Representatives to Stand with Them*, Charleston Daily Mail (W. Va.), June 24, 2009, at 4A.
26. Ken Ward, Jr., *W.Va. Chamber: Block Health Care Reform to Help Coal*, Charleston Gazette (W. Va.), Coal Tattoo Blog (Nov. 20, 2009), http://blogs.wvgazette.com/coaltattoo/2009/11/20/wva-chamber-block-health-care-reform-to-help-coal.
27. David A. Fahrenthold & Michael D. Shear, *As Obama Visits Coal Country, Many Are Wary of His Environmental Policies*, Wash. Post, Apr. 25, 2010, at A1, http://www.washingtonpost.com/wp-dyn/content/article/2010/04/24/AR2010042402711_pf.html.
28. Ry Rivard, *Maynard, Rahall Wage "War on Coal"; Candidates Work to Set Themselves Apart on Issue*, Charleston Daily Mail (W. Va.), Sept. 20, 2010, at 1A.
29. MacGillis, *Obama's Dirty, Coal-Loving Past*, *supra* note 19.
30. Porterfield, *supra* note 15.
31. Charles Owens, *Rahall, Maynard Spar*, Bluefield Daily Telegraph (W. Va.), Sept. 8, 2010, http://www.bdtonline.com/news/local_news/rahall-maynard-spar/article_6af303f8-7dc6-5165-bf3b-417d29568ccb.html.
32. Charles Owens, *Rahall Vows to Fight for Coal, W. Va. with Seniority*, Bluefield Daily Telegraph (W. Va.), Oct. 23, 2010, http://www.bdtonline.com/news/local_news/rahall-vows-to-fight-for-coal-w-va-with-seniority/article_dab0da82-7ae4-5cac-ac27-5bec2b6e0448.html.
33. Jim Workman, *Rahall is Elected to 18th Straight Term in Congress*, The Register-Herald (W. Va.), Sept. 20, 2010, http://www.register-herald.com/news/article_4f586a5d-3e9e-5dbd-9923-ab2d3c05be0a.html?mode=jqm.
34. *See* Brian Montopoli, *Has Obama Declared a "War on Coal?,"* CBSNews.com (July 16, 2012), http://www.cbsnews.com/news/has-obama-declared-a-war-on-coal.
35. Amy Harder, *Romney Opposes EPA Mercury Rule*, Nat'l J., June 19, 2012, http://www.nationaljournal.com/energy/romney-opposes-epa-mercury-rule-20120619.
36. Jason Plautz, *Is Obama Really Waging a War on Coal?*, Bloomberg, The Grid Blog, Oct. 17, 2012, http://www.bloomberg.com/news/2012-10-17/is-obama-really-waging-a-war-on-coal-.html.
37. Wall Street Journal, *Opinion: Obama's War on Coal*, YouTube (Sept. 20, 2012), https://www.youtube.com/watch?v=V0AJ886Csy0.

38. America's Power, *Home Field Advantage*, YouTube (Oct. 2, 2012), https://www.youtube.com/watch?v=_fid3NCqAdc&feature=youtu.be.
39. Dave Jamieson, *Mitt Romney: Coal Industry Crippled by Obama Policies*, Huffington Post, Oct. 3, 2012, http://www.huffingtonpost.com/2012/10/03/mitt-romney-coal_n_1937796.html.
40. Google Trends, "War on Coal," http://www.google.com/trends/explore#q=war%20on%20coal.
41. Alex Guillen, *Ready, Set, Debate—Coal Group Runs Ads Hitting EPA Regs—ITC Meets Today on Solar Tariffs—Obama Stops by Hoover Dam—Mine Investigators Get FBI Training*, Politico, Oct. 3, 2012, http://www.politico.com/morningenergy/1012/morningenergy596.html.
42. *See 2012 Election Results*, Huffington Post, http://elections.huffingtonpost.com/2012/results.
43. Dave Jamieson, *"War on Coal" Campaign Against Obama Has Failed, Coal Lobby Concedes*, Huffington Post, June 12, 2013, http://www.huffingtonpost.com/2013/06/11/war-on-coal-campaign-failure_n_3422524.html.
44. *See* Coral Davenport, *McConnell Urges States to Help Thwart Obama's "War on Coal,"* N.Y. Times, Mar. 20, 2015, at A1.
45. Ian Prior, *NRCC TV Ad Highlighting Nick Rahall's War on Coal*, NRCC Blog, Oct. 21, 2014, http://www.nrcc.org/2014/10/21/nrcc-tv-ad-highlighting-nick-rahalls-war-coal.
46. Philip Bump, *Obama's Coal Proposal Gives Alison Grimes an Excellent Way to Fight with Him*, Wash. Post, June 5, 2014, http://www.washingtonpost.com/blogs/the-fix/wp/2014/06/05/obamas-coal-proposal-gives-alison-grimes-an-excellent-way-to-fight-with-him.
47. Joseph Gerth & James R. Carroll, *With Victory, McConnell Pledges Change*, The Courier-Journal (Louisville, KY), Nov. 5, 2014, http://www.courier-journal.com/story/news/politics/elections/kentucky/2014/11/04/senate-race-boosts-turnout-kentucky-urban-areas/18474689.
48. Peter Brooks, *Narrative Transactions—Does the Law Need a Narratology?*, 18 Yale J.L. & Human. 1, 2 (2006).
49. *Id.* at 10–20.
50. *Id.* at 9.
51. *Id.* at 13.
52. Cullen Couch, *Teaching the Narrative Power of the Law*, UVA Lawyer (Fall 2005), *available at* http://www.law.virginia.edu/html/alumni/uvalawyer/f05/humanities.htm.
53. Univ. of Cal. Regents v. Bakke, 438 U.S. 265, 272–78 (1978) (Powell, J., announcing the judgment of the Court).
54. *Id.* at 275.
55. *Id.* at 270–71.

56. *Id.* at 272.
57. *Id.* at 387–88 (Marshall, J., concurring in the judgment in part and dissenting in part).
58. Couch, *supra* note 52.
59. Mitch McConnell, *Obama's Energy Policy Is Not Science—It's an Ideological Crusade*, WASH. EXAM'R, Sep. 22, 2014, http://washingtonexaminer.com/obamas-energy-policy-is-not-science-its-an-ideological-crusade/article/2553631; Joseph Bast et al., *Heartland Institute Experts React to President Obama's Power Plant Emission Rule to Fight Global Warming/Climate Change*, HEARTLAND INST., June 2, 2014, http://heartland.org/press-releases/2014/06/02/heartland-institute-experts-react-president-obamas-power-plant-emission-ru.
60. Erica Martinson, *Uttered in 2008, Still Haunting Obama in 2012*, POLITICO, Apr. 5, 2012, http://www.politico.com/news/stories/0412/74892.html.
61. *Id.*
62. Laura Barron-Lopez, *McConnell: Dems Waging "Elitist War on Coal,"* THE HILL, May 7, 2014, http://thehill.com/policy/energy-environment/205494-mcconnell-dems-waging-elitist-war-on-coal.
63. *Why Does Obama Hate Coal Miners and Appalachia?*, THE LONELY CONSERVATIVE, Oct. 17, 2012, http://lonelyconservative.com/2012/10/why-does-obama-hate-coal-miners-and-appalachia.

Chapter 3

1. J. CLARENCE DAVIES III & BARBARA S. DAVIES, THE POLITICS OF POLLUTION 44–54 (2d ed. 1975) (summarizing the history of air quality legislation through 1970).
2. JOHN C. ESPOSITO & LARRY J. SILVERMAN, RALPH NADER'S STUDY GROUP REPORT ON AIR POLLUTION, VANISHING AIR 1 (1970).
3. *Air Pollution–1969: Hearing Before the Subcomm. on Air & Water Pollution of the S. Comm. on Pub. Works on Problems and Programs Associated with the Control of Air Pollution*, 91st Cong. 55 (1969).
4. NAT'L WEATHER SERV. FORECAST OFFICE, WHAT ARE TEMPERATURE INVERSIONS?, http://www.wrh.noaa.gov/slc/climate/TemperatureInversions.php (last visited Feb. 17, 2015).
5. *Id.*
6. *Id.*
7. *Id.*
8. *See id.* (noting that the duration of an inversion is one of the factors that affects air quality).

9. Edwin Kiester, Jr., *A Darkness in Donora*, SMITHSONIAN MAG. (Nov. 2009), http://www.smithsonianmag.com/history/a-darkness-in-donora-174128118.
10. Steve Tracton, *The Killer London Smog Event of December, 1952: A Reminder of Deadly Smog Events in U.S.*, WASH. POST, Dec. 20, 2012, 10:30 AM, http://www.washingtonpost.com/blogs/capital-weather-gang/post/the-killer-london-smog-event-of-december-1952-a-reminder-of-deadly-smog-events-in-us/2012/12/19/452c66bc-498e-11e2-b6f0-e851e741d196_blog.html.
11. Arnold W. Reitze, Jr., *The Legislative History of U.S. Air Pollution Control*, 36 HOUS. L. REV. 679, 699 (1999).
12. *Air Pollution Control and Solid Wastes Recycling: Hearing on H.R. 12934, H.R. 14960, H.R. 15137, and H.R. 15192 Before the Subcomm. on Pub. Health and Welfare of the H. Comm. on Interstate and Foreign Commerce*, 91st Cong. 6 (1970).
13. THE AMERICAN PRESIDENCY PROJECT, RICHARD NIXON, REMARKS ON SIGNING THE NATIONAL ENVIRONMENTAL POLICY ACT OF 1969 (Jan. 1, 1970), *available at* http://www.presidency.ucsb.edu/ws/?pid=2446.
14. EPA, THE GUARDIAN: ORIGINS OF THE EPA (1992), *available* at http://www2.epa.gov/aboutepa/guardian-origins-epa.
15. EPA, 40TH ANNIVERSARY OF THE CLEAN AIR ACT, http://www.epa.gov/air/caa/40th.html (last visited Feb. 24, 2015).
16. THE AMERICAN PRESIDENCY PROJECT, RICHARD NIXON, REMARKS ON SIGNING THE CLEAN AIR AMENDMENTS OF 1970 (Dec. 31, 1970), *available at* http://www.presidency.ucsb.edu/ws/?pid=2874.
17. DAVIES & DAVIES, THE POLITICS OF POLLUTION, *supra* note 1, at 82.
18. J. CLARENCE DAVIES III, THE POLITICS OF POLLUTION 21–22 (1st ed. 1970).
19. EARTH DAY NETWORK, EARTH DAY: THE HISTORY OF A MOVEMENT, http://www.earthday.org/earth-day-history-movement (last visited Feb. 24, 2015).
20. *Id.*
21. Douglas Brinkley, *Can the Earth Be Saved? Walter Cronkite and the Creation of Earth Day*, THE AUSTIN CHRON., Apr. 20, 2012, http://www.austinchronicle.com/news/2012-04-20/can-the-earth-be-saved/all (describing Cronkite's environmental broadcasts); *Walter Cronkite Dies*, CBS News, July 17, 2009, http://www.cbsnews.com/news/walter-cronkite-dies/ (describing 1972 poll finding that Cronkite was "most trusted man in America").
22. EPA, WILLIAM D. RUCKELSHAUS: ORAL HISTORY INTERVIEW (1993), http://www2.epa.gov/aboutepa/william-d-ruckelshaus-oral-history-interview.
23. *Id.*
24. DAVIES & DAVIES, THE POLITICS OF POLLUTION, *supra* note 1, at 53; E. Donald Elliott et al., *Toward a Theory of Statutory Evolution: The Federalization of Environmental Law*, 1 J. L. ECON. & ORG. 313, 335 (1985).

25. Esposito & Silverman, *supra* note 2, at 304.
26. Annual Message to the Congress on the State of the Union, 1970 Pub. Papers 8, at 12-3 (Jan. 22, 1970).
27. *Id.* at 13.
28. Special Message to the Congress on Environmental Quality, 1970 Pub. Papers 96, 97 (Feb. 10, 1970), *available at* http://library.cqpress.com/cqalmanac/document.php?id=cqal70-1290732#22-A.
29. There had actually been a law called the "Clean Air Act" on the books since 1963, but the original law—and amendments passed in 1965 and 1967—had proven toothless. *See* Reitze, *The Legislative History of U.S. Air Pollution Control, supra* note 11, at 698–702. When today's scholars, politicians, and pundits speak of the passage of the "Clean Air Act," they are typically referring to the 1970 version, which established the basic regulatory structure that is still in place today.
30. Elliott et al., *supra* note 24, at 336 (quoting Alfred Marcus, Promise and Performance: Choosing and Implementing an Environmental Policy (1980)).
31. *Id.* at 337–38.
32. *Id.*
33. *Id.*
34. Reitze, *The Legislative History of U.S. Air Pollution Control, supra* note 11, at 702.
35. Davies & Davies, The Politics of Pollution, *supra* note 1, at 54–55.
36. *Id.*
37. *Id.*
38. *Id.*
39. Clean Air Act Amendments of 1970, Pub. L. No. 91-604, § 109(b)(1), 84 Stat. 1676, 1680 (1970).
40. § 109(a)(1), 84 Stat. at 1679.
41. § 110(a)(1), 84 Stat. at 1680.
42. § 110, 84 Stat. at 1680.
43. § 110(c), 84 Stat. at 1681.
44. § 111(b), 84 Stat. at 1684.
45. § 111(a)(1), 84 Stat. at 1683.
46. Jonathan Remy Nash & Richard L. Revesz, *Grandfathering and Environmental Regulation: The Law and Economics of New Source Review,* 101 Nw. U. L. Rev. 1677, 1709–10 (2007).
47. James G. Speight, The Chemistry and Technology of Coal, 671–76 (3d ed. 2012).
48. Nash & Revesz, *supra* note 46, at 1710.
49. *Id.*

50. *Id.* at 1708.
51. Standards of Performance for New Stationary Sources, 36 Fed. Reg. 24,876 (Dec. 23, 1971).
52. Richard E. Ayres, *Enforcement of Air Pollution Controls on Stationary Sources Under the Clean Air Amendments of 1970*, 4 Ecology L.Q. 441, 443 (1975).
53. *See* Bruce Ackerman & William T. Hassler, Clean Coal/Dirty Air: or How the Clean Air Act Became a Multibillion-Dollar Bail-Out for High-Sulfur Coal Producers 19, 34 (1981). Large power plants may require several scrubbers, each of which consists of a series of pipes and a tower that can be more than 150 feet tall. Spencer Hunt, *Scrubbing Air*, Columbus Dispatch, May 6, 2008, http://www.dispatch.com/content/stories/science/2008/05/06/Sci_scrubber.ART_ART_05-06-08_B6_H5A33IC.html.
54. New Stationary Source Performance Standards; Electric Utility Steam Generating Units, 44 Fed. Reg. 33,580, 33,580 (June 11, 1979) (noting that the new SO_2 standard was applicable to generating units that commenced construction after September 18, 1978). The universal scrubbing requirement created economic distortions of its own that are outside the scope of this book. For more detail, see Ackerman & Hassler, *supra* note 53.
55. New Stationary Source Performance Standards, *supra* note 54, at 33,581.
56. Rachel Cleetus et al., Union of Concerned Scientists, Ripe for Retirement: The Case for Closing America's Costliest Coal Plants 22 (2012).
57. *Id.* at 1.
58. *Id.* at 18 fig.1.
59. Steven Mufson, *Vintage U.S. Coal-Fired Power Plants Now an "Aging Fleet of Clunkers,"* Wash. Post, Jun. 13, 2014, http://www.washingtonpost.com/business/economy/a-dilemma-with-aging-coal-plants-retire-them-or-restore-them/2014/06/13/8914780a-f00a-11e3-914c-1fbd0614e2d4_story.html.
60. Cleetus et al., *supra* note 56, at 24.
61. Committee on Changes in New Source Review Programs for Stationary Sources of Air Pollution, National Research Council, New Source Review for Stationary Sources of Air Pollution 225 tbl.7-1(d) (2006).
62. *Id.*
63. *Id.*
64. *Id.*
65. *See* U.S. Gov't Accountability Office, GAO 12-545R, Air Emissions and Electricity Generation at U.S. Power Plants 12 fig.8 (2012), http://www.gao.gov/assets/600/590188.pdf.

66. *Compare id.* at 7 fig.3 (showing average SO_2, NO_x, and CO_2 emission rates for pre-1978 plants, most of which burn coal), *with id.* at 11 fig.7 (showing average emission rates for gas plants).
67. Bruce Biewald, David White, Tim Woolf, Frank Ackerman & William Moomaw, Grandfathering and Environmental Comparability: An Economic Analysis of Air Emission Regulations and Electricity Market Distortions 3 (1998), *available at* http://www.synapse-energy.com/sites/default/files/SynapseReport.1998-01.NARUC_.Grandfathering--Air-Emission-Regulation-and-Distortions..98-U06.pdf.
68. 42 U.S.C. § 7412.
69. EPA, Toxic Air Pollutants: About Air Toxics, http://www.epa.gov/air/toxicair/newtoxics.html (last updated on June 21, 2012).
70. 42 U.S.C. § 7411(d).
71. *See* Richard L. Revesz, Environmental Law and Policy 488 (2d ed. 2012); EPA, EPA 400-F-92-014, Milestones in Auto Emissions Control (1994) *available at* http://www.epa.gov/otaq/consumer/12-miles.pdf.
72. EPA, Comparison of Growth Areas and Emissions, 1970–2013, http://www.epa.gov/airtrends/images/y70_13.png (last visited Apr. 9, 2015).
73. *Benefits and Costs of the Clean Air Act: Retrospective Study*, EPA, http://www.epa.gov/cleanairactbenefits/design.html (last updated Aug. 15, 2013).
74. EPA, Benefits and Costs of the Clean Air Act: Second Prospective Study–1990 to 2020, http://www.epa.gov/air/sect812/prospective2.html (last updated Aug. 15, 2013).
75. Heidi Gorovitz Robertson, *If Your Grandfather Could Pollute, So Can You: Environmental "Grandfather Clauses" and Their Role in Environmental Inequity*, 45 Cath. U. L. Rev. 131, 132–33 (1995). The term "grandfathering" derives from a series of racially discriminatory state voting laws passed in the late-nineteenth and early-twentieth centuries. *Id.* at 131 & n.1. Those statutes imposed literacy tests and poll taxes as barriers to the ballot box but exempted anyone whose grandfather had been allowed to vote. *Id.* at 131 & n.2. The goal was to disenfranchise black citizens without violating the Fifteenth Amendment to the United States Constitution, which prohibits race-based restrictions on the right to vote. Henry L. Chambers, Jr., *Colorblindness, Race Neutrality, and Voting Rights*, 51 Emory L.J. 1397, 1431–32 (2002). The Supreme Court deemed "grandfather clauses" unconstitutional in 1915. Robertson, *supra*, at 132 n.5.
76. Richard L. Revesz & Allison L. Westfahl Kong, *Regulatory Change and Optimal Transition Relief*, 105 Nw. U. L. Rev. 1581, 1585 (2011).
77. *Id.* at 1585–87.

78. *See, e.g.*, Louis Kaplow, *An Economic Analysis of Legal Transitions*, 99 HARV. L. REV. 509, 533 (1986).
79. Revesz & Westfahl Kong, *supra* note 76, at 1590.
80. Steven Shavell, *On Optimal Legal Change, Past Behavior, and Grandfathering*, 37 J. LEGAL STUD. 37, 38–39 (2008).
81. *Id.* at 51–52.
82. *Id.* at 38.
83. Revesz & Westfahl Kong, *supra* note 76, at 1614.
84. *Id.* at 1613–14.
85. *Id.* at 1615–16.
86. *Id.* at 1617–18.
87. *Id.* at 1621.
88. *Id.* at 1623.
89. *Id.*
90. Robert N. Stavins, *Vintage-Differentiated Environmental Regulation*, 25 STAN. ENVTL. L.J. 29, 43 (2006).
91. Nash & Revesz, *supra* note 46, at 1712.
92. *See* REVESZ, ENVIRONMENTAL LAW AND POLICY, *supra* note 71, at 537–38.
93. *Id.* at 538.
94. *Id.* at 539.
95. EPA, EPA-230-11-90-083, ENVIRONMENTAL INVESTMENTS: THE COST OF A CLEAN ENVIRONMENT 10-6 (1990), *available at* http://yosemite.epa.gov/ee/epa/eerm.nsf/vwAN/EE-0294B-2.pdf/$file/EE-0294B-2.pdf.
96. Jan G. Laitos & Heidi Ruckriegle, *The Clean Water Act and the Challenge of Agricultural Pollution*, 37 VT. L. REV. 1033, 1035 (2013).
97. *See generally* ROBERT A. KATZMANN, JUDGING STATUTES 34–49 (2014) (summarizing judicial debate over the uses of legislative history).
98. *Id.* at 33–34.
99. *Id.* at 37 (quoting Abbe R. Gluck & Lisa Schultz Bressman, *Statutory Interpretation from the Inside—An Empirical Study of Congressional Drafting Delegation and the Canons: Part I*, 65 STAN. L. REV. 901, 965 (2013)).
100. DAVIES & DAVIES, THE POLITICS OF POLLUTION, *supra* note 1, at 49; *Air Pollution–1967 (Air Quality Act): Hearing on S. 780 and Related Matters Pertaining to the Prevention and Control of Air Pollution, H.R. 4279 Before the Subcomm. on Air & Water Pollution of the S. Comm. on Public Works*, 90th Cong. 749 (1967).
101. DAVIES & DAVIES, THE POLITICS OF POLLUTION, *supra* note 1, at 50.
102. *Air Pollution–1967 (Air Quality Act): Hearing on S. 780 and Related Matters Pertaining to the Prevention and Control of Air Pollution Before the Subcomm. on Air & Water Pollution of the S. Comm. on Public Works*, 90th Congress 2156 (1967) (statement of Curtis Hutchins, Chairman of Dead River Co. and representative of the U.S. Chamber of Commerce).

103. *Id.* at 2149 (statement of S.I. Goldsmith, Executive Vice President of the Aluminum Ass'n).
104. *Id.* at 1436 (statement of John B. O'Fallon, Dir. of Bldg. Inspection for Denver, Colo., Appearing for the Nat'l League of Cities).
105. *Id.* at 1435.
106. *Id.*
107. *Id.* at 1340–41.
108. *Air Pollution–1967 (Air Quality Act): Hearing on S. 780 and Related Matters Pertaining to the Prevention and Control of Air Pollution Before the Subcomm. on Air & Water Pollution of the S. Comm. on Public Works*, 90th Congress 2142 (1967).
109. *Id.* at 2330–31.
110. S. Rep. No. 90-403, at 5 (1967).
111. *Id.*
112. Air Quality Act of 1967, 81 Stat. 485, 503 (1967).
113. *Id.* at 491.
114. *Id.* at 492.
115. *Id.*
116. Arnold W. Reitze, Stationary Source Air Pollution Law 10 (2005).
117. Davies & Davies, The Politics of Pollution, *supra* note 1, at 52–53.
118. S. Rep. No. 91-63, at XVII (1970).
119. *Id.*
120. *Id.* at XVIII.
121. *Id.* at XV.
122. *Id.*
123. *Air Pollution–1970: Hearings on S. 3229, S. 3466 & S. 3546 Before the Subcomm. on Air & Water Pollution of the S. Comm. on Public Works*, 91st Cong. 1804 (1970) (statement of Fred E. Tucker, Manager of Pollution Control and Services, National Steel Corp., arguing against national emission standards "because some areas require more restrictive control than others to meet a specified air quality"; U.S. Chamber of Commerce arguing that national emission standards "are not responsive to the needs and demands of local conditions").
124. *Air Pollution–1970 Part 5: Hearings on S. 3229, S. 3446 & S. 3546 Before the Subcomm. on Air & Water Pollution of the S. Comm. on Public Works*, 91st Cong. 1573 (1970).
125. *Id.* at 1603.
126. *Air Pollution 1970–Part 5: Hearings on S. 3229, S. 3466, and S. 3546 Before the Subcomm. on Air & Water Pollution of the S. Comm. on Public Works*, 91st Cong. 1625 (1970) (statement of L.A. Iacocca, Exec. Vice President, Ford Motor Co.).

127. ESPOSITO & SILVERMAN, *supra* note 2, at 260.
128. *Id.*
129. 116 CONG. REC. 15,608 (1970).
130. Telephone Interview with Leon Billings (Apr. 17, 2014).
131. *Id.*
132. *Air Pollution–1967 (Air Quality Act): Hearing on S. 780 and Related Matters Pertaining to the Prevention and Control of Air Pollution Including Testimony on the Current Status of Control Technology Before the Subcomm. on Air & Water Pollution of the S. Comm. on Public Works*, 90th Cong. 2171 (1968) (statement of American Medical Association).
133. Telephone Interview with Leon Billings (Apr. 17, 2014).
134. *Air Pollution–1970 Part 5: Hearings on S. 3229, S. 3446 & S. 3546 Before the Subcomm. on Air & Water Pollution of the S. Comm. on Public Works*, 91st Cong. 1667 (1970) (statement of John J. Sheehan, Legislative Director for the United Steelworks of America).
135. THE PRINCETON ENCYCLOPEDIA OF POETRY & POETICS 254–55 (Roland Green et al. eds., 4th ed. 2012).
136. Isabel Hyde, *The Tragic Flaw: Is It a Tragic Error?*, 58 MOD. LANGUAGE REV. 321, 322 (July 1963).
137. *Id.* at 323–24.
138. *Id.* at 323; T.C.W. Stinton, *Hamartia in Aristotle and Greek Tragedy*, 25 CLASSICAL Q. 221, 222 (1975) (noting that in the literal sense, hamartia means "to miss the mark").
139. Nash & Revesz, *supra* note 46, at 1681–82 n.18.
140. S. REP. NO. 95-127, at 128 (1977).
141. Nash & Revesz, *supra* note 46, at 1681–82 n.12.

Chapter 4

1. Alani Golanski, *A "Time-Slice" Approach to Tort Law's Component Parts Problem*, 51 DEPAUL L. REV. 39, 48 (2005); Andre Gallois, *Identity Over Time*, STANFORD ENCYCLOPEDIA OF PHILOSOPHY (Mar. 18, 2005, rev. Mar. 17, 2011), http://plato.stanford.edu/entries/identity-time.
2. Clean Air Act Amendments of 1970, § 111(b)(1)(A), Pub. L. No. 91-604, 84 Stat. 1676, 1684 (1970).
3. *Id.* § 111(a)(2), 84 Stat. at 1683 (emphasis added).
4. *Air Pollution–1967 (Air Quality Act): Hearing on S. 780 and Related Matters Pertaining to the Prevention and Control of Air Pollution Including Testimony on the Current Status of Control Technology Before the Subcomm. on Air & Water Pollution of the S. Comm. on Public Works*, 90th Cong. 2370–71 (1967).

5. *Id.* at 2402.
6. DEP'T OF JUSTICE, CIVIL RIGHTS DIV., TITLE III HIGHLIGHTS, *available at* http://www.ada.gov/t3hilght.htm.
7. *Id.*
8. N.Y.C. Admin. Code § 28-101.4.5.1 (2014), *available at* http://www.nyc.gov/html/dob/apps/pdf_viewer/viewer.html?file=2014CC_AC_Chapter1_Administration.pdf§ion=conscode_2014.
9. DEP'T OF JUSTICE, *supra* note 6.
10. N.Y.C. Admin. Code § 28-101.4.5.1 (2014).
11. 42 U.S.C. § 7411(a)(4).
12. *See generally* Rules and Regulations, 36 Fed. Reg. 24,876 (Dec. 23, 1971).
13. *Id.* at 24,877.
14. *Id.*
15. Requirements for Preparation, Adoption and Submittal of Implementation Plans; Approval and Promulgation of Implementation Plans; Standards of Performance for New Stationary Sources, 57 Fed. Reg. 32,313, 32,316 (June 21, 1992).
16. *Id.*
17. Standards of Performance for New Stationary Sources: Modification, Notification, and Reconstruction, Determination of Construction or Modification, 40 Fed. Reg. 58,416, 58,148 (Dec. 16, 1975).
18. *Id.* at 58,416.
19. *Id.*
20. *Id.*
21. *Id.* at 58,416–17.
22. *Id.* at 58,419.
23. *Id.* at 58,420.
24. *Id.*
25. *Id.*
26. 578 F.2d 319, 328 (D.C. Cir. 1978).
27. *Id.* at 324 n.13.
28. *Id.* at 323–24.
29. Clean Air Act Amendments of 1977, Pub. L. No. 95-95, 91 Stat. 685 (1977).
30. 42 U.S.C. § 7602(j); *but see* 42 U.S.C. § 7479(1) (setting a threshold of 250 tons for some source categories in areas that have achieved the NAAQS).
31. H.R. REP. NO. 94-117, at 7 (1977) ("Only new or modified major stationary sources are required to obtain a State permit prior to construction."); S. REP. NO. 95-127, at 31 (1977) ("As part of the required procedure, the State must establish a permit program to regulate construction of new major sources.").
32. Jonathan Remy Nash & Richard L. Revesz, *Grandfathering and Environmental Regulation: The Law and Economics of New Source Review*, 101 NW. U. L. REV. 1677, 1682–83 (2007).

33. *Id.* at 1683.
34. 42 U.S.C. § 7503(a)(1)(A), (c)(1).
35. 42 U.S.C. § 7479(3) ("best available control technology" definition); *id.* § 7503(a)(2) ("lowest achievable emission rate" definition).
36. 42 U.S.C. § 7501(4) (noting that the words "modification" and "modified" mean the same thing for purposes of the New Source Review provisions as they do for New Source Performance Standards).
37. Prevention of Significant Air Quality Deterioration, 43 Fed. Reg. 26,380, 26,388 (June 19, 1978); Emission Offset Interpretative Ruling, 44 Fed. Reg. 3274, 3282 (Jan. 16, 1979).
38. 43 Fed. Reg. at 26,385 ("The plan may provide that such requirements shall apply to a proposed source or modification only with respect to those pollutants for which the proposed construction would be a major stationary source or major modification.").
39. *Id.* ("[T]he requirement of best available control technology, notwithstanding paragraph (f)(2) of this section, shall not apply if no net increase in emissions of an applicable pollutant would occur at the source, taking into account all emission increases and decrease as the source which would accompany the modification, and no adverse air quality impact would occur.").
40. *Id.* at 26,394.
41. Ala. Power Co. v. Costle, 636 F.2d 323, 402 (1979).
42. *Id.* at 400.
43. *Id.*
44. *Id.*
45. Requirements for Preparation, Adoption, and Submittal of Implementation Plans; Approval and Promulgation of Implementation Plans, 45 Fed. Reg. 52,676, 52,735 (Aug. 7, 1980) (emphasis added).
46. *Id.* at 52,737, 52,747.
47. *Id.* at 52,736.
48. Chevron U.S.A. Inc. v. NRDC, 467 U.S. 837, 840, 866 (1984).
49. LARRY B. PARKER & JOHN E. BLODGETT, AIR QUALITY: ISSUES AND OUTLOOK 76 n.28 (Lawrence S. Tooker ed., 2004) (citing LARRY B. PARKER, JOHN E. BLODGETT, ALVIN KAUFMAN & DONALD DULCHINOS, CONG. RESEARCH SERV., CRS REPORT 85-50 ENR, THE CLEAN AIR ACT AND PROPOSED ACID RAIN LEGISLATION: CAN WE GET THERE FROM HERE? 46 (Feb. 21, 1985)).
50. Thomas O. McGarity, *When Strong Enforcement Works Better Than Weak Regulation: The EPA/DOJ New Source Review Enforcement Initiative*, 72 MD. L. REV. 1204, 1218 (2013).
51. *Id.* at 1219.
52. *See id.* at 1218–20 (describing Reagan Administration's lax approach to enforcement).

53. Memorandum from Don R. Clay, Acting Assistant Adm'r for Air & Radiation, to David A. Kee, Dir., Air & Radiation Div., Region V, 2 (Sept. 9, 1988) *available at* http://www.epa.gov/region7/air/nsr/nsrmemos/wpco2.pdf.
54. *Id.*
55. *Id.*; Wis. Elec. Power Co. v. Reilly, 893 F.2d 901, 905–06 (7th Cir. 1990) [hereinafter *WEPCO*].
56. *WEPCO*, 893 F.2d at 905.
57. *Id.*
58. *Id.*
59. *Id.*
60. Memorandum from Don R. Clay, *supra* note 53, at 3.
61. *Id.* at 5–6.
62. *Id.* at 3–4.
63. *WEPCO*, 893 F.2d at 908.
64. *Id.* at 910.
65. *Id.* at 908.
66. *Id.* at 909.
67. *Id.* at 913.
68. *Id.*
69. *Id.* at 913–14.
70. *Id.* at 915–16.
71. *Id.* at 916.
72. *Id.* at 917.
73. *Id.* at 918.
74. Nash & Revesz, *supra* note 32, at 1706.
75. Subcomm. on Health and the Environment of the H. Comm. on Energy and Commerce, An Investigation of EPA's Clean Air "WEPCO" Rule, Staff Report (undated), *reprinted in Clean Air Act Implementation (Part 1): Hearings Before the Subcomm. on Health and the Env't of the H. Comm. on Energy and Commerce*, 102d Cong. 314 (1991).
76. *Id.*
77. *Id.*
78. Anne M. Skalyo, *The WEPCO-"Fix": Out of the* Wisconsin Electric Power Co. v. Reilly *Decision, and the Clean Air Act Amendments of 1990, a Pro-Utility Solution Evolved*, 10 Pace Envtl. L. Rev. 331, 376 (1992).
79. *Clean Air Act Implementation (Part 1): Hearings Before the Subcomm. on Health and the Env't of the H. Comm. on Energy and Commerce*, 102d Cong. 284 (1991) (statement of Rep. Henry Waxman).
80. McGarity, *supra* note 50, at 1226.
81. Skalyo, *supra* note 78, at 385–86.
82. McGarity, *supra* note 50, at 1226.

83. *Id.* (quoting Requirements for Preparation, Adoption and Submittal of Implementation Plans; Approval and Promulgation of Implementation Plans; Standards of Performance for New Stationary Sources, 56 Fed. Reg. 27,630, 27,637 (June 14, 1991)).
84. Skalyo, *supra* note 78, at 387.
85. Nash & Revesz, *supra* note 32, at 1689.
86. *Id.* at 1689–90.
87. *Id.* at 1690.
88. *Id.*
89. Bruce Barcott, *Changing All the Rules*, N.Y. TIMES, Apr. 4, 2004, *available at* http://www.nytimes.com/2004/04/04/magazine/04BUSH.html?pagewanted=1&pagewanted=all.
90. Nash & Revesz, *supra* note 32, at 1692–93; McGarity, *supra* note 50, at 1229.
91. McGarity, *supra* note 50, at 1230.
92. Barcott, *supra* note 89. at sec. II.
93. McGarity, *supra* note 50, at 1233.
94. *Id.* at 1232–33.
95. Elliot Eder & Robin L. Juni, *Has EPA Fired Up Utilities to Clear the Air?*, 15 NAT. RES. & ENV'T. 8, 8–9 (2002).
96. *Clean Air Act: New Source Review Regulatory Program: Hearings Before the Subcomm. on Clean Air, Wetlands, Private Prop. and Nuclear Safety of the S. Comm. on Env't and Pub. Works*, 106th Cong. 100 (2000) (statement of David Hawkins, Dir., Air & Energy Programs, NRDC).
97. *New Source Review Policy, Regulations and Enforcement Activities: Hearings Before the S. Comm. on Env't and Pub. Works and the S. Comm. on the Judiciary*, 107th Cong. 2d Sess. 175 (2002) (statement of Eliot Spitzer, Att'y Gen., N.Y.) (quoting UARG document).
98. Barcott, *supra* note 89, at sec. III.
99. *Id.*
100. *Id.*
101. Richard L. Revesz & Allison L. Westfahl Kong, *Regulatory Change and Optimal Transition Relief*, 105 NW. U. L. REV. 1581, 1630 (2011).
102. *Id.*
103. Barcott, *supra* note 88, at sec. III.
104. *Id.*
105. *Id.*
106. Revesz & Westfahl Kong, *supra* note 101, at 1631.
107. *Id.*
108. *Id.*
109. *Id.*
110. *Id.*

111. Press Release, NRDC (Natural Resources Defense Council), Data Shows Industry Had Extensive Access to Cheney's Energy Task Force (May 21, 2002), *available at* http://www.nrdc.org//media/pressreleases/020521.asp.
112. Nat'l Energy Policy Dev. Grp., National Energy Policy Report: Reliable, Affordable, and Environmentally Sound Energy For America's Future, app. 1 (2001).
113. *Id.*
114. McGarity, *supra* note 50, at 1249.
115. EPA, New Source Review: Report to the President 1, 11 (2002), *available at* http://www.epa.gov/NSR/documents/nsr_report_to_president.pdf.
116. Barcott, *supra* note 89, at sec. V.
117. *Id.*
118. Earthjustice, Paybacks Policies, Patrons and Personnel: How the Bush Administration Is Giving Away Our Environment to Its Corporate Contributors 16 (2002), *available at* http://earthjustice.org/sites/default/files/library/reports/payback_report_final.pdf.
119. Barcott, *supra* note 89, at sec. V.
120. *Id.*
121. *Id.* at sec. VI.
122. *See* Nash & Revesz, *supra* note 32, at 1702–03.
123. Barcott, *supra* note 89, at sec. VI.
124. *Id.*
125. *New Source Review Policy, Regulations and Enforcement Activities: Hearings Before the S. Comm. on Env't and Pub. Works and the S. Comm. on the Judiciary,* 107th Cong. 2d Sess. 604 (2002) (statement of John Walke, Clean Air Dir., NRDC).
126. Catherine Cash & Gerald Karey, *EPA Issues Final Rule "Clarifying" NSR Restriction,* Inside Energy with Fed. Lands, Sept. 1, 2003, at 1.
127. New York v. EPA, 443 F.3d 880, 883 (D.C. Cir. 2006).
128. McGarity, *supra* note 50, at 1269.
129. *See* Revesz & Westfahl Kong, *supra* note 101, at 1628 (noting that "beneficiaries of grandfathering will have incentives to lobby for the purpose of extending the time period during which they receive the benefit").
130. *Air Pollution–1970 Part 5: Hearings on S. 3229, S. 3446 & S. 3546 Before the Subcomm. on Air & Water Pollution of the S. Comm. on Public Works,* 91st Cong. 1575 (1970) (statement of James D. Kittleton, Director, Environmental Activities, American Mining Congress).
131. *See* Missouri Public Service Commission, *PSConnection,* June 2011, at 13, *available at* http://psc.mo.gov/CMSInternetData/PSConnection/Publications/PSConnection%20June%202011.pdf (describing how capital depreciation factors into a utility's rate case).

132. Richard L. Revesz, Environmental Law and Policy 539 (2d ed. 2012).
133. *Id.*
134. 33 U.S.C. § 1316 (2015).
135. Last Week Tonight, *Last Week Tonight with John Oliver: Net Neutrality (HBO)*, YouTube (June 1, 2014), https://www.youtube.com/watch?v=fpbOEoRrHyU.
136. Revesz, Environmental Law and Policy, *supra* note 132, at 539 (noting that the deadline for existing sources to install the "best available technology" was extended from 1983 to 1987).

Chapter 5

1. Ala. Power Co. v. Costle, 636 F.2d 323, 346 (D.C. Cir. 1979).
2. *See id.* ("The provisions for the attainment and maintenance of NAAQS were to operate primarily through controls on existing sources of pollution.").
3. *See, e.g.*, James E. McCarthy, Cong. Research Serv., R43092, Ozone Air Quality Standards: EPA's 2015 Revision ii (2014), *available at* http://fas.org/sgp/crs/misc/R43092.pdf.
4. 42 U.S.C. § 7409(d)(1).
5. 42 U.S.C. § 7409(a).
6. *Id.* § 7409(b)(1).
7. *Id.* § 7409(b)(2) (secondary NAAQS must be sufficient to protect "public welfare"); *id.* § 7602(h) (defining "welfare"); M.J. Roberts & S.O. Farrell, *The Political Economy of Implementation: The Clean Air Act and Stationary Sources*, *in* Approaches to Controlling Air Pollution 154 (Ann F. Friedlacher ed., 1978).
8. Press Release, EPA, EPA Sets National Air Quality Standards (Apr. 30, 1971), *available at* http://www2.epa.gov/aboutepa/epa-sets-national-air-quality-standards.
9. Clean Air Act Amendments of 1970, Pub. L. No. 91-604, § 110(a)(2)(A), 84 Stat. 1680 (1970).
10. EPA, *What Is a State Implementation Plan?*, *in* The On-Line State Implementation Plan Processing Manual, *available at* http://www.epa.gov/region1/topics/air/sips/REVISED_WHAT_IS_A_SIP.pdf.
11. A Legislative History of the Clean Air Act Amendments of 1977, 95th Cong., 2d Sess., August 1978, vol. 4, at 3050 (House Debate on H.R. 6161, May 24, 1977, Clean Air Act Amendments of 1977).
12. Brief for Respondents at 16 n.6, Ruckelshaus v. Sierra Club, No. 72-804 (U.S. 1973), 1973 WL 172680 (citing EPA, Background Information, State Air Implementation Plans, p. 3 (May 1972)).
13. *Id.*

14. Yvonne F. Lindgren, *The Emissions Trading Policy: Smoke on the Horizon for Takings Clause Claimants*, 18 HASTINGS CONST. L.Q. 667, 673 (1991).
15. David E. Adelman, *Environmental Federalism When Numbers Matter More Than Size*, 32 UCLA J. ENVTL. L. & POL'Y 238, 296 (2014).
16. *Id.*
17. *Id.* at 296–97.
18. Richard E. Ayres, *Enforcement of Air Pollution Controls on Stationary Sources Under the Clean Air Amendments of 1970*, 4 ECOLOGY L.Q. 441, 443 (1975).
19. NRDC v. EPA, 489 F.2d 390, 403 (5th Cir. 1974), *vacated in part by* NRDC v. EPA, 516 F.2d 488 (5th Cir. 1975).
20. *Id.*
21. Regan R.J. Smith, *Playing the Acid Rain Game: A State's Remedies*, 16 ENVTL. L. 255, 268–69 (1986).
22. *Empire State Building Fast Facts*, CNN, http://www.cnn.com/2013/07/11/us/empire-state-building-fast-facts (last updated July 22, 2015).
23. Richard L. Revesz, *Federalism and Interstate Environmental Externalities*, 144 U. PA. L. REV. 2341, 2351 n.37 (1996).
24. *Id.* at 2351.
25. Bruce A. Ackerman & William T. Hassler, *Beyond the New Deal: Coal and the Clean Air Act*, 89 YALE L.J. 1466, 1491 n.93 (1980) (citing estimate that tall stacks cost 3 to 17 percent as much as a scrubber); *Air Pollution Control and Solid Waste Recycling: Hearings on H.R. 12934, H.R. 14960, H.R. 15137, and H.R. 15192, H.R. 15848, H.R. 15847, and Related Bills Before the Subcomm. on Public Health and Welfare of the H. Comm. on Interstate and Foreign Commerce*, 91st Cong. 2555, (1969–1970) (estimating that low-sulfur coal was twenty-five times as expensive as a high stack for a Midwestern power plant).
26. *See, e.g.*, Ala. Power Co. v. Costle, 636 F.2d 323, 391 (D.C. Cir. 1979) (summarizing findings of a 1977 House report on problems associated with tall stacks).
27. Richard E. Ayres, *Enforcement of Air Pollution Controls on Stationary Sources Under the Clean Air Amendments of 1970*, 4 ECOLOGY L.Q. 441, 452 (1975) (referring to the intuitive "environmental bankruptcy" of dispersion strategies).
28. *Clean Air Act Oversight: Hearings Before the Subcomm. on Environmental Pollution of the Senate Comm. on Public Works*, 93d Cong., 2d Sess. 320, 330 (1974) (statement of Richard Ayres).
29. NRDC v. EPA, 489 F.2d 390, 410 (5th Cir. 1974), *vacated in part by* NRDC v. EPA, 516 F.2d 488 (5th Cir. 1975).
30. Stack Height Increase Guidelines, 41 Fed. Reg. 7450, 7451–52 (1976).
31. Union Elec. Co. v. EPA, 427 U.S. 246, 252 (1976).
32. *Id.*
33. Roberts & Farrell, *supra* note 7, at 165.
34. *Id.*

35. *Id.; see also* EPA, ASTHMA TRIGGERS: GAIN CONTROL, NITROGEN DIOXIDE, http://www.epa.gov/asthma/no2.html (last updated Apr. 11, 2012) (noting that nitogren oxides are odorless); NAT'L PARK SERV., SULFUR DIOXIDE EFFECTS ON HEALTH, http://www.nature.nps.gov/air/AQBasics/understand_so2.cfm (last updated Jan. 10, 2013) (noting that sulfur dioxide is colorless); EPA, PARTICULATE MATTER: BASIC INFORMATION, http://www.epa.gov/pm/basic.html (noting that some particle pollution is so small it can only be detected with an electron microscope) (last updated Mar. 18, 2013).
36. Roberts & Farrell, *supra* note 7, at 166.
37. *Id.*
38. S. REP. NO. 95-127, at 49 (1977).
39. *Id.* at 128–29.
40. Clean Air Act Amendments of 1970, Pub. L. No. 91-604, § 113(b) & (c), 84 Stat. 1680, 1687 (1970).
41. Ayres, *supra* note 18, at 473.
42. *Id.* at 473–74.
43. David McN. Olds, *Thoughts on the Role of Penalties in the Enforcements of the Clean Air and Clean Water Acts*, 17 DUQ. L. REV. 1, 9 (1978).
44. *Id.* at 17.
45. *Id.* at 16.
46. *Id.* at 9.
47. 42 U.S.C. § 7428.
48. Arnold W. Reitze, Jr., *The Legislative History of U.S. Air Pollution Control*, 36 HOUS. L. REV. 679, 710–11 (1999).
49. *Id.* at 711.
50. *See, e.g.*, Air Pollution Control Dist. of Jefferson Cty. v. EPA, 739 F.2d 1071, 1077 (6th Cir. 1984).
51. Sierra Club v. EPA, 719 F.2d 436, 440–41 (D.C. Cir. 1983).
52. *Id.* at 441; 42 U.S.C. § 7423(a).
53. Clean Air Act Amendments of 1977, Pub. L. 95-95, § 110(a)(2)(E)(i), 91 Stat. 685, 693.
54. *Id.* § 126(b), 91 Stat. at 724.
55. *Id.* § 126(b).
56. 42 U.S.C. § 7423(c).
57. *See* Arnold W. Reitze, Jr., *State and Federal Command-and-Control Regulation of Emissions from Fossil-Fuel Electric Power Generating Plants*, 32 ENVTL. L. 369, 404 (2002) (citing Sierra Club v. EPA, 719 F.2d 436, 466–68 (D.C. Cir. 1983)).
58. Reitze, *supra* note 57, at 404–05 (citing NRDC v. Thomas, 838 F.2d 1224 (D.C. Cir. 1988)).
59. 739 F.2d 1071 (6th Cir. 1984).
60. *Id.* at 1076–77.

61. *Id.* at 1077.
62. *Id.* at 1076–77.
63. *Gallagher Station*, Duke Energy, https://www.duke-energy.com/power-plants/coal-fired/gallagher.asp (last visited July 16, 2015).
64. Air Pollution Control Dist. of Jefferson Cty. v. EPA, 739 F.2d. 1071, 1076 (6th Cir. 1984).
65. U.S. Energy Info. Admin. (Glossary), British thermal unit definition, http://www.eia.gov/tools/glossary/index.cfm?id=B#brit_th_unit (last visited July 13, 2015).
66. Unlike weight- or volume-based metrics—pounds of coal, gallons of gas—measuring fuels in terms of Btus allows the EPA to meaningfully compare pollution rates across fuel types. Imagine that a pound of Fuel A generates half the pollution when burned as does a pound of Fuel B. Does this mean that Fuel A is the "cleaner" choice? Not if Fuel B generates three times as much heat—that is, contains three times as many potential Btus—as an equivalent quantity of Fuel A. Fuel A may still be dirtier on a per-pound basis, but we can use far less of it to reach the same energy-producing goal and thus generate a smaller quantity of total pollution.

    An even better measure, which the EPA uses for some of its performance standards, is pounds of pollution per kilowatt-hour generated. This takes into account not only the energy content of the fuel burned but also the efficiency with which the generating unit in question turns that heat into a final, usable product: electricity.
67. Jeremy M. Hales, Tall Stacks and the Atmospheric Environment, B-4 tbl.1 (EPA-450/3-76-007, 1976) (listing stack height for Gallagher Station).
68. Air Pollution Control Dist. of Jefferson Cty. v. EPA, 739 F.2d 1071, 1076–77 (6th Cir. 1084).
69. Mitch McConnell, Biography, http://www.mcconnell.senate.gov/public/index.cfm?p=Biography (last visited June 25, 2014).
70. 739 F.2d at 1079.
71. *Id.* at 1079 (describing the EPA's delay in responding to the petition); *see also id.* at 1077–79 (describing the EPA's reasons for rejecting the petition).
72. *Id.* at 1083.
73. *Id.* at 1077–78 (describing EPA's modeling efforts).
74. *Id.* at 1083.
75. *Id.* at 1078.
76. *Id.* at 1084.
77. *Id.* at 1090–91.
78. *Id.*
79. *Id.* at 1093 (quoting 42 U.S.C. § 7426(a)).
80. 739 F.2d at 1093.

81. *Id.* at 1085.
82. *Id.* at 1078.
83. *Id.* at 1085.
84. *Id.* at 1086 (quoting 45 Fed. Reg. 17,048, 17,049 (Mar. 17, 1980)).
85. 739 F.2d at 1087–88.
86. *Id.* at 1094.
87. Reitze, *State and Federal Command-and-Control Regulation of Emissions from Fossil-Fuel Electric Power Generating Plants, supra* note 57, at 408.
88. *See, e.g.,* Connecticut v. EPA, 696 F.2d 147, 155 (2d Cir. 1982) (noting that deference "is entirely appropriate in light of the Agency's expertise and experience with the intricate workings of the Clean Air Act and EPA's greater understanding of the pollution problem that Act is designed to control").
89. *Id.* at 156.
90. Long Island Power Auth., Electric Resource Plan 2010–2020: Appendix E-2.c: Northport/Port Jeff Repowering Study 1 (2009), *available at* http://www.lipower.org/pdfs/company/projects/energyplan10/energyplan10-e2c.pdf.
91. Connecticut v. EPA, 696 F.2d at 151–52.
92. *Id.*
93. *Id.* at 153.
94. *Id.* at 165.
95. *Id.* at 165 & n.41.
96. *Id.* at 165.
97. *Id.* at 168.
98. New York v. EPA, 710 F.2d 1200, 1202 (6th Cir. 1983) (noting that the nearest point in New York was 926 kilometers from the Kingston plant).
99. *Id.* at 1203.
100. *See* Approval and Promulgation of Implementation Plans; Tennessee: Revised SO_2, 46 Fed Reg. 61,120, 61,120 (Dec. 15, 1981) (noting prior state standard of 1.2 lbs/MMBtu); *see also* Tenn. Valley Auth., About TVA: History, http://www.tva.com/abouttva/history.htm (last visited July 16, 2015).
101. *See* 46 Fed Reg. at 61,120 (noting that the plant was out of compliance with original state standard and had "until the recent tie-in of tall stacks . . . caused violations of the sulfur dioxide ambient standards" in the surrounding county); *see also* Tenn. Valley Auth., Kingston Fossil Plant Fact Sheet (2009), http://www.tva.gov/news/kingston/kif.pdf.
102. Approval and Promulgation of Implementation Plans; Tennessee: Revised SO_2, 46 Fed Reg. at 61,120.
103. EPA, EPA-600/8-83-016A, The Acidic Deposition Phenomenon and its Effects, Critical Assessment Review Papers Volume I Atmospheric Sciences: Public Review Draft, 3-61 (1983), *available*

at http://nepis.epa.gov/Simple.html (type "600883016A" in search field and click "search").

104. New York v. EPA, 710 F.2d 1200, 1202 (6th Cir. 1983).
105. *Id.* at 1202–03.
106. *Id.* at 1204.
107. New York v. EPA, 852 F.2d 574, 576 (D.C. Cir. 1988).
108. *Id.* at 581 (Ginsburg, J., concurring).
109. Richard E. Cohen, Washington at Work: Back Rooms and Clean Air 53 (2d ed. 1995).
110. *Id.* at 55.
111. *Id.* at 51.
112. *Id.* at 53.
113. *Id.* at 54; *see also* Robin Toner, *Bush, in Enemy Waters, Says Rival Hindered Cleanup of Boston Harbor*, N.Y. Times, Sept. 2, 1988, http://www.nytimes.com/1988/09/02/us/bush-in-enemy-waters-says-rival-hindered-cleanup-of-boston-harbor.html.
114. Cohen, supra note 109, at 53.
115. *Id.*
116. Gene E. Likens & F. Herbert Bormann, *Acid Rain: A Serious Regional Environmental Problem*, 184 Science 1176 (1974).
117. Boyce Rensberger, *Acid in Rain Found to Be Up Sharply*, N.Y. Times, June 13, 1974, at 1, http://timesmachine.nytimes.com/timesmachine/1974/06/13/99170519.html.
118. *Id.* at 1, 9.
119. *Id.* at 9.
120. EPA, Sulfur Dioxide: Health, http://www.epa.gov/oaqps001/sulfurdioxide/health.html (last updated Mar. 25, 2015).
121. EPA, Nitrogen Dioxide: Health, http://www.epa.gov/airquality/nitrogenoxides/health.html (last updated Aug. 15, 2014).
122. EPA, Particulate Matter (PM), http://www.epa.gov/pm/ (last updated Mar. 18, 2013).
123. EPA, What is Acid Rain?, http://www.epa.gov/acidrain/what/ (last updated Dec. 4, 2012).
124. EPA, Effects of Acid Rain–Forests, http://www.epa.gov/acidrain/effects/forests.html#a3 (last updated Dec. 4, 2012).
125. EPA, Effects of Acid Rain–Materials, http://www.epa.gov/acidrain/effects/materials.html (last updated Dec. 4, 2012).
126. EPA, Effects of Acid Rain–Surface Waters and Aquatic Animals, http://www.epa.gov/acidrain/effects/surface_water.html (last updated Dec. 4, 2012).
127. *Acid Rain: Hearings Before the Subcomm. on Oversight and Investigations of the H. Comm. on Interstate and Foreign Commerce*, 96th Cong. 330 (1980) (statement of Douglas Costle, EPA Adm'r).

128. Larry B. Parker et al., Cong. Research Serv., Report No. 85-50 ENR, The Clean Air Act and Proposed Acid Rain Legislation: Can We Get There From Here? 7 (1985).
129. *Id.*
130. *Id.* at 22.
131. *Id.* at 41.
132. *Id.* at 17.
133. *See* EPA, Green Book: National Area and County-Level Multi-Pollutant Information, http://www.epa.gov/airquality/greenbook/multipol.html (last updated Mar. 23, 2015) (select "Whole or Part County Nonattainment Status by Year Since 1978 for All Criteria Pollutants").
134. *Id.*
135. James R. Vestigo, *Acid Rain and Tall Stack Regulation Under the Clean Air Act*, 15 Envtl. L. 711, 716, 719 (1985).
136. *Id.* at 716.
137. A. Denny Ellerman et al., Markets for Clean Air: The U.S. Acid Rain Program 19 (2000).
138. *Id.*
139. To be sure, a high level of energy demand could also indicate that energy is being used inefficiently, as a result of, for example, inadequate insulation in buildings.
140. *See Clean Air Act Reauthorization—Part 3: Hearing on H.R. 3400 and H.R. 5094 Before the Subcomm. on Health and the Environment of the H.R. Comm. on Energy and Commerce*, 98th Cong. 69–73 (1984) (table listing 200 power plants with highest SO_2 emissions as of 1980).
141. *Id.*
142. *Id.*
143. Parker et al., *supra* note 128, at 21.
144. *Id.* at 18.
145. Report of the Acid Rain Peer Review Panel II-1 (July 1984), *available at* http://nepis.epa.gov/Simple.html (type "450R84505" in the search field and click "search").
146. Parker et al., *supra* note 128, at 20.
147. *Id.* at 23.
148. *Id.* at 23–24, 49.
149. *Id.* at 50.
150. *Id.* at 55–56.
151. Ellerman et al., *supra* note 137, at 19.
152. *Id.* at 19–20.
153. Cohen, *supra* note 109, at 67.
154. Ellerman et al., *supra* note 137, at 6.
155. *Id.*

156. *Id.* at 44. Though the 1.2 lbs/MMBtu served as the general benchmark for Phase II, many plants were subject to special allocation rules that deviated somewhat from the basic formula.
157. Ellerman et al., *supra* note 137, at 6; *Bush Calls for 50% Acid Rain Cut by 2000*, L.A. Times, June 12, 1989, http://articles.latimes.com/1989-06-12/news/mn-1634_1_acid-rain-dirty-air-bush-calls.
158. *See* Gabriel Chan, Robert Stavins, Robert Stowe & Richard Sweeney, The SO_2 Allowance Trading System and The Clean Air Act Amendments of 1990 6 (2012), *available at* http://www.hks.harvard.edu/m-rcbg/heep/papers/SO2-Brief_digital_final.pdf (describing basic mechanics of emissions trading).
159. Ellerman et al., *supra* note 137, at 34.
160. *See, e.g.*, Philip Shabecoff, *Several Governors Oppose Plan on Acid Rain*, N.Y. Times, Jan. 11, 1990, http://www.nytimes.com/1990/01/11/us/several-governors-oppose-plan-on-acid-rain.html.
161. *Id.*
162. Ellerman et al., *supra* note 137, at 41; Cohen, *supra* note 109, at 185–86.
163. Ellerman et al., *supra* note 137, at 41. This figure assumes an allowance price of $200.
164. Press Release, EPA, *EPA Administrator Reilly Hails Signing of New Clean Air Act* (Nov. 15, 1990), http://www2.epa.gov/aboutepa/epa-administrator-reilly-hails-signing-new-clean-air-act.
165. *Id.*
166. *Id.*
167. *See, e.g.*, Richard Schmalensee et al., *An Interim Evaluation of Sulfur Dioxide Emissions Trading*, 12 J. Econ. Persp. 53, 55 (1998) ("In the early 1990s, analysts predicted allowance prices of about $250–350 per ton in Phase I and $500–700 in Phase II."); Ellerman et al., *supra* note 137, at 8 ("[C]ontemporary estimates were that Phase I allowances would be worth $250–350 per ton and that Phase II allowances would be worth $500–700 per ton.").
168. *See* EPA, The United States Experience with Economic Incentives for Pollution Control 81 (2001), *available at* http://yosemite.epa.gov/ee/epa/eed.nsf/webpages/USExperienceWithEconomicIncentives.html; Dallas Burtraw, *Cost Savings Sans Allowance Trades? Evaluating the SO_2 Emission Trading Program to Date* 8 (Resources for the Future, Discussion Paper 95-30-Rev, 1996), *available at* http://www.rff.org/RFF/documents/RFF-DP-95-30-REV.pdf.
169. Juha Siikamäki, Dallas Burtraw, Joseph Maher & Clayton Munnings, The U.S. Environmental Protection Agency's Acid Rain Program 6 (2012), *available at* http://www.rff.org/RFF/Documents/RFF-Bck-AcidRainProgram.pdf.

170. Ellerman et al., *supra* note 137, at 82.
171. *Id.* at 82–83.
172. *Id.* at 83.
173. *Id.*
174. Richard Schmalensee & Robert N. Stavins, *The SO_2 Allowance Trading System: The Ironic History of a Grand Policy Experiment*, 27 J. Econ. Persp. 103, 111 (2013).
175. *Id.*
176. *Id.*
177. *See* Ellerman et al., *supra* note 137, at 235–42 (summarizing innovations that reduced operating costs for scrubbers); *id.* at 243 (noting "high degree of innovation in adapting boilers built for bituminous coals to burn PRB coals").
178. EPA, Acid Rain Program: 2005 Progress Report 8 (2006), *available at* http://www.epa.gov/airmarkets/documents/progressreports/2005report.pdf.
179. *See* Jason S. Grumet, *Old West Justice: Federalism and Clean Air Regulation 1970–1998*, 11 Tul. Envtl. L.J. 375, 393 (1998) ("In 1995, roughly seventy million people lived in areas that violated the one-hour 120 ppb federal health standard for ozone.").
180. EPA, EPA-451/K-03-001, Ozone: Good Up High, Bad Nearby 2 (2003).
181. *Id.*
182. EPA, Ground Level Ozone, http://www.epa.gov/ozonepollution/ (last updated Mar. 25, 2015).
183. Am. Lung Ass'n, Nitrogen Dioxide, http://www.lung.org/healthy-air/outdoor/resources/nitrogen-dioxide.html (last visited July 17, 2015).
184. U.S. Gen. Accounting Office, Air Pollution: Emissions from Older Electricity Generating Units 3 (2002), *available at* http://www.gao.gov/assets/240/234728.pdf.
185. *Id.* at 12.
186. Grumet, *supra* note 179, at 393.
187. *Id.* at 379.
188. Congressional Budget Office, Federalism and Environmental Protection: Case Studies for Drinking Water and Ground-Level Ozone 44 (1997), *available at* http://www.cbo.gov/sites/default/files/drinkwat.pdf.
189. *Id.*
190. Findings of Significant Contribution and Rulemaking on Section 126 Petitions for Purposes of Reducing Interstate Ozone Transport, 63 Fed. Reg. 24,058, 24,071 (1998).
191. EPA v. EME Homer City Generation, L.P., 134 S. Ct. 1584, 1595 (2014).

192. Michigan v. EPA, 213 F.3d 663, 675 (D.C. Cir. 2000) ("Nothing in the text of the [Good Neighbor Provision] or any other provision of the statute spells out a criterion for classifying 'emissions activity' as 'significant.'").
193. Finding of Significant Contribution and Rulemaking for Certain States in the Ozone Transport Assessment Group Region for Purposes of Reducing Regional Transport of Ozone, 63 Fed. Reg. 57,356, 57,375 (Oct. 27, 1998).
194. *Id.* at 57,376.
195. *Id.* at 57,356, 57,377.
196. *Id.* at 57,377–78.
197. *Id.* at 57,358–59.
198. Michigan v. EPA, 213 F.3d 663, 675 (D.C. Cir. 2000).
199. *Id.* at 677.
200. Rule to Reduce Interstate Transport of Fine Particulate Matter and Ozone (Clean Air Interstate Rule); Revisions to Acid Rain Program; Revisions to the NOX, 70 Fed. Reg. 25,162 (May 12, 2005).
201. North Carolina v. EPA, 531 F.3d 896, 903–04 (D.C. Cir. 2008).
202. *Id.* at 904.
203. 70 Fed. Reg. at 25,176.
204. EPA, Clean Air Interstate Rule (CAIR): Reducing Power Plant Emissions for Cleaner Air, Healthier People, and a Strong America 18 (2005), *available at* http://www.epa.gov/airmarkt/documents/cair/cair_final_presentation.pdf.
205. North Carolina v. EPA, 531 F.3d at 901.
206. *Id.* at 908.
207. *Id.* at 907.
208. *Id.* at 901.
209. North Carolina v. EPA, 550 F.3d 1176, 1178 (D.C. Cir. 2008).
210. Lauraine G. Chesnut & David M. Mills, *A Fresh Look at the Benefits and Costs of the US Acid Rain Program*, 77 J. Envtl. Mgmt. 252, 257 (2005).
211. EPA, EPA-430-R-09-026, The NOx Budget Trading Program: 2008 Highlights 7 (2009), *available at* http://www.epa.gov/airmarkets/documents/progressreports/NBP_2008_Highlights.pdf.
212. EPA, EPA-452/R-05-002, Regulatory Impact Analysis for the Final Clean Air Interstate Rule 1-3 (2005), *available at* http://nepis.epa.gov/Adobe/PDF/P1001EZK.PDF.

Chapter 6

1. EPA, Learn About Carbon Pollution From Power Plants, http://www2.epa.gov/cleanpowerplan/learn-about-carbon-pollution-power-plants (last updated July 17, 2015).

2. Endangerment and Cause or Contribute Findings for Greenhouse Gases Under Section 202(a) of the Clean Air Act, 74 Fed. Reg. 66,496, 66,527 (Dec. 15, 2009) (noting that none of the predicted health effects of climate change are associated with direct exposure to carbon and other greenhouse gases).
3. *See* U.S. DEP'T OF COMMERCE, NOAA, EARTH SYS. RESEARCH LAB., CARBON CYCLE SCIENCE, http://www.esrl.noaa.gov/research/themes/carbon/ (last visited July 20, 2015).
4. EPA, CAUSES OF CLIMATE CHANGE, http://www.epa.gov/climatechange/science/causes.html (last updated Mar. 18, 2014).
5. EPA, CLIMATE CHANGE: BASIC INFORMATION, http://www.epa.gov/climatechange/basics/ (last updated Mar. 18, 2014).
6. CAUSES OF CLIMATE CHANGE, *supra* note 4.
7. EPA, FUTURE CLIMATE CHANGE, http://www.epa.gov/climatechange/science/future.html (last updated Mar. 4, 2014); *see also* Endangerment and Cause or Contribute Findings for Greenhouse Gases Under Section 202(a) of the Clean Air Act,74 Fed. Reg. at 66,523–66,536 (2009).
8. EPA, GLOBAL GREENHOUSE GAS EMISSIONS DATA, http://www.epa.gov/climatechange/ghgemissions/global.html (last updated Sept. 9, 2013) (global emissions); EPA, OVERVIEW OF GREENHOUSE GASES, http://www.epa.gov/climatechange/ghgemissions/gases.html (last updated May 7, 2015) (U.S. emissions).
9. PRESIDENT BARACK OBAMA, REMARKS BY THE PRESIDENT ON CLEAN ENERGY (Apr. 22, 2009), transcript *available at* https://www.whitehouse.gov/video/Seeing-Green-in-Iowa#transcript.
10. Steve Graham, *John Tyndall (1820–1893)*, NASA: EARTH OBSERVATORY (Oct. 8, 1999), http://earthobservatory.nasa.gov/Features/Tyndall/.
11. *The Discovery of Global Warming: The Carbon Dioxide Greenhouse Effect*, AM. INST. OF PHYSICS (Mar. 2015), https://www.aip.org/history/climate/co2.htm.
12. *Id.*
13. *Id.*; *Keeling Curve*, WIKIPEDIA, http://en.wikipedia.org/wiki/Keeling_Curve (last updated Aug. 20, 2015).
14. *How Much Will Earth Warm if Carbon Dioxide Doubles Pre-Industrial Levels?*, NAT'L OCEANIC & ATMOSPHERIC ADMIN. (Jan. 24, 2014), https://www.climate.gov/news-features/climate-qa/how-much-will-earth-warm-if-carbon-dioxide-doubles-pre-industrial-levels.
15. ENVTL. POLLUTION PANEL, PRESIDENT'S SCI. ADVISORY COMM., RESTORING THE QUALITY OF OUR ENVIRONMENT (1965), *available at* http://dge.stanford.edu/labs/caldeiralab/Caldeira%20downloads/PSAC,%201965,%20Restoring%20the%20Quality%20of%20Our%20Environment.pdf.
16. *Id.* at 126.

17. *Id.*
18. *Id.* at 127.
19. Staff of Subcomm. on Sci., Research, & Development of the H. Comm. on Sci. & Astronautics, 89th Cong., Rep. on Environmental Pollution: A Challenge to Science and Technology 22 (Comm. Print 1966).
20. *Id.* at 24.
21. Leon G. Billings, *The Obscure 1970 Compromise that Made Obama's Climate Rules Possible*, Politico (June 2, 2014), http://www.politico.com/magazine/story/2014/06/the-obscure-1970-compromise-that-made-obamas-climate-rules-possible-107351_Page2.html#ixzz3VtZRcM5F.
22. *See, e.g., Air Pollution Control and Solid Wastes Recycling: Hearing on H.R. 12934, H.R. 14960, H.R. 15137, and H.R. 15192 Before the Subcomm. on Pub. Health and Welfare of the H. Comm. on Interstate and Foreign Commerce*, 91st Cong. 300 (1970) ("There are two schools of thought and whether or not we are going to heat up the atmosphere so that we melt the ice caps and have flooding of our land or whether we are going to do the reverse in terms of holding out radiant energy, the carbon dioxide balance might result in the heating up of the atmosphere whereas the reduction in the radiant energy through particulate matter released in the atmosphere might cause reduction in radiation that reaches the earth."); *Air Pollution 1970–Part 4: Hearings on S. 3229, S. 3466, and S. 3546 Before the Subcomm. on Air and Water Pollution of the S. Comm. on Pub. Works*, 91st Cong. 1279–80 (1970) ("[O]ne scientist theorizes that air pollution could, by trapping energy from the sun, cause the polar icecaps to melt and bring on earthquakes, volcanic eruptions, flooding and other calamities. Another is reported to have reached the opposite conclusion—that air pollution, by reflecting the sun's rays away from the earth, would cool the earth and lead to the formation of glaciers, icebergs and ice. . . . Thus the effect of different pollutants were thought to counteract each other to some extent.").
23. Bill Chameides, *What's Global Dimming?*, Envtl. Def. Fund: Climate 411 (Apr. 3, 2007), http://blogs.edf.org/climate411/2007/04/03/global_dimming/.
24. Clean Air Act Amendments of 1970, Pub. L. No. 91-604, § 111(b)(1), 84 Stat. 1676, 1684 (1970) (requiring the EPA to regulate any stationary source category that "may contribute significantly to air pollution which causes or contributes to the endangerment of public health or welfare").
25. *Id.* § 302(g), 84 Stat. at 1710.
26. 42 U.S.C. § 7602(g). Explaining the change, a report from the House Committee on Interstate and Foreign Commerce noted that the Clean Air Act was "the comprehensive vehicle for protection of the Nation's health from air pollution" and that "[i]n the committee's view, it [was] not appropriate to

exempt certain pollutants or certain sources from the comprehensive protections afforded by the Clean Air Act." H. REP. NO. 95-254, at 42 (1977).

27. *See* Thomas C. Peterson, William M. Connolley & John Fleck, *The Myth of the 1970s Global Cooling Scientific Consensus*, BULL. OF THE AM. METEROLOGICAL SOC'Y, Sept. 2008 at 1325, 1332 tbl.1, *available at* http://journals.ametsoc.org/doi/pdf/10.1175/2008BAMS2370.1 (surveying peer-reviewed climate science from 1970s and finding that more publications pointed toward global warming than cooling, particularly in later years of the decade); *see also* David Biello, *Could Cleaning Up Air Pollution Actually Speed Up Global Warming?*, SCI. AM. (Apr. 23, 2009), http://www.scientificamerican.com/article/could-cleaning-up-air-pollution-hasten-global-warming/ (describing atmospheric residence times of particulate matter and carbon dioxide).
28. *Environmental Implications of the New Energy Plan: Hearings Before the Subcomm. on the Env't & the Atmosphere of the H. Comm. on Sci. & Tech*, 95th Cong. 454–55 (1977).
29. *Id.* at 544–45.
30. *Id.* at 427.
31. *Id.* at 426.
32. NAT'L ACAD. OF SCIENCES, STUDIES IN GEOPHYSICS: ENERGY AND CLIMATE 3 (1977).
33. *Id.* at viii.
34. *Id.* at 5.
35. National Climate Program Act § 5, 15 U.S.C. § 2904.
36. *Government: The View from Washington, D.C.*, AM. INST. OF PHYSICS (Feb. 2015), https://www.aip.org/history/climate/Govt.htm.
37. *Greenhouse Effect and Global Climate Change: Hearing Before the S. Comm. on Energy and Natural Res.*, 100th Cong. 39 (1988) (statement of James Hansen, Director, NASA Goddard Inst. for Space Studies).
38. *Id.*
39. NAT'L OCEANIC & ATMOSPHERIC ADMIN., GLOBAL ANALYSIS—ANNUAL 2014: VARIOUS GLOBAL TEMPERATURE TIME SERIES, UPDATED THROUGH 2014, http://www.ncdc.noaa.gov/sotc/global/2014/13/supplemental/page-4 (last visited July 20, 2015).
40. G.A. Res. 43/53, ¶ 5, U.N. Doc. A/RES/43/53 (Dec. 6, 1988).
41. CLIMATE CHANGE: THE IPCC SCIENTIFIC ASSESSMENT xi (J.T. Houghton, G.J. Jenkins & J.J. Ephraums eds., 1990), *available at* https://www.ipcc.ch/ipccreports/far/wg_I/ipcc_far_wg_I_spm.pdf.
42. *Id.*
43. United Nations Framework Convention on Climate Change, May 9, 1992, S. Treaty Doc. No. 102–38, art. 2, 1771 U.N.T.S. 107, *available at* http://unfccc.int/resource/docs/convkp/conveng.pdf; *see also* Massachusetts v. EPA, 549 U.S. 497, 508–09 (2007).

44. United Nations Framework Convention on Climate Change, *supra* note 43, art. 3.
45. Larry Parker, John Blodgett & Brent D. Yacobucci, Cong. Research Serv., RL30024, U.S. Global Climate Change Policy: Evolving Views on Cost, Competitiveness, and Comprehensiveness 3 (2011), *available at* https://www.fas.org/sgp/crs/misc/RL30024.pdf.
46. United Nations Framework Convention on Climate Change, Fact Sheet: The Need for Mitigation 3 (2009), https://unfccc.int/files/press/backgrounders/application/pdf/press_factsh_mitigation.pdf.
47. Massachusetts v. EPA, 549 U.S. at 508–09.
48. Parker, Blodgett & Yacobucci, *supra* note 45, at 3–4.
49. Steven Greenhouse, *Clinton's Economic Plan: The Energy Plan; Fuels Tax: Spreading The Burden*, N.Y. Times, Feb. 18, 1993, http://www.nytimes.com/1993/02/18/us/clinton-s-economic-plan-the-energy-plan-fuels-tax-spreading-the-burden.html.
50. Parker, Blodgett & Yacobucci, *supra* note 45, at 5–6.
51. Gary Lee, *Clinton Offers Package to "Halt Global Warming,"* Wash. Post., Oct. 20, 1993, http://www.washingtonpost.com/archive/politics/1993/10/20/clinton-offers-package-to-halt-global-warming/957a479c-c9cf-433d-baa6-7343b702396a/ (quoting criticism of Clinton climate plan by Sierra Club and Greenpeace leaders).
52. Intergovernmental Panel on Climate Change, IPCC Second Assessment: Climate Change 1995, at 5 (1995), *available at* https://www.ipcc.ch/pdf/climate-changes-1995/ipcc-2nd-assessment/2nd-assessment-en.pdf.
53. *Id.*
54. *Id.* at 23.
55. *Id.*
56. Framework Convention on Climate Change Conference of the Parties, Berlin, Mar. 28–Apr. 7, 1995, *Report of the Conference of the Parties on Its First Session*, 4 (1995) U.N. Doc. FCCC/CP/1995/7/Add.1, *available at* http://unfccc.int/resource/docs/cop1/07a01.pdf (concluding that developed countries' voluntary commitments in the original convention are "not adequate"); *Making Those First Steps Count: An Introduction to the Kyoto Protocol*, United Nations, Framework Convention on Climate Change, http://unfccc.int/essential_background/kyoto_protocol/items/6034.php (last visited July 20, 2015) (describing adoption of Kyoto Protocol).
57. *Making Those First Steps Count*, *supra* note 56.
58. Eric Pooley, The Climate War 92–93 (2010).
59. S. Res. 98, 105th Cong. (1997).

60. Statement by Vice President Gore on the United States' Signing of the Kyoto Protocol (Nov. 12, 1998), *available at* http://clinton4.nara.gov/CEQ/19981112-7936.html.
61. *U.S. Carbon Dioxide Emissions Jump in 2000*, L.A. Times, Nov. 11, 2001, http://articles.latimes.com/2001/nov/11/news/mn-2985.
62. Pooley, *supra* note 58, at 93 (see note at bottom).
63. David E. Sanger, *Bush Will Continue to Oppose Kyoto Pact on Global Warming*, N.Y. Times, June 12, 2001, http://www.nytimes.com/2001/06/12/world/bush-will-continue-to-oppose-kyoto-pact-on-global-warming.html?pagewanted=1.
64. National Association of Clean Air Agencies, Background and History of EPA Regulation of Greenhouse Gas (GHG) Emissions Under the Clean Air Act & National Association of Clean Air Agencies' Comments on EPA GHG Regulatory and Policy Proposals (2011), *available at* http://www.nwcleanair.org/pdf/ClimateChange/Misc/History_%20EPA_Regulation_GHGs-July2011-post.pdf.
65. Memorandum from Jonathan Z. Cannon, EPA Gen. Counsel, to Carol M. Browner, EPA Adm'r (Apr. 10, 1998), *available at* http://www.law.umaryland.edu/faculty/bpercival/casebook/documents/epaco2memo1.pdf.
66. EPA, Notice of Denial of Petition for Rulemaking: Control of Emissions From New Highway Vehicles and Engines, 68 Fed. Reg. 52,922 (Sept. 8, 2003).
67. *Id.* at 52,925.
68. *Id.*
69. *Id.* at 52,929–32.
70. Massachusetts v. EPA, 549 U.S. 497, 501 (2007).
71. *Id.*
72. *Id.*
73. *Id.*
74. Intergovernmental Panel on Climate Change, Climate Change 2007 Synthesis Report 1, 30, 39 (2007), *available at* https://www.ipcc.ch/pdf/assessment-report/ar4/syr/ar4_syr.pdf.
75. Stephen Johnson, Draft Outline of Proposed Summary of Endangerment Finding in Preamble 10 (Dec. 5, 2007), *available at* http://insideclimatenews.org/sites/default/files/2007_Draft_Proposed_Endangerment_Finding.pdf.
76. *Id.* at 12–13.
77. *Id.* at 13.
78. *See* Juliet Eilperin, *White House Tried to Silence EPA Proposal on Car Emissions*, Wash. Post, June 26, 2009, http://www.washingtonpost.com/wp-dyn/content/article/2008/06/25/AR2008062502713.html.
79. *See* Felicity Barringer, *White House Refused to Open Pollutants E-Mail*, N.Y. Times, June 25, 2008, http://www.nytimes.com/2008/06/25/washington/25epa.html.

80. *Id.*
81. Press Release, EPA, EPA Finds Greenhouse Gases Pose Threat to Public Health, Welfare/Proposed Finding Comes in Response to 2007 Supreme Court Ruling (Apr. 17, 2009), *available at* http://yosemite.epa.gov/opa/admpress.nsf/0/0ef7df675805295d8525759b00566924.
82. President Barack Obama, Remarks by the President on Clean Energy (Apr. 22, 2009), transcript *available at* https://www.whitehouse.gov/video/Seeing-Green-in-Iowa#transcript.
83. *Id.*
84. An Introduction to the Law and Economics of Environmental Policy: Institutional Design 20, at 335 (Timothy Swanson ed., 2002).
85. Bill Chameides, *On the Climate Bill Fence: What Sen. McCain Is Thinking*, Duke Univ.: The Green Grok (July 3, 2009), http://blogs.nicholas.duke.edu/thegreengrok/fencesitter-mccain/.
86. Jim Efstathiou Jr., *Air-Pollution Market Debut Tests Cap-and-Trade Model (Update 1)*, Bloomberg, Sept. 23, 2008, http://www.bloomberg.com/apps/news?pid=newsarchive&sid=a7fmAZqdHrW0&refer=home.
87. Cal. Air Res. Board, Climate Change Scoping Plan, ES-1, ES-3 (2008), *available at* http://www.arb.ca.gov/cc/scopingplan/document/adopted_scoping_plan.pdf.
88. U.S. Climate Action P'ship, A Blueprint for Legislative Action (2009), *available at* http://www.c2es.org/docUploads/USCAP-legislative-blueprint.pdf.
89. *See* Petra Bartosiewicz & Marissa Miley, The Too Polite Revolution: Why the Recent Campaign to Pass Comprehensive Climate Legislation in the United States Failed 3–4, (2013), *available at* http://www.journalism.columbia.edu/system/documents/684/original/CLIMATE_CHANGE_FULL_WITH_COVER.pdf.
90. U.S. Climate Action P'ship, *supra* note 88, at 5.
91. *Id.* at 11–15.
92. *See generally* Pew Ctr. on Global Climate Change, Greenhouse Gas Emissions Allowance Allocations (2007), *available at* http://www.c2es.org/docUploads/Allowance-Allocations-Policy-Brief-DDuke.pdf.
93. *Id.* at 1.
94. U.S. Climate Action P'ship, *supra* note 88, at 11.
95. *Id.* at 13, 15.
96. Obama for America, Barack Obama and Joe Biden: New Energy for America, 3–4 (undated), *available at* http://energy.gov/sites/prod/files/edg/media/Obama_New_Energy_0804.pdf.
97. *See* Pooley, *supra* note 58, at 334–35.
98. *Id.*

99. *Rick Boucher: Top 20 Contributors, 2007–2008*, OPEN SECRETS, https://www.opensecrets.org/politicians/contrib.php?type=C&cid=N00002171&newMem=N&cycle=2008 (last visited July 21, 2015) (listing Duke Energy as Boucher's fifth-largest contributor in 2008 election cycle); POOLEY, *supra* note 58, at 142–43 (noting that Duke Energy is the United States' third-largest carbon emitter and that the company generates 70 percent of its electricity with coal); John M. Broder, *Obama's Greenhouse Gas Gamble*, N.Y. TIMES, Feb. 27, 2009, http://www.nytimes.com/2009/02/28/science/earth/28capntrade.html (featuring comment from Duke spokesman regarding "coal state stickup").
100. U.S. ENERGY INFO. ADMIN., DOE/EIA-0226 (2009/02), ELECTRIC POWER MONTHLY: FEBRUARY 2009, at 110 tbl.5.6.B (2009), *available at* http://www.eia.gov/electricity/monthly/archive/pdf/02260902.pdf (showing average retail price of electricity in each state as of November 2008).
101. POOLEY, *supra* note 58, at 346, 375–76.
102. Anne C. Mulkern, *Free Carbon Emissions Permits Could Create Added Costs*, N.Y. TIMES, May 29, 2009, http://www.nytimes.com/gwire/2009/05/29/29greenwire-free-carbon-emissions-permits-could-create-add-73326.html.
103. *Id.*; POOLEY, *supra* note 58, at 347–48.
104. Darren Samuelsohn & Katherine Ling, *"Fragile Compromise" of Power Plant CEOs in Doubt as Senate Climate Debate Nears*, N.Y. TIMES, Aug. 5, 2009, http://www.nytimes.com/cwire/2009/08/05/05climatewire-fragile-compromise-of-power-plant-ceos-in-do-68966.html?pagewanted=all.
105. *Id.*
106. POOLEY, *supra* note 58, at 376.
107. John M. Broder, *With Something for Everyone, Climate Bill Passed*, N.Y. TIMES, June 30, 2009, http://www.nytimes.com/2009/07/01/us/politics/01climate.html.
108. Editorial, *New Energy Bill Reflects Commitment to Cleaner Coal*, WASH. POST, June 25, 2009, http://www.washingtonpost.com/wp-dyn/content/article/2009/06/24/AR2009062403266.html (emphasis added).
109. *The Waxman-Markey Bill: A Good Start or a Non-Starter?*, ENVIRONMENT 360, June 18, 2009, http://e360.yale.edu/feature/the_waxman-markey_bill_a_good_start_or_a_non-starter/2163/.
110. Memorandum from Senate EPW Staff to House, Senate Energy/Environment Staff 2 (May 14, 2009), *available at* http://www.politico.com/static/PPM116_gop_memo.html.
111. POOLEY, *supra* note 58, at 346–47 (noting that the oil sector was allocated only 2 percent of allowances).
112. Steven Mufson, *ConocoPhillips, BP and Caterpillar Quit USCAP*, WASH. POST, Feb. 17, 2010, http://www.washingtonpost.com/wp-dyn/content/

article/2010/02/16/AR2010021605543.html; Clifford Krauss & Jad Mouawad, *Oil Industry Backs Protests of Emissions Bill*, N.Y. Times, Aug. 18, 2009, http://www.nytimes.com/2009/08/19/business/energy-environment/19climate.html (describing American Petroleum Institute's orchestration of rallies).

113. Ctr. for Climate & Energy Solutions, 111th Congress Climate Change Legislation, http://www.c2es.org/federal/congress/111 (last visited July 21, 2015); *see also* Pooley, *supra* note 58, at 417–18 (describing failed Senate bill).

114. John M. Broder, *"Cap and Trade" Loses Its Standing as Energy Policy of Choice*, N.Y. Times, Mar. 25, 2010, http://www.nytimes.com/2010/03/26/science/earth/26climate.html.

115. *See* Brian H. Potts, *Trading Grandfathered Air—A New, Simpler Approach*, 31 Harv. Envtl. L. Rev. 115, 121 (2007) (explaining that plants built in 1971 and later must restrict sulfur dioxide emissions, while plants built in 1978 and later must restrict both sulfur dioxide and nitrogen oxides emissions); Utility Air Regulatory Group v. EPA, 134 S. Ct. 2427, 2437 (2014) (noting that the EPA began to subject some new sources to restrictions on their carbon emissions in 2011).

116. U.S. Gov't Accountability Off., GAO-12-545R, Air Emissions and Electricity Generation at U.S. Power Plants 11 fig. 7 (2012), *available at* http://www.gao.gov/assets/600/590188.pdf (metric tons have been converted to pounds).

117. U.S. Energy Info. Admin., Most Electric Generating Capacity Additions in the Last Decade Were Natural Gas-Fired (July 5, 2011), http://www.eia.gov/todayinenergy/detail.cfm?id=2070 (percentages calculated using underlying CSV data).

118. *Id.*

119. *Id.*

120. Richard J. Campbell, Cong. Research Serv., R43343, Increasing the Efficiency of Existing Coal-Fired Power Plants 7 (2013), *available at* https://fas.org/sgp/crs/misc/R43343.pdf.

121. *Id.* at 14; IEA Clean Coal Centre, *Upgrading and Efficiency Improvement in Coal-Fired Power Plants*, Profiles, Aug. 2013, *available at* http://www.iea-coal.org.uk/documents/83185/8784/Upgrading-and-efficiency-improvement-in-coal-fired-power-%20plants,-CCC/221.

122. Envtl. Integrity Project, Dirty Kilowatts: America's Most Polluting Power Plants 6 tbl.1 (2007), *available at* http://www.dirtykilowatts.org/Dirty_Kilowatts2007.pdf (listing fifty plants with highest emission rates for carbon dioxide); Standards of Performance for Greenhouse Gas Emissions From New Stationary Sources: Electric Utility Generating Units, 79 Fed. Reg. 1430, (proposed Jan. 8, 2014) (listing

estimated emission rates of different types of new coal-fired generating units).

123. MOST ELECTRIC GENERATING CAPACITY ADDITIONS IN THE LAST DECADE WERE NATURAL GAS-FIRED, *supra* note 117 (percentages calculated using underlying CSV data).
124. Garth Heutel, *Plant Vintages, Grandfathering, and Environmental Policy*, 61 J. ENVTL. ECON. & MGMT. 36, 47, 49–50 (2011).
125. *See, e.g.*, POOLEY, *supra* note 58, at 369–71.
126. Emission rate data obtained from "Dirty Kilowatts" 2007 Report Database, ENVIRONMENTAL INTEGRITY PROJECT, http://www.dirtykilowatts.org/index.cfm (last visited July 27, 2015) (download plant data for both "Duke Energy Corp" and "Duke Energy—Cincinnati Gas & Electric Co"). Plant in-service dates obtained from SOURCE WATCH, THE CTR. FOR MEDIA & DEMOCRACY, CATEGORY: EXISTING COAL PLANTS IN THE UNITED STATES, http://www.sourcewatch.org/index.php/Category:Existing_coal_plants_in_the_United_States (last updated on Apr. 25, 2015).
127. U.S. GOV'T ACCOUNTABILITY OFF., *supra* note 116, at 28 tbl.5.
128. POOLEY, *supra* note 58, at 384–85.
129. Tim Dickinson, *Climate Bill, R.I.P.*, ROLLING STONE, July 21, 2010, http://www.rollingstone.com/politics/news/climate-bill-r-i-p-20100721.

Chapter 7

1. *Duke Energy to Retire Coal Operations at Its W.C. Beckjord Station*, DUKE ENERGY (Aug. 28, 2014), http://www.duke-energy.com/news/releases/2014082801.asp.
2. *W.C. Beckjord Station Retirement Plans: Beckjord Station Through the Years*, DUKE ENERGY, http://www.duke-energy.com/beckjord/through-the-years.asp (last visited Jan. 27, 2014).
3. SOURCE WATCH, EXISTING U.S. COAL PLANTS, http://www.sourcewatch.org/index.php?title=Existing_U.S._Coal_Plants (last updated Aug. 26, 2015).
4. *See* Cleveland Elec. Illuminating Co. v. EPA, 572 F.2d 1150, 1165 (6th Cir. 1978) (appendix summarizing content of 1972 plan).
5. *Id.* at 1156.
6. *Id.*
7. *Id.* at 1165 (appendix summarizing content of 1973 plan).
8. *Id.* at 1156.
9. *Id.* at 1165.
10. *See id.* at 1160–61.
11. *Id.* at 1165.

12. *Id.* at 1156.
13. *See* Designations of Areas for Air Quality Planning Purposes; Attainment Status Designations; Ohio, 53 Fed. Reg. 9112, 9113 (Mar. 21, 1988) (describing results of emissions testing at Beckjord).
14. Arnold W. Reitze, Jr., *State and Federal Command-and Control Regulation of Emissions from Fossil-Fuel Electric Power Generating Plants*, 32 Envtl. L. 369, 381 (2002).
15. *Id.*
16. Interstate Pollution Abatement, Proceedings Under Section 126 of the Clean Air Act and Hearing, 46 Fed. Reg. 24,602, 24,603 (May 1, 1981).
17. Interstate Pollution Abatement, Final Determination, 49 Fed. Reg. 48,152, 48,152, 48,153, 48,156 (Dec. 10, 1984).
18. Third Amended Complaint ¶¶ 172–175, No. 1:99-cv-1693-LJM-JMS, United States v. Cinergy Corp. (S.D. Ind. 1999), 1999 WL 34744777.
19. United States v. Cinergy Corp., 495 F. Supp. 2d 909, 916–18 (S.D. Ind. 2007).
20. *Id.* at 911.
21. Press Release, N.Y. State Att'y Gen., Second Major Utility Agrees to Cut Acid Rain Emissions (Dec. 21, 2000), *available at* http://www.ag.ny.gov/press-release/second-major-utility-agrees-cut-acid-rain-emissions.
22. Eric Schaeffer, *Clearing the Air: Why I Quit Bush's EPA*, Wash. Monthly (July/Aug. 2002), http://www.washingtonmonthly.com/features/2001/0207.schaeffer.html.
23. Verdict Form, United States v. Cinergy Corp., No. 1:99-cv-1693-LJM-JMS (S.D. Ind. 1999), *available at* http://indianalawblog.com/documents/Cinergy%20verdict.pdf.
24. Emission rates and rankings obtained from Envtl. Integrity Project, "Dirty Kilowatts" 2007 Report Database, http://www.dirtykilowatts.org/index.cfm (last visited July 22, 2015). According to this database, in addition to placing in the top 50 for total emissions, the plant placed in the top 50 for SO_2 (in terms of both its per megawatt-hour emission rate and its total emissions), in the top 100 for NO_x and mercury (again, in terms of both rate and total emissions), and in the top 200 for CO_2 (both rate and total).
25. Clean Air Task Force, The Toll from Coal: An Updated Assessment of Death and Disease from America's Dirtiest Energy Source 14 tbl.6 (2010), *available at* http://www.catf.us/resources/publications/files/The_Toll_from_Coal.pdf.
26. Paul Wojoski, *Duke Announces 2015 Closing of Beckjord Coal Plant*, Greenpeace (July 20, 2011), http://www.greenpeace.org/usa/duke-announces-2015-closing-of-beckjord-coal-plant/.
27. Tatum Hunter, *Duke Energy Repurposes Former Local Coal Plant*, Cincinnati Bus. Courier, May 26, 2015, http://www.bizjournals.com/cincinnati/

news/2015/05/26/duke-energy-repurposes-former-greater-cincinnati.html.

28. *Id.*
29. U.S. Gov't Accountability Office, GAO-14-672, EPA Regulations and Electricity 19 (2014), available at http://www.gao.gov/assets/670/665325.pdf.
30. U.S. Energy Info. Admin., AEO2014 Projects More Coal-Fired Power Plant Retirements by 2016 than Have Been Scheduled (Feb. 14, 2014), http://www.eia.gov/todayinenergy/detail.cfm?id=15031.
31. *Id.*
32. 40 C.F.R. § 60.43Da (b)(2) (explaining requirements for gas-fired plants); EPA, Air Emissions, http://www.epa.gov/cleanenergy/energy-and-you/affect/air-emissions.html (last updated May 22, 2014).
33. *See* U.S. Energy Info. Admin., Most Electric Generating Capacity Additions in the Last Decade Were Natural Gas-Fired (July 5, 2011), http://www.eia.gov/todayinenergy/detail.cfm?id=2070 (showing gas-fired capacity dating back to 1940s); U.S. Energy Info. Admin., Fuel Competition in Power Generation and Elasticities of Substitution, at fig.1 (June 2012), http://www.eia.gov/analysis/studies/fuelelasticities (showing market shares of coal and gas from 1950 to 2010).
34. *See* Richard J. Pierce, Jr., *Natural Gas Regulation, Deregulation, and Contracts*, 68 Va. L. Rev. 63, 65 (1982) (describing supply effects of the Natural Gas Act of 1938).
35. Am. Petroleum Inst., Oil and Natural Gas Overview: Natural Gas and Its Uses, http://www.api.org/oil-and-natural-gas-overview/exploration-and-production/natural-gas/natural-gas-uses (last visited July 27, 2015).
36. Mass. Inst. of Tech., The Future of Natural Gas 3 (2011), *available at* http://mitei.mit.edu/system/files/NaturalGas_Report.pdf.
37. N.Y. State Energy Research & Dev. Auth., New York's Natural Gas and Oil Resource Endowment: Past, Present, and Potential 8 (2007), *available at* http://www.dec.ny.gov/docs/materials_minerals_pdf/nyserda2.pdf (stating that first commercial gas well was drilled in Fredonia, NY, in 1821); Robert W. Kolb, The Natural Gas Revolution: At the Pivot of the World's Energy Future 47 (2014) (describing development of interstate pipelines in early twentieth century).
38. Pierce, *supra* note 34, at 79–80.
39. 15 U.S.C. § 717c(a) (2015).
40. Phillips Petroleum Co. v. Wisconsin, 347 U.S. 672 (1954).
41. *Id.* at 685.
42. IHS Cambridge Energy Research Assocs., Fueling America's Energy Future: The Unconventional Natural Gas Revolution

and the Carbon Agenda I-7 (2010), *available at* https://www.gov.uk/government/uploads/system/uploads/attachment_data/file/43227/1296-ihs-cera-special-report.pdf.

43. W.M. Burnett & S.D. Ban, *Changing Prospects for Natural Gas in the United States*, 244 Science 305, 305 (Apr. 21, 1989).
44. Paul L. Joskow, *Natural Gas: From Shortages to Abundance in the United States*, 103 Am. Econ. Rev. 338, 338 (2013).
45. Burnett & Ban, *supra* note 43, at 305.
46. Fuel Competition in Power Generation and Elasticities of Substitution, *supra* note 33.
47. Joskow, *supra* note 44, at 338–39.
48. IHS Cambridge Energy Research Assocs., *supra* note 42, at I-7, I-8.
49. U.S. Energy Info. Admin., Repeal of the Powerplant and Industrial Fuel Use Act (1987), http://www.eia.gov/oil_gas/natural_gas/analysis_publications/ngmajorleg/repeal.html (last visited July 23, 2015).
50. *Id.*
51. Burnett & Ban, *supra* note 43, at 305.
52. Repeal of the Powerplant and Industrial Fuel Use Act (1987), *supra* note 49.
53. IHS Cambridge Energy Research Assocs., *supra* note 42, at I-8.
54. Michael Arndt, *Possibilities Are Truly Electric for Natural Gas*, Chi. Trib., May 14, 1989, http://articles.chicagotribune.com/1989-05-14/business/8904120560_1_gas-reserves-electric-generation-gas-fired.
55. Hillary Durgin, *Shift to Gas Is No Death Blow*, The Financial Times, Sept. 23, 1999, at 2.
56. Mass. Inst. of Tech., *supra* note 36, at 73 fig.4.1.
57. *Id.*
58. U.S. Energy Info. Admin., Demand for Electricity Changes Through the Day (Apr. 6, 2011), http://www.eia.gov/todayinenergy/detail.cfm?id=830; U.S. Energy Info. Admin., Electricity Demand Patterns Matter for Valuing Electricity Supply Resources (Aug. 27, 2013), http://www.eia.gov/todayinenergy/detail.cfm?id=12711.
59. U.S. Energy Info. Admin., Electric Generator Dispatch Depends on System Demand and the Relative Cost of Operation (Aug. 17, 2012), http://www.eia.gov/todayinenergy/detail.cfm?id=7590.
60. *Id.*
61. *Id.* (noting that coal's "fuel cost advantage was sufficient to overcome the efficiency advantage of the new vintage of gas-fired generators built beginning in the 1990s").
62. U.S. Energy Info. Admin., U.S. Natural Gas Power Price (June 30, 2015), http://www.eia.gov/dnav/ng/hist/n3045us3a.htm (showing decline

of gas prices for electricity providers); PPI Energy and Chemicals Team, *The Effects of Shale Gas Production on Natural Gas Prices*, Beyond the Numbers (May 2013), http://www.bls.gov/opub/btn/volume-2/the-effects-of-shale-gas-production-on-natural-gas-prices.htm#ednref3 (explaining how boom in shale production affected gas prices); U.S. Dep't of Energy, Office of Fossil Energy, Natural Gas from Shale: Questions and Answers 3 (2013), *available at* http://energy.gov/sites/prod/files/2013/04/f0/complete_ brochure.pdf (describing formation of shale gas).

63. U.S. Dep't of Energy, Office of Fossil Energy, *id.* at 9.
64. EPA, Plan to Study the Potential Impacts of Hydraulic Fracturing on Drinking Water Resources 15 (2011), *available at* http://www2.epa.gov/sites/production/files/documents/hf_study_plan_ 110211_final_508.pdf.
65. *Id.*
66. U.S. Energy Info. Admin., Shale Gas Provides Largest Share of U.S. Natural Gas Production in 2013 (Nov. 25, 2014), http://www.eia.gov/todayinenergy/detail.cfm?id=18951.
67. *See* U.S. Energy Info. Admin., *U.S.* Natural Gas Marketed Production (June 30, 2015), http://www.eia.gov/dnav/ng/hist/n9050us2a.htm (showing annual U.S. production of natural gas from 1900 to 2014).
68. Tom Murphy, *Natural Gas Edges Past Coal to Become Biggest U.S. Electricity Source for First Time Ever*, U.S. News & World Report, July 13, 2015, http://www.usnews.com/news/business/articles/2015/07/13/natural-gas-surpasses-coal-as-biggest-us-electricity-source.
69. *Id.*
70. *Id.*
71. *See, e.g.*, U.S. Energy Info. Admin., Scheduled 2015 Capacity Additions Mostly Wind and Natural Gas; Retirements Mostly Coal (Mar. 10, 2015), http://www.eia.gov/todayinenergy/detail.cfm?id=20292 (noting that the coal units scheduled for retirement in 2015 "operate at a lower capacity factor than average coal-fired units in the United States").
72. Adam Liptak, *Justices Hear Case on Cross-State Pollution Rules*, N.Y. Times (Dec. 11, 2013), http://www.nytimes.com/2013/12/11/us/justices-hear-arguments-on-cross-state-air-pollution-rules.html.
73. EPA v. EME Homer City Generation, 134 S. Ct. 1584, 1596 (2014).
74. *Id.* at 1596–97.
75. Federal Implementation Plans: Interstate Transport of Fine Particulate Matter and Ozone and Correction of SIP Approvals, 76 Fed. Reg. 48,208, 48,271 (Aug. 8, 2011).
76. *Id.* at 48,271–72.

77. *Id.*
78. 134 S. Ct. at 1598–99.
79. 134 S. Ct. at 1590, 1594.
80. EPA, CROSS-STATE AIR POLLUTION RULE (CSAPR), http://www.epa.gov/airtransport/CSAPR (last updated June 3, 2015).
81. EPA, CROSS-STATE AIR POLLUTION RULE (CSAPR): BASIC INFORMATION, http://www.epa.gov/crossstaterule/basic.html (last updated Apr. 14, 2015).
82. *Id.*
83. EPA, FACT SHEET: MERCURY AND AIR TOXICS STANDARDS FOR POWER PLANTS, at 1, http://www.epa.gov/mats/pdfs/20111221MATSsummaryfs.pdf (last visited July 23, 2015).
84. *Id.* at 2–3.
85. Alan Jay Goldberg, Note, *Toward Sensible Regulation of Hazardous Air Pollutants Under Section 112 of the Clean Air Act*, 63 N.Y.U. L. REV. 612, 613 (1998) (quoting 42 U.S.C. § 7412 (1982)).
86. *See* New Jersey v. EPA, 517 F.3d 574, 578 (D.C. Cir. 2008).
87. *Id.*
88. *See* 42 U.S.C. § 7412(b)(1), (c)(1), (e)(1)–(3) (2015).
89. *See* 42 U.S.C § 7412(n)(1)(A) (2015).
90. *See id.*
91. *See* New Jersey v. EPA, 517 F.3d at 579.
92. Regulatory Finding on the Emissions of Hazardous Air Pollutants from Electric Utility Steam Generating Units, 65 Fed. Reg. 79,825, 79,827 (Dec. 20, 2000) (describing findings of the "Study of Hazardous Air Pollutant Emissions from Electric Utility Steam Generating Units—Final Report to Congress").
93. *Id.*
94. *Id.*
95. Standards of Performance for New and Existing Stationary Sources: Electric Utility Steam Generating Units, 70 Fed. Reg. 28,606 (May 18, 2005).
96. *Id.* at 28,609.
97. *See* New Jersey v. EPA, 517 F.3d 574, 581–82 (D.C. Cir. 2008).
98. National Emission Standards for Hazardous Air Pollutants from Coal- and Oil-Fired Electric Utility Steam Generating Units and Standards of Performance for Fossil-Fuel-Fired Electric Utility, Industrial-Commercia l-Institutional, and Small Industrial-Commercial-Institutional Steam Generating Units, 77 Fed. Reg. 9304, 9304 (Feb. 16, 2012).
99. *Id.* at 9306.
100. EPA, AIR EMISSIONS, http://www.epa.gov/cleanenergy/energy-and-you/affect/air-emissions.html (noting the EPA's conclusion that "regulating natural gas-fired [power plants] was not appropriate and necessary because

the impacts due to [hazardous air pollutant] emissions from such units are negligible") (last visited Mar. 2, 2015).

101. EPA, EPA-452/R-11-011, Regulatory Impact Analysis for the Final Mercury and Air Toxics Standards 3-14 to 3-15 (2011), *available at* http://www.epa.gov/ttn/ecas/regdata/RIAs/matsriafinal.pdf [hereinafter MATS Regulatory Impact Analysis] (predicting the controls that plants will install to satisfy MATS); EPA, Cleaner Power Plants, http://www.epa.gov/airquality/powerplanttoxics/powerplants.html (last updated Feb. 11, 2014) (estimating that MATS will reduce SO_2 emissions by 41 percent beyond the level required by the Transport Rule).
102. EPA, Mercury and Air Toxics Standards: Benefits and Costs of Cleaning Up Air Pollution from Power Plants 1 (undated), *available at* http://www.epa.gov/mats/pdfss/20111221MATSimpactsfs.pdf.
103. EPA, Fact Sheet: Overview of the Clean Power Plan, http://www2.epa.gov/cleanpowerplan/fact-sheet-overview-clean-power-plan (last updated Aug. 6, 2015).
104. Keith Goldberg, *Carbon Rule Sends EPA Into Uncharted Legal Territory*, Law360 (June 13, 2014), http://www.law360.com/articles/547456/carbon-rule-sends-epa-into-uncharted-legal-territory.
105. Robert R. Nordhaus & Avi Zevin, *Historical Perspectives on § 111(d) of the Clean Air Act*, 44 Envtl. L. Rep. News & Analysis 11,095, 11,100 (2014), *available at* http://64.106.168.122/files/10710_article_2014_11_44.11095.pdf.
106. Endangerment and Cause or Contribute Findings for Greenhouse Gases Under Section 202(a) of the Clean Air Act, 74 Fed. Reg. 66,496 (Dec. 15, 2009).
107. Light-Duty Vehicle Greenhouse Gas Emission Standards and Corporate Average Fuel Economy Standards, 75 Fed. Reg. 25,324 (May 7, 2010).
108. EPA Settlement Agreement (Dec. 2010), *available at* http://www2.epa.gov/sites/production/files/2013-09/documents/boilerghgsettlement.pdf.
109. *Id.*
110. EPA, 2012 Proposed Carbon Pollution Standard for New Power Plants (Mar. 27, 2012), http://www2.epa.gov/carbon-pollution-standards/2012-proposed-carbon-pollution-standard-new-power-plants.
111. Exec. Office of the President, The President's Climate Action Plan (2013), *available at* http://www.whitehouse.gov/sites/default/files/image/president27sclimateactionplan.pdf.
112. *Id.*
113. Standards of Performance for Greenhouse Gas Emissions from New, Modified, and Reconstructed Stationary Sources: Electric Utility Generating Units, http://www.epa.gov/airquality/cpp/cps-final-rule.pdf

(Aug. 3, 2015) (not yet published in Federal Register); Carbon Pollution Emission Guidelines for Existing Stationary Sources: Electric Utility Generating Units, http://www2.epa.gov/sites/production/files/2015-08/documents/cpp-final-rule.pdf (last updated Aug. 3, 2015) (not yet published in Federal Register).

114. EPA, Fact Sheet: Final Limits on Carbon Pollution from New, Modified and Reconstructed Power Plants 2–3 (Aug. 3, 2015), http://www.epa.gov/airquality/cpp/fs-cps-overview.pdf.
115. Standards of Performance for Greenhouse Gas Emissions from New, Modified, and Reconstructed Stationary Sources: Electric Utility Generating Units, *supra* note 113, at 29.
116. *Id.* at 28.
117. *Id.*
118. *Id.* at 29.
119. EPA, Fact Sheet: Overview of the Clean Power Plan 2-3 (Aug. 3, 2015), http://www2.epa.gov/sites/production/files/2015-08/documents/fs-cpp-overview.pdf.
120. *Id.* at 4.
121. *Id.* at 3-4.
122. *Id.* at 2-3.
123. MATS Regulatory Impact Analysis, *supra* note 101, at 2-9 n.2 (noting that selective catalytic reduction is primarily used for NO_x control but can also reduce mercury); *id.* at 2-9 (explaining that a "wet" scrubber can reduce both SO_2 and mercury).
124. *See* Cleaner Power Plants, *supra* note 101 (noting that newer plants already control their emissions of mercury, heavy metals, and acid gases).
125. EPA, Regulatory Impact Analysis for the Federal Implementation Plans to Reduce Interstate Transport of Fine Particulate Matter and Ozone in 27 States; Correction of SIP Approvals for 22 States 15 (2011), *available at* http://www.epa.gov/airtransport/pdfs/FinalRIA.pdf.
126. MATS Regulatory Impact Analysis, *supra* note 101, at 3-35.
127. EPA, EPA-452/R-15-003, Regulatory Impact Analysis for the Clean Power Plan Final Rule 3-30 (2015), *available at* http://www2.epa.gov/sites/production/files/2015-08/documents/cpp-final-rule-ria.pdf [hereinafter Clean Power Plan Regulatory Impact Analysis].
128. Jennifer Macedonia & Colleen Kelly, Bipartisan Policy Ctr., Projected Impact of Changing Conditions on the Power Sector 9 (2012), *available at* http://bipartisanpolicy.org/wp-content/uploads/sites/default/files/CAA_Modeling_Staff_Paper.pdf; Jennifer Macedonia et. al., Bipartisan Policy Ctr., Insights from Modeling the

Proposed Clean Power Plan 15 (2015), http://bipartisanpolicy.org/wp-content/uploads/2015/04/BPC-Clean-Power-Plan-Slides.pdf.

129. EPA, EPA Analysis of the Proposed Clean Power Plan, http://www.epa.gov/airmarkets/programs/ipm/cleanpowerplan.html (last updated Aug. 4, 2015) (download.zip file for "Base Case" and open "ssr" spreadsheet; see row 79); U.S. Energy Info. Admin., Electric Power Annual 2013, at tbl.4.2.A (2015), *available at* http://www.eia.gov/electricity/annual/pdf/epa.pdf (showing total coal-fired generation capacity as of 2013).
130. *See* Clean Power Plan Regulatory Impact Analysis, *supra* note 127, at 1-5 (noting that "base case" includes MATS and the Transport Rule).
131. Larry B. Parker et al., Cong. Research Serv., 85–50 ENR, The Clean Air Act and Proposed Acid Rain Legislation: Can We Get There From Here? 78 (1985).
132. Calculated using data from U.S. Energy Info. Admin., Total Energy at tbl.7.2B, http://www.eia.gov/beta/MER/index.cfm?tbl=T07.02B#/?f=A&start=200001 (last visited July 24, 2015).
133. U.S. Gov't Accountability Office, GAO-14-672, EPA Regulations and Electricity: Update on Agencies' Monitoring Efforts and Coal-Fueled Generating Unit Retirements 19 (2014), *available at* http://www.gao.gov/assets/670/665325.pdf.
134. IHS CERA, Fueling the Future with Natural Gas: Bringing It Home at ES-1 (2014), *available at* https://www.fuelingthefuture.org/assets/content/AGF-Fueling-the-Future-Study.pdf.
135. Macedonia et al., Insights from Modeling the Proposed Clean Power Plan, *supra* note 128, at 33–34.
136. Michigan v. EPA, 576 U. S. ____, 135 S. Ct. 2699, 2711–12 (2015).
137. MATS Regulatory Impact Analysis, *supra* note 101, at ES-2 tbl.ES-1.
138. Michigan v. EPA, 135 S. Ct. at 2714 (Kagan, J., dissenting).
139. *Id.*
140. *Id.* at 2711–12 (majority opinion).
141. *See, e.g., In re* Murray Energy Corp. v. EPA, 788 F.3d 330, 333–34 (D.C. Cir. 2015); Oklahoma v. McCarthy, No. 15-CV-0369-CVE-FHM, 2015 WL 4414384, at *5 (N.D. Okla. July 17, 2015); Ann Carlson, *As Predicted, Premature Suit to Block Clean Power Plan Implementation Fails*, Legal Planet (Sept. 9, 2015), http://legal-planet.org/2015/09/09/as-predicted-premature-suit-to-block-clean-power-plan-implementation-fails.
142. *Murray Energy*, 788 F.3d at 334.
143. 42 U.S.C. § 7607 ("Any petition for review . . . [of an EPA rulemaking under the Clean Air Act] shall be filed within sixty days from the date notice of such promulgation, approval, or action appears in the Federal Register.").

144. Logan Layden, *EPA In the Crosshairs as Oklahoma's Inhofe Gains Sway Over Climate Policy*, NPR: State Impact (Nov. 20, 2014), https://stateimpact.npr.org/oklahoma/2014/11/20/epa-in-the-crosshairs-as-oklahomas-inhofe-gains-sway-over-climate-policy/.
145. John Siciliano, *White House Slams GOP Spending Bill Targeting Climate Rules*, Wash. Examiner (July 7, 2015), http://www.washingtonexaminer.com/white-house-slams-gop-spending-bill-targeting-climate-rules/article/2567784; Rebecca Shabad, *GOP Sharpens Ax for Regulations*, The Hill, June 29, 2015, http://thehill.com/policy/finance/246361-gop-sharpens-ax-for-regulations.
146. Coral Davenport, *McConnell Urges States to Defy U.S. Plan to Cut Greenhouse Gas*, N.Y. Times, Mar. 4, 2015, http://www.nytimes.com/2015/03/05/us/politics/mcconnell-urges-states-to-defy-us-plan-to-cut-greenhouse-gas.html?_r=0.
147. Devin Henry, *Oklahoma Takes Aim at Climate Plan*, The Hill, Apr. 30, 2015, http://thehill.com/policy/energy-environment/240696-oklahoma-takes-aim-at-climate-plan.
148. Daniel Selmi, *States Should Think Twice Before Refusing Any Response to EPA's Clean Power Rules*, Columbia Law School Sabin Ctr. for Climate Change Law 3 (Mar. 2015), https://web.law.columbia.edu/sites/default/files/microsites/climate-change/selmi_-_states_should_think_twice_before_refusing_any_response_to_epas_clean_power_rules.pdf.
149. Carbon Pollution Emission Guidelines for Existing Stationary Sources, *supra* note 113, at 38.
150. Eric Wolff, *Supreme Court's Eventual MATS Ruling Will Be (Mostly) Moot*, SNL (May 14, 2015), https://www.snl.com/InteractiveX/Article.aspx?cdid=A-32620730-13109.

Conclusion

1. Coral Davenport, *Laurence Tribe Fights Climate Case Against Star Pupil from Harvard, President Obama*, N.Y. Times, Apr. 6, 2015, http://www.nytimes.com/2015/04/07/us/laurence-tribe-fights-climate-case-against-star-pupil-from-harvard-president-obama.html (describing Tribe's background and retention by Peabody); Peabody Energy, About Us, http://www.peabodyenergy.com/content/101/about-us (last visited July 24, 2015) (stating that Peabody is the world's largest private-sector coal company).
2. Laurence H. Tribe & Peabody Energy Corp., Comments on Carbon Pollution Emission Guidelines for Existing Stationary Sources: Electric Utility Generating Units, at 10 (Dec. 1, 2014), http://www.masseygail.com/pdf/Tribe-Peabody_111(d)_Comments_(filed).pdf.

3. New Jersey v. EPA, 517 F.3d 574, 581 (D.C. Cir. 2008) (quoting 42 U.S.C. § 7412(c)(9)).
4. Notice of Regulatory Finding, 65 Fed. Reg. 79,825, 79,827 (Dec. 20, 2000).
5. Massachusetts v. EPA, 549 U.S. 497, 534 (2007).
6. Lisa P. Jackson, Remarks to the United Nations Climate Change Conference in Copenhagen, As Prepared (Dec. 9, 2009), *available at* http://yosemite.epa.gov/opa/admpress.nsf/a883dc3da7094f97852572a00065d7d8/2e2fc405206fb50d85257687005493c2!OpenDocument.
7. Robert Meltz, Cong. Research Serv., R40984, Legal Consequences of EPA's Endangerment Finding for New Motor Vehicle Greenhouse Gas Emissions (2009).
8. Edith Wharton, A Backward Glance 147 (1934).
9. Elizabeth Belfiore, *Aristotle and Iphigenia, in* Essays on Aristotle's Poetics 359, 359 (Amélie Oksenberg Rorty ed., 1992); *see also* Justina Gregory, *Euripidean Tragedy, in* A Companion to Greek Tragedy 251, 253–54 (Justina Gregory ed., 2005).

INDEX